STREETWISE®
MEETING AND EVENT PLANNING

From Trade Shows and Conventions to Fundraisers and Galas—Everything You Need for a Successful Business Event

Joe LoCicero

ADAMS MEDIA
AVON, MASSACHUSETTS

To the lovely

Lori, who makes

every day an

amazing event

Published by Adams Media, an F+W Publications Company
57 Littlefield Street
Avon, MA 02322

ISBN-10: 1-59869-271-2
ISBN-13: 978-1-59869-271-6

Printed in the United States of America.

J I H G F E D C B A

Library of Congress Cataloging-in-Publication Data
LoCicero, Joe.
Streetwise meeting and event planning / Joe LoCicero.
     p.   cm.
   Includes bibliographical references.
   ISBN-13: 978-1-59869-271-6 (pbk.)
   ISBN-10: 1-59869-271-2 (pbk.)
   1. Business meetings—Planning. 2. Special events—
Planning. 3. Advertising—Planning. 4. Sales
promotion—Planning. 5. Marketing—Planning. I. Title.
II. Title: Meeting and event planning.
HF5734.5.L63 2007
658.4'56—dc22   2007030948

This publication is designed to provide accurate and authoritative information with
regard to the subject matter covered. It is sold with the understanding that the publisher is not engaged in rendering legal, accounting, or other professional advice.
If legal advice or other expert assistance is required, the services of a competent
professional person should be sought.

      —From a *Declaration of Principles* jointly adopted by a Committee of the
American Bar Association and a Committee of Publishers and Associations

Many of the designations used by manufacturers and sellers to distinguish their
product are claimed as trademarks. Where those designations appear in this book
and Adams Media was aware of a trademark claim, the designations have been
printed with initial capital letters.

This book is available at quantity discounts for bulk purchases.
For information, please call 1-800-289-0963.

CONTENTS

Acknowledgments

Seeds for professional success are often planted in college, and that's when my enthusiasm for and success in event planning took root. In that, I want to thank my brother Ricky, Robin Clark, Pete Cunningham, Ken Halliburton, Mark Mahoney, and Bill Thorne for encouraging my creativity with a plethora of events for various organizations, especially Tau Kappa Epsilon.

Professionally, I owe gratitude to some outstanding colleagues, including Cyndie Pershing, Lynn Brockman, Shawn Sites, Lisa Murray, and Kristy Wylie. I'm so proud of both the work we did for companies and clients and am especially grateful for having the opportunity to work with—and learn from—each of you. For this book particularly, I appreciate the time, enthusiasm, and smarts of Brad Packer, Jennifer Hess, and Jennifer Capler for sharing your workplace experiences.

I'm always in awe of my amazing agent Jacky Sach and feel so fortunate to have her as my advisor and advocate.

I also want to thank my most-excellent editors at Adams, Nikki Van Noy, Shoshanna Grossman, and Peter Archer for their enthusiasm and because they've been a dream to work with.

Finally, at Practical Whimsy, my heartfelt, continual thanks goes to Sarah Kent and Julie Jones for their indefatigable work and spirit.

And, of course, to my wife and children, who provided constant inspiration for this book and for all kinds of endeavors.

Introduction

As companies strive to cut through the clutter of messages that bombard their customers' and clients' lives, executives and entrepreneurs have increasingly been turning to events—the simple and the sublime—to elevate their business' brand, prospects, and profits. Meetings, Webinars, cocktail parties, conferences, and the many guises of events don't just connect with a target audience for your company's sales, they can also curry favor with investors and colleagues; impress the media; win over vendors; and train, laud, and unite employees.

In these pages I've brought lessons learned and showcased the advantages of each kind of event, how it can benefit your business and what you need to know to make one happen—any kind happen—swiftly, inventively, efficiently, and economically.

Events don't have to be confined by venues, the number of attendees, or budget. The only limits are your imagination and a dedication to success. In my background they've ranged from the black-tie gala that took over a chic department store to another in the middle of a zoo, from dozens of mall-based restaurant grand openings to one on a main square in a small Southern village, from a fashionable hotel chain's star-studded celebration in Chicago to another single resort's jubilee in a remote desert town, from the intimate dinner party extolling a company's first-quarter earnings to the Beverly Hills luncheon feting a CNN anchor.

Unlike many corporate initiatives, events can be tailor-made for any budget: from lavish receptions to imaginative guerrilla tactics, from massive trade shows to sales by e-mail. You'll be astounded at what will advance your company's marketing plan and overall objectives, and how efficiently and effectively you can make it happen.

In my meeting and event planning experience with Fortune 500 companies, entertainment conglomerates, hospitality chains, restaurants, retail stores, nonprofit organizations, tourist attractions, Internet start-ups, and my own enterprises I've witnessed the substantial impact and the sheer verve that events can contribute to a company's stature, internal morale, community and media relations, and, yes, the bottom line.

In designing and executing events for that multitude of entities, I've seen firsthand the impressive way that all kinds of events bring people together for the good of a company: the accomplishments and learning that arise out of a well-planned meeting; the good fortune and goodwill that emanate from a fundraiser and its attendant activities like auctions and bazaars; the triumphant success of an electrifying product launch that translates into enormous sales; the festivities of a grand opening that augur a business' long run; the grandeur of a convention that draws crowds, teaches, and pumps up sales; the genial simplicity of an open house; the creativity of an incentive program; the vision of a press conference; the low-tech ease of creating a cross-promotion with another noncompeting business; and the high-tech (but also easy) moves of putting on a podcast and coordinating a Web conference.

Once you've got some event experience under your belt, you'll be amazed at how you can call on it, learn from it, and expound upon it for an array of other subsequent events be they in a grand ballroom, in your company's conference room, at a hip local hotspot, or over the Web. In lining up budgets, deciding on staffing, laying out logistics, brainstorming activities, setting up action plans, determining equipment, finding talent, creating content, and defining mission statements for an event—all handily and expressly laid out in these pages—you'll realize how fruitful a single endeavor is and how your experience from it multiplies, allowing you to easily segue to manage, handle, and execute all kinds of other events.

That's because events, happily, cross over in a sense. Planning a meeting for twelve can give you the starting foundation to organize one for 1,200. A company retreat is simply a series of meetings. A banquet is several small luncheons assembled together. A Webinar is a cross between a seminar and Web conference. Once you bring the basics of event planning to life, you'll be amazed at how you can create events that play such an integral role in growing your business, extending its reach, establishing or building upon its reputation, and relating to your internal and external audiences.

As you embark on your event-planning ventures—and particularly once you discern the significance of the final outcomes—you'll realize that few experiences can bring you such fulfillment, enjoyment, and rewards in catapulting your business to new heights.

What's in an Event?

PART 1

Types of Events for Your Business

While the umbrella term *events* covers a wide range of occasions, experiences, and planned episodes, all of them can have a positive, mighty impact on your business.

As the business world embraces a global economy and thousands of new businesses set up shop each year, events can make a thriving, driving impact that gives your company a unique identity, separates your enterprise from the pack, streamlines your operation, improves communication internally and externally, and adds profit to your bottom line.

No matter what business you're in, an event will undoubtedly make its way into your goals, objectives, and plans. You may not even realize that you're calling on an event to enhance your image or strengthen sales. But when you realize the forms and formats events can take, and the success they can bring to your enterprise in a variety of ways, you'll be clamoring to integrate them regularly into your ventures.

The Importance of an Event

In a 2005 study cosponsored by Meeting Professionals International (MPI), 700 decision-making marketing executives from such industries as automotive, technology, healthcare, financial, associations, and manufacturing were interviewed. Among the findings: 96 percent of the respondents make events part of their marketing mix; nearly that many regard the importance of events as constant or increasing; and a majority consider events as a "lead tactic" or a "vital component" in their marketing campaigns.

Events conjure up many different meanings and images depending on what your company does and its goals. Grand openings, a Web site promotion for free shipping, inviting the boss over for dinner, a guerrilla marketing campaign, a trade show—these all qualify as events. Each may be different from the other in size, scope, and audience, but in each case the overarching goal is to improve your business in some way to impact sales and image. (You'll learn about more specific goals later on in the next section.) In their many differences, they can be one-time-only affairs, annually held, or conducted on a regular basis. You may be planning them for your company, or you may be participating in one hosted by a trade group or sponsored by one or more organizations.

What's the Goal of Your Event?

To make an event have its most extensive impact, you must first determine its goals. Those goals should be clear, precise, tied in some way to your company's objectives, and measurable. Just because it sounds like a good idea to have a sale or conduct a seminar isn't enough to sink time, money, energy, and other resources into it.

You may be drawn to some sort of event because it will create buzz for your business. While buzz is certainly alluring, it's not meaningful to your big financial picture unless you're creating buzz for a specific reason. You must ask and answer: What is your specific reason for having this event?

Tabbing a Goal

In answering that question, many possibilities may stand out: to generate sales, to increase profits, to engender name recognition, to foster goodwill in the community, to attract media attention and publicity, to target a specific market, or to establish or continue loyalty to a product or service.

Events break down into three categories relevant to goals:

➲ To amp up marketing and sales
➲ To start or enhance awareness
➲ To increase productivity

Further Defining and Refining

Even within those categories, your goals must be sharply defined. For instance, will the sale specifically target moving unsold merchandise to make room for new collections? Or will it bring exposure to a new line that was designed in-house?

Some events will cross over into all categories: Your company may be at a trade show where a new product launches well, attracting several orders; publicity for the trade show raises awareness for your new product.

Subsequently, employees take pride in the success of the new item and productivity increases.

As you come up with the goal of a particular event, canvass all potential possibilities for objectives that could be served. For instance, in the case of a grand opening, don't be shortsighted and just state your goal as: "Let's make a good impression on the community with this grand opening." Instead, also resolve to generate strong sales, attract media coverage, and sample new products.

Tailor the Event to Your Company

While you'll find several of the same kinds of events, remember that every company is different. You can certainly learn from other company's events, but you can't use their blueprint as your own.

What's Your Company's Big Idea?

While events can revolve around a big idea or the next big thing, many of the most effective kinds of events are actually, at their base, simple and common ones that benefited from a company infusing the event with its own inimitable spin. If you're trying to come up with that perfect idea—or a twist on a traditional one—visit Web sites such as *www.forbes.com* and *www.inc.com* for profiles of businesses that were so adept in orchestrating an event that it made the news (and many of the most impressive ones are quite cost-conscious). Further, use a Google search to find public relations agencies, and peruse case studies of some of the events they've completed for clients. Although the events you find won't be "one-size-fits-all" affairs, the accomplishments of those agencies can provide inspiration, a loose framework, and a firsthand account for getting the event job done well.

Understanding Your Event's Audience

For an event to achieve its maximum potential, you must also be specific about the audience you're trying to reach with the event. Don't be satisfied with the "I-want-to-appeal-to-everyone" approach. That tack tends to accomplish the exact opposite: Appealing to everyone prompts a generic outlook that will both soften your focus and cause any intended audience to feel they're not being spoken to. Sometimes your audience will be obvious: the employees at a company retreat, the participants at a business expo, your town's chamber of commerce at an upcoming meeting. But often—and particularly if you're the one conceiving, designing, and executing the event—your potential audience might be a bit fuzzy.

Sharpening Your Focus

Even if you think you're clear on the audience you want your event to appeal to, ask yourself these five questions:

1. Who are the people I'm trying to attract, reach, motivate, or influence with this event?
2. Why will they care about this event?
3. What are their wants and needs?
4. What specific action do I want that intended audience to take by coming to the event or after the event's over?
5. How will my event create that response?

Getting the Audience There

Now that you're specific about the audience you want to have at your event, how will you get them there? Different audiences respond to different kinds of invitations. As events are described and detailed in the following chapters, you'll get an idea of the ways audiences should be invited. But know that a one-size-fits-all approach can't be taken. Since you want the maximum response rate to your invitation (whatever form it may take) and the maximum attendance at your event, you have to come up with the optimal way to draw in your intended audience.

Events for Amping up Marketing and Sales

These events are the most obvious ones, so obvious, in fact, you might not consider them events. They are linked to occasions that spur sales—either directly or indirectly. They don't have to be overt in nature, but they should either drive traffic to your Web site or store, prompt product orders, or otherwise cause buying to surge.

Inside Track	Making Your Purpose Part of a Bigger One

No matter what business you might be in, I'm always struck by how events can play a reliable and starring part. Ideas for your company's events can come from companies anywhere and everywhere. For instance, for the past ten years National Construction Week (NCW) in the United Kingdom has offered a string of events for young people to see a variety of positions in the construction industry. In so doing, NCW offers a high-profile opportunity for businesses that want to be involved in it. For instance, this year enterprises such as nursery schools, construction and design firms, museums, and factories have sponsored events that are part of the week, allowing youths of all ages to participate in such projects as building a skyline out of newspaper, creating outdoor ping-pong tables out of concrete, and taking on-site tours.

Sponsored by a nonprofit organization, the multinational NCW (with companies of all sizes in England, Scotland, and Wales) generates interest and media coverage and is a big recruiter for the construction industry. With the overall event's success, NCW also positions itself to be a perfect alternative for companies that might not have the resources, time, and money to sponsor an event on their own to link in with this bigger cause.

Obviously the concept of NCW—wherein several companies come together for a greater cause—is nothing new. Consider big events that might be planned in your area. Can you make a name for your company by tying in with an event? It can be as simple as providing a company-sponsored float for a hometown parade (that both garners name recognition and inspires customer loyalty) or opting to have a booth to sell products at a local fair that benefits a worthy cause. (Your company, in turn, can donate part of the day's profits to the cause.)

These types of events include:

Sales—Categorized as "start of the season" or "new model" debuts; seasonal as in holiday or summer; time-of-day, such as "midnight madness" or "early bird"; or a simple discount, such as 10 percent off.

Trade shows—Participating in trade shows triggers sales with the trade audience. For instance, you would display your line of cards at a show that brought in retail gift store owners or your water softening system at a plumbers' conference.

Coupon giveaways—Through the media (such as in a newspaper) or a direct mailing, you encourage traffic or sales by offering a coupon for a discount or a free gift with purchase.

Direct mail—Use this strategy for an announcement to your intended audience, such as a store opening, a special rate decrease, or a coupon offer.

Radio promotions—In this event your company teams up with a media partner for an on-air contest or the station makes an appearance at your business for an upcoming happening; the crossover may involve buying advertising time on the outlet or providing some in-kind service for the exposure.

Web site promotions—If you run a Web site in tandem with your business (or your business is exclusively a Web site), events can do brisk business in the form of such enticements as free shipping, e-mailing coupons to previous and current customers, and buy-two-get-one-free offers.

Sampling and demonstrations—Either at your place of business or off-site at an expo or fair, you provide samples of your product for consumers to try or demonstrate your product's features in front of an audience.

Events to Start or Enhance Awareness

Most people tend to associate the word *events* with this category. These events are the ones that are often showy and require complex logistics, big budgets, and often incorporate such elements as theme, food, décor, and entertainment. They include:

Grand openings—They integrate food and festivities into an enterprise opening its doors for the first time.

Charity or fundraising initiatives—Working with a philanthropic organization to raise funds for its cause, these activities can take the shape of such diverse occasions as a sporting event, fair, or ball.

Black-tie affairs and galas—While these can also be associated with charity efforts, they may also be award ceremonies honoring an individual or an entire company, or the celebration for a company milestone.

Product launch parties—Simple or sublime, these introduce a new product to the audience most likely to generate buzz for it.

Banquets—Be they breakfasts, luncheons, or dinners, they usually include speakers and presentations and often honor an individual or all the attendees, celebrate a cause, or both.

Open houses—While they can have elements of a grand opening (such as food), they are sometimes goodwill gestures for a company, giving tours and fostering community interest. They are also a sales tool for real-estate agents to show homes on the market looking for buyers.

Receptions—A wide category, these are often hosted before or after larger events to cement networking efforts and honor individuals.

Press conferences—Hugely popular for businesses of all kinds, these are held to launch products, deal with sensitive company matters that need to be explained, and make important announcements to the media.

Events to Increase Productivity

With these events you're looking to expand your own knowledge base to better your business, gain contacts that will propel your business, inform employees, or foster enrichment and deeper understanding in employees of the company and its practices, customers, or products and services. The realm of productivity events includes:

Meetings—These regularly held events, usually for internal staff, are agenda driven and focus on a single topic. Depending on their importance, they can be off-site but typically occur on company property

Retreats—These are a series of interconnected meetings that, because of their sensitive nature, importance, or both, are held off-site so that distractions are kept to a minimum

Seminars—These educational sessions should address key issues facing employees to help them, for instance, connect with customers better or gain a deeper vision of their industry

---

The Name Game

As you can tell, events can take on many a name and mien. They don't all have to be "special events," but they also don't have to be the rote and routine. Whatever name they go by—meetings, seminars, clinics, promotions, galas— they should work individually and cumulatively to build, market, and showcase your business. The word *event* can be traced back to 1573 and, appropriately enough, is derived from words that mean "outcome."

Crossover Events

These events can take on enormous proportions and often draw on and include components of the other event categories: meetings, banquets, seminars, galas, and even trade-show elements.

Sometimes the terms *conventions*, *conferences*, and *expositions* (or expos) are used interchangeably. And, in fact, they do have many similarities—particularly since they almost always incorporate lots of those events from other categories.

Big-Picture Events

With these types of events, your company or enterprise (with you as the planner) may be charged with organizing an entire one, or your responsibility may entail organizing a meeting or minievent that's a part of a bigger one. (Or, at the very least, you'll be invited to one.) Learning about these grand-scale events is incalculably helpful in conceiving, designing, planning, and executing smaller ones.

Conventions and Conferences

Both conventions and conferences tend to be trade focused, meaning only people in a certain industry, belonging to the same organization, or who are employees of one company are invited to participate in the proceedings. Both conventions and conferences usually involve large meetings with many members present that then break up into many smaller meetings. Conventions can be very focused on industry matters, trends, and regulations and can often involve votes regarding certain issues.

Conferences, which can also involve both large and smaller meetings, are typically more focused on educating members on various topics that are both central and corollary to business at hand.

In both instances there is usually a theme that conveys the focus of the gathering and guides the event's varied components. In either case outside companies with products, goods, or services related to the convention or conference's agenda may be invited to set up vendor booths. Their participation is considered valuable for conference or convention attendees. (In many cases their participation, which includes a registration fee, helps defray costs for the convention or conference host or sponsor.)

Depending on the size and number of attendees, conventions and conferences are usually held in such venues as larger hotels, city convention centers, and on college campuses. They typically need a mix of large and small-size rooms for meetings, food services for meals and receptions, and sometimes a dance hall or ballroom for an entertainment event. In addition, they may need a large hall or space for vendors to set up booths or tables to show or sell products and display literature.

Expos

While expos concentrate on one theme or industry, they are open to the public. You don't have to be a member of the trade, industry, or company to attend. You'll often see them advertised in the Saturday newspaper for home building and home decorating, baby goods, and the like. While they may include seminars on trends and demonstrations of many products, they're usually focused on providing booths from many companies that have products pertaining to a certain industry that the general public can find out about and either buy on-site or obtain information to buy from a select supplier.

Identifying the Scope and Size of the Event

Once you've decided on the event you're planning on having or if you're surveying a few that you're considering, your next step will be crucial. As you give shape to your event, determining its focus, audience, and content, you'll need to be very clear about how much you want to cover or accomplish and how big or small the event should be. These components will be vastly affected by budget (which you'll learn about in Chapter 2), time (both yours and the date or dates of the event), and personnel.

While you may want to sponsor an industry-wide summit, be realistic, particularly if it's the first event you're attempting. Be ruthless in first assessing your goals, then in considering the necessary resources.

Where events are concerned, big isn't always better, and small isn't always piddling. While you'll want your reach to be considerable if you're conducting a Web site promotion, a dinner party will be more effective if it's done in a more intimate setting and on a smaller scale.

Social Versus Business Aspects

Companies regard events as social because many can be deemed "fun." Many events take employees out of the workplace, occur in stimulating environments, foster learning and enrichment, and center on meeting with community leaders and colleagues. But don't let the "fun" distract you from the business at hand. **As you begin drawing up your plans for the event, remember professionalism is always paramount.** You always want your company to shine in events that you undertake. While many events clearly have social aspects, that should encourage you to employ both professional acumen and personal panache.

In many of these events, if you're the host as well as the planner, your personality will be front and center. No matter how big or small, if it's at an industry lecture or a colleague's dinner party, never let go of your professional decorum. While many events will take place out of the office setting, you must still be on guard professionally or you'll lose the impact you're expecting the event to make.

Outlining Your Needs

Once you've got an idea of the event you're planning, start jotting down a loose structure for it. This document that you create shouldn't be viewed as the permanent be all and end all; it will serve as a working document you can continue to add to, edit, and refine. Whatever your event, this outline should include the following:

- The event's name, type, and goal
- The event's audience
- The budget
- A timetable
- Staffing
- How the event's results will be measured

You'll learn more about the budget, timetable, staffing, and measurable results in upcoming chapters and how to write a comprehensive action plan in Chapter 3. For now, keep in mind that this working document will be the guiding force for an event that will be well designed and adeptly implemented to enhance one or more company goals.

▶▶ Test Drive

Look at the business section of today's newspaper (or the home page of a news Web site). Identify an event that a company just had that impacted its business:

- Is the article favorable or not?
- What was the event?
- What was it designed to do? What were the goals?
- Did it succeed?
- Would the same kind of event have worked for your company? Why or why not? If it would, how would you tailor it specifically for your company?

PART **1**

What's in an Event?

The Budget's Purpose

Where events are concerned—and undoubtedly many other business initiatives, too—the budget can be the one component that sends the project off course, mitigates its success, or stops it from taking flight to begin with. Obviously while they're not always fun to contend with, budgets are necessary for events. They have plenty of purposes, the overriding one being that they will keep your event grounded in reality!

Like many ventures in a sound, well-run company, a budget must be implemented for an event. Never think that winging it financially is an appropriate course in tackling an event. **In the realm of events, you'll soon learn that unexpected costs arise—even when the budget's being vigorously tracked.** Without a budget tracker at the helm, line items can quickly spiral out of control, other ideas may be tossed in with abandon, and those previously mentioned unexpected costs (that will surely pop up) can throw the whole project asunder.

The budget can work in one of two ways: You can decide that you want to allocate a certain dollar figure to events, or you can devise some event ideas that seem to fit your company well and investigate what kind of money will be needed to make them work. The latter tactic is a smarter move because events have many sizes, shapes, factors, and—as you learned in Chapter 1—purposes, so simply assigning a budget (no matter how big) would be random. The only reason to take that tack would be to follow a past year's budget allocations for specific events that you will be tackling again in the new budget year. However, outside of trade shows and conventions that you are certain are regular annual events, you'll most likely want to vary your event schedule often from year to year to keep it fresh so that you can smartly target your customers and other audiences and reflect any changes in your business, products, or services.

Budget Line Items

As events vary, so will the budget line items that will be required for the event. Following is an extensive breakdown of categories—and the items within—that may be considered for your next event. As you look at each section, you'll realize that events can require many components all of which (unfortunately, sometimes) must be paid for.

Site Fees

Obviously if an event is on company property you have much more control over it and can eliminate the cost of renting another space. However, your office or property might not be big enough or conducive to an event's activities. In that case you'll have to scout out other locations, which may include a civic auditorium, a hotel meeting room, a community hall, or a complex's hospitality center.

Depending on the venue, other costs may be folded into this fee. For example, the site's management may also charge for city permits needed to hold the event, rental fees for equipment the site will need to host the event, parking, wages for additional labor, security detail, and, of course, the location's base rental fee. When considering a location you must ask questions about "hidden" fees; you don't want to be surprised when the final bill comes.

Remember, you can also think outside the box when it comes to a setting for your event. If you're holding your event at night, think about places that close at 5:00 P.M. but might be amenable to staying open and renting out their space to you for a small fee. Or you may know an art gallery owner who may enjoy the publicity an event might bring her place of business. Particularly if your budget is tight, be creative in brainstorming for venue possibilities.

Rentals

Unless your place of business hosts events regularly, you'll often need to supplement with items that may include registration tables, chairs, tents, staging (such as risers or stairs), stanchions, fans, and heaters.

When drawing up the budget, break down your event. Use a map of your event's site to determine what equipment you'll need to bring in to carry out your event's activities and to make all the participants comfortable.

Catering or Food Services

Will your event have food as a component? Will it feature a meal, cocktail hour, snacks, a dessert buffet? Food takes an event up a notch, making it more interactive for participants. Plus, when you're feeding guests, they tend to believe that you're taking extra care where they're concerned. Depending on the food you elect to serve, it can make an event more memorable.

However, food can get expensive, and besides the food and drink itself, other costs are associated with serving food. You'll have to also consider:

➲ Bartending fees
➲ Catering fees
➲ Equipment rental such as chafing dishes and ice coolers
➲ Furniture such as banquet tables, round tables, and chairs
➲ Accessories such as china, silverware, linens, and chair coverings
➲ Wait staff, cook staff, and gratuities for those personnel
➲ Health permits

Don't let those possibilities deter you from including food in your event. Even if you don't serve a seven-course meal, you can think about such budget-friendly foods as hot dogs and popcorn, a taco spread, an ice cream sundae bar, and chocolate fountains.

One caveat: Don't run out of food. Make sure your budget allows for having enough for everyone expected to attend. Not having enough food creates a memorable event of a different kind—one you don't want your company associated with.

Audio-Visual Needs

This takes in all the equipment you'll need to demonstrate a product for a large group of people, use materials for instruction, or listen to a speaker. These components include television monitors, DVD players, overhead projectors, PowerPoint assets (such as computer interfaces), slide projectors, lecterns, microphones, sound systems, digital cameras, digital photo presentations, and even flip charts and blackboards.

Depending on the complexity of the presentation and your own skills, you may also need to hire technical support to operate the equipment. (If so, that support will require a line item in this section as well.) Audio-visual equipment for events is addressed in its entirety in Chapter 5.

Entertainment

This line item refers to any fees relative to speakers, models who may be showcasing your product, a celebrity who's making an appearance, or a band or DJ you hire.

In addition, if you will be incurring costs associated with bringing that talent to your event or putting them in a hotel, make sure you account for that (although that will be in your transportation category). Your talent may have special requests you'd like to accommodate: tickets to a nearby attraction or a meal after a performance. Any request you fulfill should get a line item in the appropriate budget section.

Promotion, Advertising, and Publicity

No matter what your event, you will likely be calling on at least one—or possibly all—of the aspects of this trio in preparing or executing your event. For instance, to garner better attendance you may rely on newspaper, magazine, trade, radio, or television ads. You may also decide to send a direct-mail piece to increase exposure.

For the event itself you may want media in attendance, in which case you'll need to budget for press release distribution and possibly hiring a publicist to contact the media and conduct follow-up. You will also most likely need signage and banners, plus you may decide to have promotional items as a giveaway.

Design and Printing

For your event you may need such elements as a press kit, brochures, registration packets, posters, flyers, invitations, tickets, and programs. An event directly and powerfully benefits from a graphic identity that is created for it. So you may come up with a logo specifically for this event that will grace letterhead, business cards, nametags, and thank-you notes.

Even if you don't go with the recommended logo you will most likely need a graphic designer to conceive, illustrate, flesh out, and finalize some or all of those components. And, of course, you'll have to employ a printer to bring all those creations to life.

Cost Cutting for Design and Printing

The Internet brims with possibilities for budget-conscious printing. While it may not look like an engraved wedding invitation or feature raised copy, digital printing can be a shockingly inexpensive and good-looking alternative. Such companies as *www.vistaprint.com* and *www.4by6.com* provide a multitude of options. If you don't see exactly the piece you need, look at your choices from different angles. For instance, can your invitation actually be printed on a high-quality, satin finish postcard? In addition, many of these companies that cater to entrepreneurs and businesses with smaller staffs offer low-priced design services. Despite the reasonable prices and varied services, you'll be impressed with the polished, professional pieces. Just make sure to research beforehand any company you consider and get samples of their work to make sure their quality is commensurate with your standards.

Decorations

The décor that will enhance your event and create a festive environment belongs in this category, which includes centerpieces, flowers, backdrops for the stage and photo opportunities, candles, and balloons.

Again, scrupulously poring over your site's floor plan will help you determine what areas need to be dressed, where activities will occur, what space should be devoted to dining, and so on.

Transportation and Parking

Depending on the site of your event, you may have to make arrangements for parking, including valet service or lot attendants. In addition, you may also have to shuttle employees, VIPs, labor, or yourself to and from the site.

Travel and Accommodations

This area could possibly be one of your most expensive. If you are planning an event such as a training conference or promotional party in another city, you'll have to factor in such expenses as airfare, hotel stays, taxis, and car rentals. If you're flying people in for the event in your city, you'll have to factor in those costs to your event as well.

Personnel

In addition to those who are actually helping execute the particulars of the event—such as security guards, wait staff, or computer technicians—you may have fees relevant to consultants, registration staff, or an event manager. And you may be calling on the services of a lawyer, accountant, or photographer—all people who may be linked to event planning and implementation.

Administration

Finally, don't overlook the costs associated with organizing the event, distributing information for it, and conducting meetings to keep it on track. Have a budget that includes faxing, copying, overnight services, mileage, fees if you're using a service to distribute e-mail blasts, postage, and cell phone use (just to name some administrative items). You may tend to overlook these costs as just part of doing everyday business, but if they have to do with your event, put them in the budget.

Other Costs to Consider

Though the line item descriptions will give you a concrete idea of the myriad costs that could be involved, realize that—because every event is different—this list should only serve as your launch pad. Take the time to brainstorm about the other fees you may face that are specific to your event. For instance, you may be constructing an area—or an entire site—in hosting your event. In that case you'll need to take into account the cost of hiring a contractor and an electrician. If you want to provide a demonstration and need a sink to do so, but there isn't one in the space provided, you'll have to check with a plumber to determine your options and the costs associated with those options.

Contingency plans (discussed in Chapters 13 and 26) need to be accounted for in the sample line-item budget. For instance, if you need an alternate plan for your event if it rains, you need to find out the costs for a tent in which to host the event.

For most events you must secure event insurance. Some liabilities may be covered by your company's insurance. However, some may not, and you don't want to be at risk if your event suffers a calamity. Insurance can also help you avoid problems associated with event-specific inconveniences and catastrophes. For instance, if the speaker—the star of your event—is detained by a delayed flight, insurance will mitigate your financial obligations and give you peace of mind.

Extras Add Up

Not only should you have a budget that you plan to stick to, remember that unexpected instances will pop up. Allocate part of the budget to cost overruns and the like. Don't forget to put the extras in your budget that all too often are overlooked and stretch a tight budget beyond its means. Check and double-check estimates you receive, and ask about hidden costs that may show up later on a bill under such listings as a "surcharge," "service fee," or an "access fee." Don't forget such common items as tips, sales taxes, and shipping costs. These categories can add up quickly.

Angling for Income

Now the flipside: You may be designing your event in hopes of breaking even or making money. If so, on what are you pinning your hopes for income? Some possibilities may include:

- Sales of booth space for participants to reach your audience
- Ticket sales for admission to your event
- Registration fees for your event
- Sponsors or underwriters who have contributed money to have their name associated with the event

➢ Merchandise sales, such as books, T-shirts, or paraphernalia featured at the event

➢ Donated items that are auctioned off at the event

➢ Sales of advertisements in the event's program

If income is a part of your budget, you'll need to project how much money those profit centers will reap. While they may offset your costs, they will command a considerable amount of time and resources.

Drafting a Budget

As you comb through the list, pinpoint the line items you know will be necessary for your event. Stick to the categories listed here as that will help streamline your budget. Then ask colleagues—particularly those who have planned events—to look at your list. They may provide new insight and help allay your concerns about costs.

When you add items to your budget, you'll then need to assign estimated costs to them. Be thorough and do your research. If you're looking for a site that will hold 300 people, call different venues and ask for the availability and cost for the date you have in mind. Better yet, see if you can find the information online to whittle down possibilities. Then call your top choices to ask more specific questions.

If someone you know has executed a similar event, see if he or she will discuss the experience with you. That approach can provide a window into realistic costs.

Researching the various categories may seem tedious, but it's necessary. Fortunately the Web can be a valuable source for much of the information. If you can't reach people with information by phone, get e-mail addresses; sometimes they yield a much quicker response.

While assigning cost estimates to each category, be as specific as possible with those from whom you're trying to glean information. Give them such details as:

➢ Date, time, and approximate length of event

➢ Number of people you expect

➢ Event's purpose

➲ What you need from the vendor (for example, six banquet tables, graphic design services to create a logo, a keynote speaker, three dozen balloons for a store entrance, and so on)

Remember that the more specific you can be, the more accurate the quote you'll get. While you don't need to get too specific about balloons (besides their size and color), get very specific about a keynote speaker. Discuss the length of her talk, her preferred topic, and her past experience.

Don't Go It Alone

When it comes to setting up your budget, don't gather up a legal pad and a calculator. Embrace technology! Format your line items, estimates, and actuals into a grid using a program you already have—such as Microsoft Excel—or (if your budget allows) a product specifically designed to track money for events. Your accountant may have some suggestions about current options. Also check for the latest software at a computer superstore. Before purchasing it, do some research and ask questions of sales personnel about its ease of use and whether it fits in to your specific event or range of events, and visit both consumer and professional Web sites to garner feedback on the product.

Activating a Budget

Once you've made estimates in all your categories, add the numbers and see if the proposed budget is commensurate with your company's finances. At this juncture you must determine your priorities and may have to eliminate or scale back certain items. Interview potential vendors to decide which ones you want to work with and which will be most effective in helping you carry out your event.

Work Deals

In selecting vendors (further discussed in Chapter 4), you may find some that can fulfill the needs of an entire category. In that case you may be able to leverage lower rates or discounts. Besides saving money, you'll have fewer people to keep tabs on.

A Luxurious—and Inexpensive—Approach   `Inside Track`

A luxury gift company, catering to executives by sending its salespeople to meet with them, operates a Web site and wanted to maximize its holiday sales potential, though its business has no storefront. While it had a slim budget to try out a new venture, the company dealt creatively with the funds it had. The company held a holiday show to drum up increased business for executives and their colleagues—presenting the newest lines it represented and some popular current ones—the first weekend of November. The company secured a modestly priced suite at a trendy hotel for that Friday, Saturday, and Sunday. For its exposure to the company's clientele, the hotel even offered a discounted rate for the suite.

A few weeks beforehand the business sent snappy (but inexpensively produced) invitations to a list of current and potential clients, luring them with a promised look at the hottest gifts for Christmas and the New Year. Further enticements included a special weekend-only sale and the chance for customers to get all their shopping done in a comfortable environment before the season even started.

The company's line items were few. It paid for the suite and for refreshments, but tables to feature products were provided by the hotel at no extra charge. Additionally, companies the event organizers approached about showing products for the holiday show were all too happy to send samples for display. More business for the gift company meant increased orders for them, too!

The weekend was such a resounding success, sparking multiple orders and allegiance from several new clients, that the company made the event an annual affair and was often approached by additional potential customers about invitations to the next one.

Get All the Details in Writing

Once you decide on a vendor or vendors, get all details in writing. Make sure both parties know what they're agreeing to. Don't just sign a contract; read and review it. Get legal counsel if necessary. Make sure that you understand the monies agreed to, as well as the payment schedule. The contract should also specify deadlines, responsible parties, and contingency plans. (Contracts are discussed further in Chapter 4.)

Keeping a Budget on Track

Sticking to your event's budget means you have to be proactive. Ruthlessly stay on top of the budget in all aspects and categories. Hold regular meetings with those involved to assure yourself that line items aren't spiraling out of control. If costs are rising, be prepared to make cuts and prioritize further.

If these tasks seem overwhelming, you have two options:

1. If you can afford it, hire an outside professional who can make this his or her priority, freeing you up to be concerned with other event aspects.

2. Assign the job of budget tracker to someone trustworthy within your organization who shows aptitude in this area.

▶▶ **Test Drive**

Is money preventing your company from staging an event that could reap needed exposure and possible profits? Consider this approach:

➲ If money weren't an object, what's an event that you'd want to host or sponsor?

➲ What is the most expensive proposition involved in the event: location costs, entertainment, the sheer scale of the event because of the number you want to invite?

➲ Is there a way to hold the event in a less expensive but equally enthusiastic manner?

➲ For the next event you hold, use this exercise to scrutinize your costs and evaluate your line items.

Setting Up an Action Plan

An event never gets off the ground without crafting a master document—the action plan—that completely, descriptively, and concisely delineates the step-by-step process and an entire list of responsibilities that will turn the well-articulated concept into a successful event. An event action plan is your blueprint for making the event a reality. It's more than just a to-do list. **The best action plans include sections that delineate goals and objectives; describe the tasks to be completed before, during, and after the event; track budget and expenses; and measure results.** The event action plan is your all-in-one passport to your event, and it lets everyone in on how the event is being created, designed, and executed.

Getting Everyone on Board

Staffing (and hiring vendors) is discussed at length in Chapter 4, but for the purposes of your action plan, it's vital to have everyone working together as a unit to get the event up, running, and—in the end—successful. Too often people involved in an event operate in a vacuum. Certainly everyone involved doesn't need to know every detail, every bit of minutiae or confidential information. However, the success of your event will be greatly enhanced if people know how their task contributes to the overall execution. Unless you're arranging for a presidential visit, your event tasks don't need to be secret. Foster open communication between yourself and your employees who are helping plan the event. If you are spearheading an effort that requires you to separate event responsibilities under committee heads, institute frequent contact with them, and encourage them to communicate among themselves and within their own committees.

To-Do Lists

Much as you separated out budget line items, you should break your to-do lists into sections such as site needs, advertising and promotion, rentals, administration, and so on. From there categorize them under target time frames (nine to twelve months ahead, one week ahead). The to-do lists arranged by time frame later in this chapter provide an ample foundation for the event's action plan.

Assigning Tasks, Attaching Due Dates

Once you've assembled the team that will carry out the event and the myriad tasks that lead up to it, you'll need a detailed task list that includes the assignment or responsibility, the person responsible for accomplishing it, and—very important—the deadline for completing the task. Checklists must not only have a what; they must have a who and a when to accompany each item or the whole project will go off-course.

You'll get more information on staffing in Chapter 4, but for now, when putting together the definitive, ultraimportant to-do list, consider the team you've assembled. Does each person involved have at least one task? Does that person understand the importance of the task assigned and how it fits into the big picture? Is he or she the best person for a particular task?

In doling out due dates to each person, institute a logical order for the responsibilities to be completed. For instance, you can't set a menu until you hire a caterer; you can't determine decorations unless you have your site nailed down. Be cognizant of how other list items will be impacted if a deadline isn't met. Explain to everyone the repercussions of missing deadlines.

In addition, when you compile your master list, break out separate "per person" lists, which should include all the tasks and due dates for each person. This breakdown will allow you to determine if any one person on your team is overloaded, and it will give you an overview of assignments for each team member. These personalized lists are also important when conducting individual meetings with your team members to keep them focused and on task, and the lists allow you to see where they are in their progress and how this fits in with the overall picture.

| Inside Track | A Zoo of a Time |

In one of my first event-centered jobs I worked in the marketing/creative services department for Zoo Atlanta, now one of the nation's top zoos. At the time the zoo had just received an infusion of millions of dollars from the city and several corporations. Events were key in generating and continuing interest in the zoo's myriad planned exhibits and programs. A master timeline was conceived with the zoo's fundraising arm, which pinpointed when new exhibits would open, the celebrations that would herald each opening, and the fundraising events—such as an annual black-tie gala, "The Beastly Feast."

A zoo presents several unique challenges for event planning. In the zoo's case, the marketing department oversaw the planning of such events, but regular meetings had to be held with departments as diverse as education, veterinary, horticulture, physical plant, and maintenance to ensure that everyone was aware of their responsibilities and the timelines involved. For instance, to host a party for the opening of Flamingo Plaza, we had to make sure that—among other items on our checklist—the flamingos would be there, the landscape and waterfall would be completed, and the exhibit's entryway would be finished.

One timeline that we circulated was a ten-year projection for the zoo's exhibits and ensuing celebrations. Not that we held regular meetings about the entire upcoming decade, but that vision—though far ahead—kept us on course. We all knew successful events that pointed to the zoo's progress kept donors happy, kept more corporations inquiring how they could help, and were a point of pride for the city.

While events you're mulling over or planning don't have to have such far-reaching implications, be open to seeing how an event might create a long lasting impression for your enterprise. That vision—and having your entire team on board from the get-go—will bring order and triumph to your event plan.

Creating a Calendar

Once you have the action plan completed with all its separate to-do lists, convert the dates from the lists into a master calendar. The calendar will give a complete bird's-eye view of the project and make it easier for you to keep track of all the components. You can use blank pages from a hanging wall calendar or set up a dry-erase board. Either way, everyone can see—and you can keep track of—all the pieces of the event puzzle and how they are coming together in site, catering, vendors, entertainment, and other areas. This will help you head off possible conflicts and make sure all responsibilities have been assigned.

Maintaining the Schedule

Once that calendar is set, be ruthless in keeping on schedule. Check in with committee heads weekly. At the end of each week, conduct a thorough evaluation to monitor progress on all levels. Be vigilant and strengthen weak spots. The action plan should be a firm document, but it may change. Incorporate revisions as soon as possible, and refer to the action plan often. When changes are made to the plan, make sure they are reflected in the master calendar as well.

The Master Plan

The schedule that follows represents an optimal setup for to-do lists in your action plan. However, you may have to plan an event in a crunch, compressing this timeline of responsibilities. Depending on your event, you may not have to consider some of these, but review this entire list. In its breadth it may suggest responsibilities, areas, considerations, or items that you now realize you should include. This plan is general and offers both a wide-angle view and close-up look at the many needs you must keep in mind. The more—and the sooner—you nail down specifics, the greater chance you have of ensuring event success and keeping yourself good-natured in the process.

Get Real

In plotting out your action plan, listing out tasks and details, and putting down dates for completion, you'll have to estimate the time involved. Be as realistic as possible. Don't cram too much into a short time or expect a fast turnaround for a complex assignment. Keep in mind who you have assigned the tasks to: Does that person work at a methodical pace with few mistakes, or is he or she a speedy worker who sometimes has to revise his or her work?

Planning with Purpose: Six to Twelve Months Out

In these months your plan will be dedicated to establishing a hearty base to support your event's tactics and components.

Overall: Decide the event purpose. Choose a theme. Register the event date with the city.

Budget: Procure cost estimates across all categories. Get bids for such big-ticket items as entertainment, possible sites, catering, audio-visual (A/V) equipment, and design/printing. Draft the budget. Finalize bids and begin securing contracts.

Site: Visit potential venues and secure a written contract. Procure an enlarged site plan or room diagram for planning purposes.

Graphics: Select a graphic artist. Begin invitation design. Create the event logo. Order save-the-date cards.

Advertising/promotion/public relations: Set the schedule for placing ads, direct-mail pieces, e-mail blasts, and press release distribution. Make plans and secure a URL for the event Web site.

Administration: Determine and compile a mailing list for invitees. Investigate needs for permits, licenses, and insurance. If applicable, select committee chairpersons and committee members. Start meetings. Distribute save-the-date cards.

In the Throes: Three to Six Months Out

Duties and responsibilities will segue from the conception phase to work on elements for actual implementation.

Budget: Track the budget at weekly (if not daily) intervals.

Site: Finalize details pertinent to the event, such as designated ballrooms or meeting space and guest room allocations.

Food: Set the menu with the caterer.

Graphics: Review the invitations, programs, posters, and tickets with the graphic artist. Secure a printer.

Entertainment: Finalize the contract(s) for entertainment.

Content: Brainstorm, decide, and finalize all equipment entertainment will need.

A/V: Determine all A/V resources needed. Secure a vendor and finalize a contract.

Advertising/promotion/public relations: Follow the schedule previously set. Brainstorm and finalize pitch angles for media coverage. Distribute intermittent announcements to encourage attendance. Place ads in long-lead publications. Secure placements in calendar listings. Have the event Web site up and running.

Administration: Finalize the event mailing lists. Secure the permits and insurance.

Consider a Time Cushion

While all your action plan's endeavors should progress at a steady pace with competent people performing their tasks well, rarely does everything go as planned. In that spirit, consider implementing "catch-up" or "dark" days or weeks. Weekday television talk shows are usually in production for a few weeks then go "dark." During this week hiatus they generate ideas, tape segments for future shows, and catch up. In your month-to-month and week-by-week time-lines, insert a few days at strategic points to allow some breathing room and build in a cushion for tasks that have taken longer than expected or unexpected responsibilities that arise and need to be handled.

Stay the Course: Two Months Ahead

During this time you should keep a proactive, head-above-water approach in outlining your action plan's steps. If you feel you're juggling too many responsibilities, seek assistance and delegate to trusted parties.

Let your vendors know you need their help and want their assurances that responsibilities on their end are being tracked.

Budget: Keep rigorous track of the budget.

Atmosphere: Take note of all rentals and decorations needed. Secure vendors. Place preliminary orders.

Content: Set a tentative timeline for the day of the event and for the event itself.

Site: Conduct a walk-through. Address concerns that arise. Confirm times of the event—from setup to strike-down—with the site.

Travel and accommodations: Finalize these for the entertainment and, if necessary, staff involved.

Graphics: Review needs for signs at registration table or for directions. Order signs.

Advertising/promotion/public relations: Distribute releases regarding any celebrity or VIP involvement. Continue e-mail blasts.

Personnel: Determine your staffing needs. Sign up additional staff or recruit volunteers.

Administration: Finalize plan for sending out invitations.

The Countdown Begins: One Month to Go

At this point a relative calm should set in, and your action plan should be weighted toward confirmations. All your big decisions have been made regarding site, rentals, entertainment, and presentations, and you should focus on garnering and confirming attendance and publicity for the event. Still, keep frequent contact with those to whom you've delegated responsibilities and, of course, keep tracking the budget.

Food: Give estimates to the caterer.

Graphics: Receive delivery for all programs, posters, and other collateral. Check to ensure their accuracy.

Entertainment: Confirm details of their participation.

Travel and accommodations: Prepare itineraries to include dates, arrival and departure times, confirmation numbers, and phone numbers for airlines and hotels.

A/V: Confirm the equipment list.

Atmosphere: Confirm rentals and the decorations list and the time these items will be delivered on-site.

Content: Set the final agenda. Have all scripts written. Determine the welcome packet contents, and assemble them.

Advertising/promotion/public relations: Place newspaper ads. Follow up with the news media. Submit copy for public service announcements (PSAs).

Personnel: Confirm staff/volunteer participation.

Administration: Meet with all outside vendors to coordinate all details. Follow up on the invitation list to track attendance and RSVPs. Compose a complete day-of-the-event itinerary detailing arrivals and departures, program elements, setup and cleanup.

The Days Leading Up to It

During this phase your action plan still concentrates on confirmations but is moving toward the execution of your event.

One week before the event you should include plans to:

- Hold committee meetings
- Confirm the number attending
- Hold a final walk-through of the site and schedule rehearsal
- Go over the event diagram, and make sure each area will be set up properly and adequately staffed
- Schedule pickups and deliveries of rentals, decorations, and A/V equipment
- Finalize the catering guarantee
- Distribute e-mail blasts

➲ Distribute timelines, itineraries, and scripts to program participants

➲ Confirm media attendance

➲ Establish amount of petty cash for event day, and prepare checks for vendors

The Event Day

For this day, focus on checking and double-checking all equipment arrivals. Make sure that all program participants and staff have arrived, review final details with the caterer, ensure that all A/V equipment is in working order, and conduct a mental and physical walk-through of the event's entire schedule.

Your action plan should include a complete itinerary for the day of the event. It's not uncommon for odds and ends to pop up on event day that weren't included in your action plan. Because of that your best recourse is to be as organized as possible so that when an emergency or inconvenience does occur you have the time and attention to devote to it.

Immediately after the event, check all equipment that is to be returned, pack and inventory all your event supplies, undertake a financial reconciliation that includes reviewing all invoices to make sure you were billed correctly, and prepare a list for thank-you letters that need to be written and sent.

It's Not Over Til It's Over

Once the actual event is over there are postevent activities that can't be overlooked. On the master plan, make sure a person is assigned to complete those as well. Prepare for these tasks before the event occurs. For instance, in the case of such responsibilities as writing and sending thank-you notes, draw up a list of names and addresses for those that will be receiving one. Consider having the stationery for them preprinted with your event's (or company's) logo when you have other materials designed and printed.

After the Event

It's easy to breathe a sigh of relief and consider the event over once the last attendee leaves. However, some of your most important work will occur once the event's over. This work is in addition to breaking down backdrops, returning equipment, and making sure all vendors are paid—tasks that are also important.

To extract every benefit from your event, make sure that your action plan includes a date for a thorough debriefing of the event. While that doesn't have to take place at midnight on event day when everyone's fatigued, this evaluation should occur within a few days (and not more than a week) after the event's finished. All the details should be fresh on everyone's minds. For this meeting include all key top personnel involved in planning and execution.

An event analysis is discussed at length in Chapter 12. The meeting will collect opinions and information about the success of the event:

➲ Were expectations met?
➲ Was the budget met, and where might money have been saved?
➲ What were attendees' reactions?
➲ How was media coverage?
➲ Were the vendors competent?
➲ Should the company hold such an event again?

Tailor These to Your Event

Timeline elements in this chapter are suggestions. A caterer you're working with may need an estimate a week (rather than a month) before. A popular hotel may need much more notice to book a meeting room. And some vendors may accept a credit card, while others need to be paid with a money order. In addition, responsibilities listed here may be exactly what your event needs and may need to be fleshed out or scaled down. As you create your own action plan, keep in mind your company's goals and objectives for the event and how the event will help your company in the long run.

▶▶ Test Drive

Think about an event you recently attended, such as a store sale, a grand opening, or a meeting:

- ➲ For everyone to be there, which task would have had to be planned the furthest in advance?
- ➲ Is there a task that you noticed that if performed would have enhanced or elevated the event?
- ➲ Is this an event that you might want to explore having for your business?
- ➲ If it is an event that would work for your business, what responsibilities or tasks would have to be revised, added, or deleted to make it successful?

Breaking Down the Event

While you may be personally responsible for an event on a small scale—such as a meeting for twelve or a luncheon for six—many events would be impossible to carry out without the help of others. Once you have the responsibilities carved out and clearly delineated in a to-do list, you have to determine who can accomplish tasks, whom you can delegate to, what responsibilities can be outsourced for maximum effectiveness, and which ones should be turned over to a vendor. This chapter looks at the best way to staff your event with employees, volunteers, vendors, and temps.

First you need to look at your master to-do list.

➲   Which duties do you know will be assigned to a vendor?
➲   Which responsibilities are you the only person who can fulfill?
➲   Which tasks can be delegated to your staff?

Now consult your master calendar. Looking at the responsibilities you've delineated as your own, can you complete them in the time allocated to your and the event's satisfaction?

Outsourcing Strategies

In analyzing your action plan, pinpoint areas that you know are beyond your realm. Even those responsibilities you think you can handle for a one-time-only occasion may require more knowledge than you expected. They'll most certainly include an array of costs you might not have realized would have to be factored in. For instance, while it may sound fun to come up with a menu and serve 100 people, and you think you can do it more cheaply out of your own kitchen, caterers have already done much of the homework that you'd be attempting for the first time. They have proven dishes to choose from, know how much food is needed, own necessary equipment such as chafing dishes, and have available staff for serving.

An Entrepreneur's Dilemma

On more than one occasion I've been called to help in the following scenario: an entrepreneur of a thriving retail store/ice cream shop/printing business/spa/Italian restaurant/real-estate office (I could go on) has planned an amazing event to spotlight his or her enterprise with an occasion such as a grand opening, an open house, or a tour for the media.

In each instance the entrepreneur—though sterling in his or her business sense and savvy—had taken on far too many responsibilities for the upcoming event. In fact, each had decided he or she could take on the entire event alone with no help. With the event fast approaching, each one discovered there was no way the event could be successfully accomplished: too many people were coming, too little food was being prepared, no programs were arranged, A/V equipment was unordered, and signage was inadequate.

If you're ever in a situation like this, remain calm. Even with just a few days left before an event, all is not lost. In each of these situations I first assessed the current state of affairs. I determined what was missing, what was in crisis mode, and what would turn out fine as is. Similarly, someone you call in can lend you that all-important objective view and help you make quick—but responsible—decisions to hire temps and necessary vendors, and locate and schedule needed equipment.

Above all, try to get people on board who can help out sooner than later. A team approach frees you from the burden of carrying an entire event and enables you to determine needs you may not have considered. Even if you feel like you have little or no budget for help, at least try to call in some favors with friends. Remember too that an unprofessional looking event impacts negatively on your business while a wonderful one will more than likely pay you back for any expenses you doled out for hiring.

For your event to be successful you must be realistic about your time and capabilities. While some tasks seem ultraeasy, they may also be time-consuming. For instance, you could handle putting together 100 press kits, but you could turn that over to an intern (or hourly temp). Your time is better suited to devising the program agenda, writing a speech, and deciding who should sit next to whom at the head table—tasks you'd have a harder time farming out.

Possible Duties to Outsource

First concentrate on those areas on the to-do lists of your action plan that require outside vendors, such as:

➲ Graphic design for the logo, invitations, and collateral material
➲ Catering, including food, beverages, and dessert
➲ Entertainment, such as a speaker or music, to be featured as part of the program or in the background
➲ Technical services, including setting up and running Power-Point presentations, video, and the necessary A/V equipment involved
➲ Mass-produced giveaways to be used as party favors or for promotion during the event

Next consider if the following responsibilities can be passed onto someone else. You may be able to delegate these tasks or bring temporary help on board:

➲ Soliciting ticket sales
➲ Confirming attendance and collecting RSVPs
➲ Distributing e-mail invitations and reminders
➲ Handling publicity
➲ Assembling/collating invitations, welcome packets, itineraries

Outsourcing Sources

Where do you turn if you've decided to outsource some responsibilities? Collect referrals vigilantly. Every city has more than one company that rents tables and chairs, provides background music, sets up A/V equipment, and publicizes events. If you're having trouble getting referrals for trusted companies, consider this tack: Suppose you've been to an event and admired how it was presented. Find out who was in charge of it and talk to that person about vendors he employed. People appreciate their work being noticed. More than likely, all you have to do is pick up a phone and ask for a few moments of that person's time and her knowledge and referrals will come tumbling out.

If you're still stumped for ideas, consult ads and the Yellow Pages. But don't just hire someone on the spot or over the phone without conducting a thorough interview. After explaining your needs, consider asking the potential hire these questions:

- ➲ Have you had experience with a similar event?
- ➲ If so, what was it and what were your responsibilities?
- ➲ Did you stay within budget parameters? Did you meet deadlines?
- ➲ What's typically the biggest challenge you face?
- ➲ How long have you been in business?
- ➲ Who would be your company's primary contact?
- ➲ Do you have suggestions or ideas within your area of expertise for making the event better?
- ➲ Can you provide three references to contact?

Listen to the potential vendor's responses, and—if meeting in person—watch his or her body language. If the vendor seems resistant or too busy to answer your questions, interview others. Even if someone comes highly referred, if you feel the vendor isn't a good fit, check in with your instincts and don't force the issue.

Is Your Vendor Listening?

For certain vendors—such as graphic designers, sign and banner makers, and even rental companies—you should peruse a catalog, portfolio, or Web site containing their work or products. These materials should include highlights or information about past events they've been involved with. When reviewing, decide if his or her work has a generic feel to it, meaning that the vendor has relied on the same style, feel, or color in his or her efforts and keeps a look that isn't specific to any client, just continually warmed over for a new one. In your planning and execution you want energetic, spirited, committed vendors who are intent on making contributions that make the event your own.

Soliciting Bids for Vendors

Depending on the size of the job, you may decide to collect bids from more than one vendor to do a certain job. If so, consider issuing a RFP (request for proposal). The RFP is discussed in detail in Chapter 10. An RFP includes all the services and products that you require from a vendor in a specific area (such as rentals, catering, or venue). The document will outline your needs, ask the potential vendor how he would fulfill those needs, and include a submission of the proposed cost. To keep your timing on track, the RFP—or any request for a bid—must include a deadline for bid submission. If a potential vendor doesn't come through in this aspect, you already know that it would be undependable for an event.

Recruiting Other Help

For those responsibilities you've tagged for outsourcing but that need someone with less professional experience you can call on temp agencies. If you go this route, explain the type of work you need performed and your expectations for the temps who are sent to you.

In addition, consider college interns to help with your event. Many can be exceptionally adept; they're further motivated by getting hands-on experience in an area or for a company that dovetails with their major.

A Professional Event Planner to the Rescue?

If you're so inclined and in a time crunch, you can turn the entire project over to a professional event planner. If you decide to go that route, be prepared to factor her fees into your event cost. In addition, you should follow the same hiring practices as you would to employ any vendor: ask questions about her experience that would be particularly pertinent to your event, find out if she or a member of her staff will be your primary contact, and check referrals. More so than other vendors, you'll be working with the event planner very closely. Make sure your personalities mesh and that she has a clear vision for the event, its goal and purpose, and its place within your company objectives. Finally, ascertain from the start whether the event planner is listening to your needs. Confirm that she is intent on designing and executing an event that is consistent with your image and company, not creating one that the planner has simply been determined to add to a portfolio.

Working with Vendors

Particularly for bigger events, you will most likely be using at least one vendor, so you should rigidly stick to a few guidelines in finding and employing them.

Check References

When you decide to hire a vendor, don't underestimate the need to check references. A vendor may be friendly and seem fun to work with, but that doesn't necessarily speak to his or her past work experience. Unfortunately many good-natured vendors don't do their job well; conversely, many vendors with muted personalities are stars when it comes to outperforming contract responsibilities, handling crises, and overall exceeding expectations.

Contact references and ask specifics regarding the vendor's duties: how they were fulfilled, if deadlines were met, if final billing was consistent with estimates, and if the reference would recommend the vendor to others. Keep the conversation professional and grounded in facts. Aside from vetting that this vendor is worthy to carry out tasks, references can also alert you to potential problem areas.

Vendors Are Your Freelancers

When outsourcing you can't abdicate responsibility for the task on your action plan just because it's been assigned. You have to treat all freelancers as employees, checking in with them, holding them to deadlines, and ensuring they share an overall vision for the event.

To that end, make sure that you establish regular check-in times: weekly meetings, e-mails, or phone calls that monitor progress. The meeting doesn't have to be long, but you should get assurances that they're handling tasks assigned and look (or listen) for red flags. Usually those will make themselves known if the vendor doesn't have an answer for a question or some task is continually put off from week to week. Use your common sense in sussing these culprits out. If a vendor seems unproductive, don't ignore it. Delve more deeply. Firmly, but gently and professionally, analyze the situation and devise a solution for getting the work done.

If a vendor isn't meeting your standards, don't jump to conclusions and threaten legal action right away. Vendors have bad weeks and may take on too many projects at once, stretching themselves too thin. More than likely they want to keep you as a happy customer who will employ them again and refer them to others. Give them the chance to rectify the situation.

The Importance of a Backup Plan

If things go wrong with a vendor, escalate your concern and involvement and come up with a backup plan. Often you won't need to use the plan, but be prepared to switch vendors if the warning signs light up.

In the end, you hire vendors, but the success of the event rests with you. When the event happens, no one will want to hear you play a blame game for a situation that went awry—particularly one that could have easily been averted with some foresight and dedication to charting assessments.

Negotiating Tactics

While you never want to use strong-arm tactics or low-balling in signing on vendors, you are completely within your right to examine some possibilities concerning discounts.

Treat your vendors as allies, not adversaries. From the get-go you should be fair and professional; this will help you manage your vendors and contribute to the success of the event. Imagine if you both feel as if you had been dragged through the mud to reach a deal. That hardly sets the stage for a healthy working relationship.

Give the potential vendor a thorough (but brief) review of your event. Are there other areas that the vendor has experience in? Obviously the more business you're willing to give the potential vendor, the more areas he or she is likely to find that can be discounted or thrown in for free. Securing a hotel as a site offers the easiest example of an economies of scale approach. While you approach the hotel (a proposed vendor) with at least one goal in mind—securing a space big enough for an awards reception—hotel management may be able to fulfill other event needs you have. The hotel has a meeting room you can use, access to a catering department, guest rooms for people to stay in if need be, and a shuttle to and from the airport if necessary. Staff at the hotel may also know of an opportunity for you to share in A/V costs with another organization that is booking a ballroom or meeting space before or after your event.

A party supply company you contact will have chairs and tables you can rent, and it may also have balloons and helium tanks for your decorations and a music system for your entertainment.

Try to use each vendor to its fullest extent. When you do, you should be able to leverage costs. If you agree to give a vendor as much business as possible, you can entice that vendor to give you a discount on certain fees or agree to perform some services at no charge.

If a vendor can only fulfill one item on your to-do list, consider other tactics for discounts or reduced fees. Perhaps you can give her an ad in your event's program, have her provide a sign you can put up in your place of business for free advertising, or provide a hot link to her Web site on yours.

While you should be open to novel—and always fair—arrangements, be organized in your approach. Be certain of your needs, then negotiate from there.

More than likely, if you're committed to keeping costs in line you'll be able to find some solution that both parties agree will be mutually beneficial. Finally, make sure that the end result of the negotiation is in writing and that both parties have signed off.

Negotiating Further

Since negotiating the best deal to keep costs in line and find mutually beneficial opportunities can be an integral part of event planning, you may want to delve deeper and brush up on your tactics even further. The books *Getting to Yes*, by Roger Fisher, William L. Ury, and Bruce Patton, and *Bargaining for Advantage: Negotiation Strategies for Reasonable People*, by G. Richard Shell, offer advice and examples on real world negotiating strategies. The latter contains a section on conducting highly effective negotiating through e-mails and instant messaging.

Accountability and Responsibility

When dealing with staff delegation and vendor hiring, make sure you have made every person's responsibilities clear. As you assign responsibilities, be cognizant of any warning signs or red flags that may indicate your communication isn't being understood. Ask questions. Pick up on any body language or questions from those receiving assignments that make you think someone may be confused or unsure.

When you sign on a vendor, you must have a signed paper. Don't trust specifics and agreements to a phone call or an e-mail. Put down in writing in a contract such details as expected responsibilities, the particulars of fulfillment, a payment schedule, and all deadlines.

For vendors, staff members, or volunteers, you can also consider incentives—financial or otherwise—tied in to deadlines. If you have a particularly aggressive timeline, incentives are extremely motivating. In the end, they can keep you sane as you see vendors repeatedly meet deadlines in a timely manner.

To make sure that everyone's on track, conduct regular meetings leading up to the event. Each meeting should have a clear agenda; ask for status reports on each area. Similarly, have regular check-in calls (or e-mails) to address concerns, track progress, and ensure everyone is steadily working toward completing their mission for event day.

Dealing with No-Shows

On the day of an event, no-shows can be a particularly woeful problem. Staff presents one area of concern, and a missing vendor can throw an entire part of your program off track.

Plan for What You Can

It often seems as if the one area you didn't cover, or the person who was your most reliable, is the component that falls through. While having a backup plan to deal with every conceivable mishap is impossible, you need to plan ahead. Your vendor contracts should stipulate backup plans in case of an emergency. If the vendor can't fulfill his responsibilities the day of the event, what will be the alternate course of action? Does the vendor have a colleague who you can call upon? If the equipment that is delivered malfunctions, who can you contact to replace it?

Recruit a few volunteers who can help out at a moment's notice on the day of the event if they are called. If you have the budget to pay them, do so. At the very least, offer them meals, and follow up with a small gift or a token of appreciation for coming through for you at the last minute.

Confirmations and Call Times

On the day prior to the event, assign someone to call and e-mail all staff and vendors to confirm the specifics of arrivals and delivery times. For a cushion, issue call times that are at least fifteen minutes before that person or vendor is actually supposed to arrive.

For the event day, assign someone to contact people immediately who aren't present at their call time. Emergencies do happen; alarm buzzers don't go off. Sometimes people just need a few extra minutes to show up. However, if contact isn't made with the missing person or vendor within a half hour, you can call in backup that you've previously arranged. For other suggestions and discussions on the particulars of contingency plans, consult Chapters 13 and 26.

▶▶ Test Drive

In preparation for your next event, consider your and your company's strengths and weaknesses in determining the vendors you would need:

- ➲ What capabilities and resources already exist within your company that could be efficiently used?
- ➲ Is there an event you can think of that wouldn't need any outside help?
- ➲ What event-related needs are completely out of your company's realm?
- ➲ To meet those needs, begin collecting a list of possible vendors to call in when your next event starts to take shape.

PART **1**

What's in an Event?

Surveying Your Event's Prime Elements

Having broken your event down into its components, you'll undoubtedly realize at least one or two (and possibly several) opportunities to use audio, video, or both. While you may not feel technologically proficient, don't eliminate these elements from your event because they intimidate you. On the most basic level remember a speaker will need a lectern and microphone to present and be heard. If the audience is large, you'll need monitors so they can see the presentation.

Think of any visual or audio mode that may enliven or enhance your event. For instance:

- Collect ideas using a flipchart during a meeting.
- Illustrate your point with a video presentation.
- Add zest with enlarged photos for a new product launch.
- Punctuate a scene through background music at a reception.

Incorporating Images to Make an Impact

Your event may be a simple one-hour meeting or a four-day industry conference. However long and involved or short and brief it is, you should be very succinct in assessing and analyzing the event's focus, reach, and audience. Then determine the best ways to bring your message across to that audience. **Don't settle for only words when they can make more of an impact accompanied by images.** Don't rely on a handout when a voice giving life to the words on the page will make them more memorable.

To make the most use of your time, the participants' time, and the money being spent on your event, figure out the audio and visual elements that will take your presentation to the next level.

The Initial Assessment

As you head into the A/V territory, review your agenda and pick it apart to examine where equipment may fit in. You'll have to ask both general and specific questions to ascertain your needs. Initially you'll need the event's location, the room's size, the date or dates of the event, and a rough idea of the number of people who will attend. More specifically, pinpoint possibilities for A/V equipment. Are you:

- ➲ Delivering a particularly complicated message, explanation, or instruction?
- ➲ Featuring a demonstration of some kind?
- ➲ Seeking to spotlight a particular person, product, or cause?
- ➲ Attempting to foment excitement for a cause?
- ➲ Building camaraderie or rapport among peers?
- ➲ Trying to impress your audience?
- ➲ Navigating audiences with different agendas in the same room?
- ➲ Covering several topics in a single session?
- ➲ Working to seamlessly segue from one topic to the next?
- ➲ Presenting a single speaker, more than one speaker, or an entire panel?
- ➲ Facilitating questions from an audience?

Making Technology Work for You

Within each of the points of your agenda, do you see possibilities for introducing an A/V element? In your review, think about events, meetings, and presentations that you've attended. Which have been most effective? Why were they successful? Which completely lost you or bored you? What prevented you from being drawn in? Now that you've got a handle on different facets of your event that could benefit from audio-visual equipment, you can identify the kinds of equipment that will best suit your purposes.

You'd be amazed at the ways in which technology can enhance an event. You may have rusty notions of overhead and slide projectors and reel-to-reel tape recorders, or a whiz-bang perspective of panoramic video views, thundering booming sound, and whirling lights.

Don't go for break-the-bank components just because they sound like a good idea or may look impressive. Have a game plan, and stick with the elements that will best get the message across to your audience.

A Technology Primer

You might not realize the technology available to beef up or complement your event, or you may be overwhelmed by the choices. Unless your company is in the A/V business, you'll likely use a vendor to supply your needs. Before you hire such a vendor you need to become familiar with key terms and equipment. Doing so will save you time and money. And remember, technology is ultraspeedy. While microphones and projectors may never be out of vogue, models and features update frequently. To fully understand how and where the A/V components could best serve and enhance your event, review this rundown of popular equipment.

Audio Equipment

When people think about the audio for events, meetings, or programs, microphones typically come to mind. In selecting the appropriate microphone, you have several options. For instance, a portable lectern may include its own microphone and sound system. If the presenter will be walking around the room or among the audience, he or she will need a wireless mic. If you're taking questions from audience members, you may need to station standing microphones in each aisle. If you're hosting a panel discussion with panelists seated behind a table, you will need tabletop microphones. If the panelists are simply seated in chairs, they will most likely use lavaliere microphones that fasten to their clothing.

But your audio needs may not stop at the microphone. You may need to consider:

- Amplifiers and speakers
- Conference/speaker phone for hands-free telephone conferencing
- Cassette tape recorders
- Sound mixers, for using multiple microphones
- Sound systems for music
- Walkie-talkies

Visual Equipment

Visual gear can be divided into low tech and high tech. Low-tech visual aids don't need to be plugged in to show off to your audience.

On the low-tech end you may want to use a blackboard or a flip chart to list ideas or notes. You may need a stationary podium for someone to stand behind to make a speech. To give someone a clear picture of the inner workings of a new product you may need to enlarge a diagram or a photo. Or you may use a laser pointer to highlight a detail in a map or drawing.

On the other end of the spectrum, high-tech visual paraphernalia is usually more complex and exciting in its awesome capabilities, but it can be confusing to operate. Some visual components you might call on for your event or meeting include:

➲ Camcorders or mini DV cameras for recording
➲ Electronic whiteboards for converting what's written on a whiteboard into printable text
➲ DVDs or VCRs for playing video footage
➲ Laptop computers for displaying PowerPoint presentations and projecting images and copy
➲ Overhead projectors for presenting transparencies
➲ Portable document cameras for projecting documents through projectors or on monitors
➲ Scan converters, which changes the video output from a computer to standard TV signals, allowing a regular television to be used as a computer
➲ 16 mm projectors to showcase film footage

While some projectors were previously mentioned (such as overhead and film projectors), projectors of very different kinds have become a routine fixture for events and meetings. Slide projectors, which would show slides from 35 mm prints, were previously the standard visual. Although they are still used, projectors have entered a new age and the category is often referred to as "image projectors."

A speaker with a computerized or multimedia presentation may use an LCD (liquid crystal display) projector, which hooks up to a computer and then displays a program in bright, clear images. Rear screen projectors are positioned behind the screen so the projector is invisible to the audience. Other recent advances include DLP (digital light processing) projectors and LCOS (liquid crystal on silicon) models. While you could become well versed in the properties that differentiate them—which include spinning mirrors, glass panels, color panels, crystals, and more—you should be more familiar with the size and dimension of your room, location of the venue, presentation area, and the number of people in the audience (aspects of which are examined more thoroughly later in this chapter). You should also know that projectors have a wide range of superior features, such as digital zoom, capabilities that allow a computer card to take the place of a laptop to run a presentation, and keystone correction, which negates the flare or skewing of a projected image.

For the projector itself, be prepared to talk with your vendor or supplier about such aspects as how bright or dim the room will be, if the projector needs to be portable, and how sharp or detailed the images presented will need to be. Brightness, resolution, and weight are the three components that will determine the type of projector you'll need and what the cost will be.

Licensing Music and Video

As you determine your A/V equipment, consider any intricacies your content may present. For instance, if you use music or video for your event from another source, you must get permission to feature it in a public venue. If you want to welcome attendees to a conference by playing a former Top 40 hit, copyright laws dictate that you'll need to pay a usage fee. If you're in this situation, check out the Web sites for BMI (*www.bmi.com*) and ASCAP (*www.ascap.com*), which collect and distribute royalty fees to the recording artists and songwriters they represent.

Similarly you can't just pop in a DVD to show an audience a scene from a movie to illustrate one of your points. Sometimes a fee to use a video will be waived if the clip is being rebroadcast for an educational purpose or if it garners publicity for whomever the clip's rights belong to. For rights, check with the DVD's distributor (their information can usually be found right on the DVD's packaging).

Costs and the Extras That Add Up

Not surprisingly, cost may affect your choices in audio and visual equipment. Wireless mics are more expensive than corded ones. An LCD projector will cost more than a slide projector. As you procure estimates to determine your A/V budget, review your options and set priorities. Don't sacrifice quality for cost. If the least expensive projector doesn't crisply display an important set of charts, your entire presentation suffers and negates any savings on rentals.

Don't forget the essentials that may seem so routine you don't realize that they cost, too. Items such as VCR carts, easels for flip charts, tripods for digital cameras, and stands for projectors aren't likely to be included in an item's rental; it will be broken out separately in a bid, estimate, and invoice.

Positioning and Dressing

In Chapter 6 you'll delve into the particulars of logistics and staging. For now, be cognizant of how some of your A/V equipment will need to be set up. In your site's diagram, map out where equipment will be stationed (and where the people who will be operating it will stand or sit).

You may need bunting (or drapes) for a monitor's stand so that unsightly wires don't detract from what's shown on screen. To address this problem you may also want to go for wireless technology as often as possible so you don't have to hide cords or keep them out of harm's way.

Focusing on Audio-Visual Needs

With knowledge about the different kinds of equipment available, you can start to piece together a list of the necessities for your event or meeting. Make notes for each part of your agenda, deciding which of the above audio-visual equipment will help you have a more successful, impactful event. Don't become wedded to your notes just yet, but brainstorm to create this first pass on your A/V needs. Don't be overly concerned with specifics at this stage. You may know that you need

| Inside Track | The Power of A/V |

The sheer capabilities of A/V technology and equipment—when used appropriately—can satisfy many a goal for an event. In fact, without A/V some events can't fulfill their goals at all.

My most intensive A/V experiences have been in network presentations for TCA, a semiannual convention of the nation's television critics. During each three-week event, networks take turns presenting programming highlights for the upcoming months, which are often designed to wow and dazzle but most of all to inform.

Each of these presentations is a production in its own right. They often consist of video clips or trailers (or both) of the network's upcoming sitcoms, dramas, telefilms, reality shows, or specials followed by panel discussions in which stars, producers, and network executives take questions from critics in the audience. The presentations require monitors (sometimes very large ones) to screen the clips, a projector to show the clips, a podium and mic for the executive introducing the presentation, lavaliere mics for the panelists, and cordless mics for the critics to ask questions from wherever they're sitting in the audience. That doesn't include the sound mixers, speakers, and computer programs that have to be figured into the equation.

Occasionally a sought-after celebrity for a high-profile project won't be available to fly to Los Angeles for TCA. In those instances a satellite hookup is arranged during the session that serves as a video conference call of sorts so that the critics in Los Angeles can ask questions and the talent can answer them (in wherever location he or she may be).

Needless to say, because of the varied, integral components involved in such a presentation production, rehearsals are a necessity, as is capable, competent staff (and vendors) to operate the equipment and—very importantly—troubleshoot. While your next event might not rely quite this heavily on A/V, figure out if it will achieve a goal in a way you hadn't considered and if it will elevate your event in any way. Make sure its functioning is smooth and precise, using rehearsals and superior tech support.

microphones and an image projector of some sort; you don't have to know which one right now.

Once you have that preliminary list in hand, you'll be ready to take the next step in getting help to fulfill it.

Examine the Area, Analyze the Program

In exploring the equipment you'd like to have at your meeting or event, you must thoroughly assess the space that will host it. In a conference room, which way will everyone be facing? In a banquet hall, in what configuration will the tables be set up, and how far apart will they be spaced? Where will the speaker or entertainment be presenting?

Diagram the room for an optimal look. Determine sightlines for all the participants. How can your program be presented for maximum effectiveness? Will there be multiple program components, each requiring its own audio-visual needs?

Next check out the actual space available. If you're considering a projection screen, is there room for it? If you're planning to project large-screen images, will there be enough distance from the projector to the screen?

How many people should be accommodated? Will any presentation have more than one speaker? If you're holding a panel discussion, how many people will need microphones?

Finally be creative but don't feel the need to reinvent the wheel. If possible, procure ideas, diagrams, and notes from previous events held in the space to determine the components and parameters that worked for them.

The A/V Vendor

As previously discussed, you will most likely be hiring an A/V vendor who can guide you through an assortment of audio and visual options for your meeting or event. When interviewing potential vendors, be prepared. Have a list—at least a rough one—already mapped out of equipment you think you'll need, your room's dimensions, a diagram of the space if possible, and questions that address any of your concerns or interests in certain equipment you'd like to know more about.

Ideally—and certainly if you don't have a working knowledge of A/V equipment—the vendor can analyze your event's needs. Event experts simply hand the vendor a list of A/V needs. However, if events aren't a routine part of your job or responsibilities, you'll benefit from finding a vendor who becomes an active participant in your event planning, not just an order taker.

A/V equipment technology regularly advances; think about how often new computers come out. So unless you're a tech head, be open to others' expert advice in this field.

In addition to procuring the equipment, you may—particularly if you're not comfortable running A/V equipment yourself—need to hire a technician who will be available the day of your event and for rehearsals before the event as well. You may even want to invest in a consultant who can instruct you on the most effective equipment to rent (and hopefully save money for you in the long run, too).

Finding the Right Vendor

As in finding and hiring other vendors, do your homework. This is important in the A/V arena because a presentation will collapse for everyone if the audio goes silent, the computer images are distorted, or the video never comes on.

If possible, hire a vendor who was responsible for the A/V needs at an event you attended that was hugely successful. Get recommendations from your city's chamber of commerce. If your event is at a hotel or regular meeting site, the staff there may have their own A/V department or work with a preferred vendor who will fill the bill and know the venue. Whomever you decide to hire, check references. Make sure the vendor completed the job he said he would, had working equipment, employed competent technicians, was punctual, and handled snafus with calmness, expertise, and aplomb.

If your event is at a venue that has its own A/V department, you may be locked in to using it. If you feel you can get a better deal elsewhere, collect bids and see if the A/V department will match it. If the site allows you to use your own A/V vendor, ask if you will have to pay a fee for doing so.

Technical Staff

After you've hired your A/V vendor, make sure the person assigned to your event is at planning meetings and rehearsals. These elements will be crucial to your event's success, and you want a person aware of the vision for the event and how the A/V elements fold into it.

Planning for and Creating Written Materials

Many of your audio-visual needs may call for you to supplement them with written materials. Don't make the A/V components work too hard or expect too much from them. At some point an A/V presentation will only be complete with a handout, one that will either provide the finer points, offer additional details, or furnish information for future reference.

One of the advantages of using A/V aids is to prompt a recall from audience members and participants of what they saw or experienced during an event. While a visual or piece of audio makes a great statement, you might need a physical representation—such as a brochure, press release, or sales sheet—to go back to the office with each attendee. Instead of a handout or in addition to it, you can also consider an e-mail message that provides follow-up, contact information, and an additional visual.

Keeping Communication Top of Mind

Finally, at the core of the event, remember communication. The primary point of almost all A/V equipment—with the possible exception of a sound system or audio that is used for background music—is to enhance communication. **That communication strengthens your organization's image and builds unity at the meeting or event.** It drives up sales and educates the audience.

Don't ever allow an audio-visual component to drown out your event's true meaning, impede the exchange of ideas or flow of conversation, or be such the starring part of the event that people forget the company or cause that brought them there.

PowerPoint Presentations

Certainly one of the most ubiquitous A/V components at events is the PowerPoint presentation. PowerPoint presentations have their own set of rules. You'll use an image projector and a laptop to present your PowerPoint, and it may include stunning graphics, flash animation, links to live Web sites, a traditional succession of information-loaded Power-Point cards, or a combination of all those elements.

With PowerPoint presentations—as with whichever communication mode you choose—don't depend on the audio-visual aspect to save the day. The presentation has to be solid and thoughtfully composed, with an articulate message geared toward a specific audience.

By some estimates professionals see hundreds of PowerPoint presentations a year. Therefore, unfortunately, your event could suffer from the "just another PowerPoint presentation" syndrome. But it doesn't have to be that way. Increase your event's impact by making a featured Power-Point presentation visually stand out. Instead of using images that are included in the PowerPoint computer program on your desktop, find ones that haven't been seen before—either that you have digitally shot or that you obtain (for a small fee) from such Web sites as *www.corbis.com* and *www.flickr.com*. You might also read *Beyond Bullet Points*, by Cliff Atkinson, which suggests trading in the traditional PowerPoint bullet point cards for a storytelling approach, replete with moving images and a three-act structure.

A Reel Video Production of Another Kind

You may be looking into featuring a crisp video presentation at your event. If so, that's a whole other A/V ballgame and an entire other set of expenses. For those kinds of visuals you or your vendor must hire talent. You need to line up a crew such as a writer, director, and editor; determine locations; and handle a myriad of other details. Be prepared to thoroughly investigate video and commercial production firms for the one that understands your business and is in line with your budget. For an overview of what a production on this scale might entail, check out *www.la411.com*, a comprehensive site that lists an array of companies that provide production services, locations, sets, stages, and the like. You may just instantly think of Los Angeles or New York for such a video production company to help you out, but chances are a resource is closer than you think. For starters or a referral, contact an advertising agency in your area; they likely have connections to produce such a piece.

The High Points of Low Tech

Not every visual at your event has to be high tech. While a laser show or a slickly produced promotional reel will be memorable for a while, will they make a lasting impact? An array of low-tech elements may be just as—or more—effective.

Never discount the value of demonstrations. Showing firsthand how a new product works—maybe even getting members of the audience to join in—is an interesting, powerful way to provide a visual. To get audience members involved in memorable ways you can always depend on a lively Q&A session or writing ideas on a blackboard or colorful dry-erase board.

A Final Evaluation

Once the equipment is ordered but before the show goes on, take stock of the A/V inventory you're using at your event by reviewing these six areas:

1. Does every piece of equipment have a purpose?

2. How will that audio or visual implement make a difference?

3. If the piece of equipment wasn't there, would that component of the event be less successful or even useless? If it would be useless, can you arrange an easy backup to present that component?

4. Does the equipment complement the event and fit in, or is it there for a flash-in-the-pan effect?

5. Is there a better piece of equipment to carry out that part of the presentation? If so, why aren't you using it? Is it too expensive, too bulky, unavailable?

6. In thinking about each part of the event, has any portion been overlooked that would benefit from an A/V device?

▶▶ Test Drive

In preparation for your next event, consider how you might be able to use A/V to make it more impactful, successful, and memorable:

➲ If you frequently rely on PowerPoint presentations as your A/V support in a meeting or event, can you change it for a mix of other methods?

➲ Can you spice up your visual presentation with music or snippets of recorded dialogue?

➲ How many people who need to be reached will be at an event's presentation?

➲ Is your A/V sense stuck in another era? Could an image projector be a better means than an overhead projector? Could a computer-generated slide show be more exciting than posters full of pictures?

Coordinating the Endeavor

Once you've fine-tuned your event's purpose, assembled your staff, and surveyed the nuts and bolts of making it run, you'll need to give it shape and shading. You'll need to find the place to host it, set the tone, and take care of both the necessities and extras that will make it most effective.

Whether the event is a meeting for ten or a conference for 500, you must take account of several aspects that will make your endeavor successful. The more successful, the more impact it will have on your organization's image and productivity.

Coordinating the scope, and relevant logistics and staging of your event will depend on all of the following:

- ➲ The event's site, conducive to the purpose, tenor, and audience for the event
- ➲ Signage, giving directions to the event, as well as announcing the event itself through banners and podium signs
- ➲ Collateral material, which can be brochures, handouts, photos, or sell sheets
- ➲ Decorations, ranging from balloons and floral arrangements to wall-sized posters and elaborate backdrops
- ➲ Supplies, including pens, pencils, notepads, clipboards, and nametags

Staging for Success

The word *staging* has become a popular phrase in real estate. In that industry, staging refers to bringing in top dollar for a home on the market by revamping and redesigning its rooms to highlight the home's most attractive features—like removing heavy curtains to spotlight sunny windows or repainting a room's shocking color with a more neutral tone. For your event, think of how can you "sell" it. How can you stage it so that it's welcoming, inviting, and attractive? Thinking about your event in those terms will give you a frame of reference for the attendees' perspective and enable you to present a powerful atmosphere.

Do Your Research!

When laying out the logistics, take time to determine components you will need, then gather up means to fulfill those needs. For instance, if your event is taking place off company property, you'll have a range of choices to select where your event should occur. The Web makes research tantalizingly swift and easy. In addition, the speed of e-mail can usually give you quick responses when making inquiries on such aspects as availability and services.

Break Down the Event Beforehand

From the outset the event planner must focus on many needs.

- How will the environment foster participants' learning, input, enthusiasm?
- How will attendees glean information, learn about your company, or better understand their reason for attending?
- How can the setup be comfortable for the attendees?
- How can the setup help participants see and hear?
- How will the start and agenda order be clear to attendees?
- How will you encourage participation?
- How can you ensure the environment reflects positively on your company and its products or services?
- What is the event's duration: an hour, a day, a weekend, three business days?
- Is the event one happening or several related ones?
- Are you responsible for other aspects, such as how attendees will get there and where they will stay? (These will be covered in Chapters 11 and 12.)

You have several ways to answer those questions. Don't take the first choice that comes along. Brainstorm and gather others who are in the know for this event or who may offer you valuable input from their own event-planning experiences.

Don't Overlook the Obvious

Particularly if you're an entrepreneur or small business owner, you're strapped for time in event planning. Don't reinvent the wheel. While you want to make choices that are specific to your event and will create a unique experience for participants, take advantage of information that's already out there.

For instance, the Las Vegas Convention and Visitors Authority can quickly supply you with information regarding meeting space, banquet rooms, and accommodations at most of the city's hotels, as well as sources for balloons and florists, and even how to arrange for golf reservations if your event will have a break for recreation.

In addition to a city's convention and visitor's bureau, check in with a city's chamber of commerce. A chamber can offer a vast collection of information about a city's attributes and resources.

Both of these entities are intent on making a city—and its businesses—attractive for both companies and individuals. Since they strive to point out advantages for doing business there, they welcome your questions and requests for assistance in meeting needs you may have. They hope this in turn will prompt you to hire businesses in their area.

How to Find Venues

You'd be amazed at the venues available. Many times people focus on a particular location or company site, or they restrict themselves to conventional places such as hotel banquet rooms or civic auditoriums. Certainly some events you host—such as your company's grand opening—have to happen at your place of business; that is important to capitalize on your location, increase your commerce, and ensure the event's success. However, it is perfectly acceptable to have some events off-site. Others, because of their size, function, or purpose, will have to be held off-site.

In mulling over considerations for places not on company property, don't be afraid to think about possibilities that are out of the ordinary. Many times the location you select will be a tip-off to potential participants or invitees that yours will be an exciting event worth attending. While you will have to gauge if the appropriateness and atmosphere is commensurate with your company and its goals, you could consider having your event at such locations as:

- An aquarium
- A movie theatre
- A pet store
- A park
- A library
- A college's historic building
- A zoo's observation area

- A train station
- A cowboy museum
- A garden nursery
- An amusement park

Make sure the atmosphere matches the tenor of the event. If everyone's in their finery, stay away from a pet store; if you're asking your guests to come in beachwear, steer clear of a five-star restaurant.

Make the Calls

In determining the best venue, you should have questions in a well-organized list. It's possible to find out the answers via e-mail as well as over the telephone. Your questions should be about the venue's capacity, available date, fees, and other details. Your initial set of questions should include:

- Is the site available on the date of the event?
- How many people does the site accommodate?
- Is the site in a fixed configuration or can equipment and rentals move around?
- What are the charges for renting the space?
- If food is part of your event, what is the minimum catering fee?
- Can you use your own vendors, or do you have to use the site's preferred or on-site ones?
- If you use outside vendors, is there a fee?
- Are certain services, rentals, space offered at a reduced fee or given discounts?
- What is the fee schedule?
- What is the cancellation policy?

A Department Store Soiree

When the producers of a long-running television show were intent on creating a stir, they decided to stage a party that would enhance their image by pairing with a trend-setting, high-end department store. In Los Angeles, event planners are always on the hunt for an innovative use of space, and this occasion provided an exceptionally fun setting: The party was to occur after-hours in a chic Beverly Hills department store.

The date was set for a Sunday, when the store's hours were shorter. The second floor—usually home to women's couture—was rearranged with some racks kept and some removed; clothes were still part of the mix and added to the atmosphere. To ward off potential damage the event organizers served no red wine or cranberry and tomato juices. Banquet tables for buffets, bars for cocktails, and even a dance floor were positioned. The entertainment included music, store tours, and even private shopping excursions.

The event was a heady hit, with coverage in national magazines. While the show created the buzz they were hoping for, the host store garnered publicity and new customers as well.

Look for win-win opportunities such as this when considering locations for your event. If you need to make your event stand out, sometimes an atypical—but desirable—location may be just the fix. On the flip side, if you run a business with an unusual location, reach out to event planners to let them know of your available space.

While you may have your heart set on one particular site, give yourself more than one option. You may be locked into a certain date that a venue can't accommodate, or the site you had in mind may be beyond your budget range. Collect information from several places to make an informed decision.

Ask for References

Don't be afraid to ask for references from organizations and individuals who have rented the space. Find out from other companies who have used the site what worked and what didn't. Those hoping that your company will rent their space certainly want the experience to be excellent for all concerned, but it helps to get a vantage point from someone who has been in the trenches and actually handled an event at that location. This person's experience can give you an insight into the preparations, the event itself, and the aftermath and can tip you off to any issues you should be particularly mindful of. People are usually willing to share information about particularly good and especially bad experiences.

Inspect the Site

In selecting the site, don't take someone else's word for it. Even virtual tours on the Web of some venues are no substitute for actually being in a room, space, or location that will host your event.

Unless the venue is prohibitively expensive to visit, take the time to go see it for yourself. Once you're actually in a room or setting, you can gauge much more effectively the space that will be in use. Take a digital camera with you to remind yourself of all the angles in the space you'll be working with. You can also use those shots—along with your commentary—to inform those working the event with you (who may not have visited the site), as well as vendors you'll hire. Getting this first-hand look and feel will inform your vision and make your work much easier.

Even if the venue is out of town, consider scheduling a visit. If that's impractical from a time or budget standpoint, see if you know someone in the area who can take a look for you. At the very least, have your contact at the venue e-mail you a visual scrapbook that includes a selection of images, capturing all the angles of the space. Ask the site vendor to supply accompanying descriptions and dimensions.

Putting a Theme to Work

Every event must have a theme. The theme is different than an overarching message for the event—that would be your event's goal or purpose. A theme provides a hook for the event, allowing you to draw in more people, heighten interest, and increase involvement.

A hook also gives your event continuity and a more cohesive approach. While theme is discussed in other chapters as well, at this juncture realize a theme informs the entire design of the event. The theme starts with the event's purpose, inception, and invitations. It guides your program content and is supported by your logistics and staging: where the event is held and how the site is decorated.

Take stock of every area, piece of equipment, and apparatus that you're using to execute your event. How can it be enhanced? How can it be dressed or shown off to heighten your organization's image? While you don't want to pile on logos willy-nilly or plaster your venue with signs and decorations until it's unrecognizable, figure out how to use the theme in placement and staging in a way that will bolster the event and your company's association with it.

Producing Signage and Collateral Materials

You want to make sure people stay focused on where and why they've come to a certain event. The focus you engender among participants, guests, or an audience will translate into a stronger message. By drawing on support from some prime and easily produced materials you can foster name recognition and provide your guests with valuable information to leave with.

Signs for Their Time

Take a look around your venue. You'll want signage on your podium and on placards or banners in the room that announce the event. Other signage may include printed tent cards for tables, nameplates in front of panelists, and place cards to announce where people are sitting for a meal. Don't forget directional signage to guide attendees to your event's site if, for instance, you're nestled in the back banquet room of a sprawling complex.

Signs must have a purpose. They should both dress the event space and provide information for your attendees.

If you don't have a vendor you've used before to create signs, you can check the Internet for a variety of sign makers and suppliers (as long as you get and check references before you hire them). You may be able to make some signage yourself with the help of a desktop publishing program and using either lamination or widely available sign holders to make them sturdy.

Give your signage a uniform look. Put your event's logo on it, or give it some other identifying characteristic that makes it uniquely associated with the occasion.

More than Propaganda

Collateral means the illustrative components that both support and supplement the event's happenings. This can include but isn't limited to sell sheets, brochures, press releases, postcards, and newsletters. For an event, these pieces can also take on such forms as programs, itineraries, and brainstorming pads. Don't pass up any opportunity for a printed piece of material to showcase your enterprise and tie in with your event. Don't inundate attendees with paper, but plan to distribute pieces that will give them information they can use while also serving as a permanent reminder of your company and the event once the event is over.

If you don't already work with a graphic designer to produce collateral, now would be a great time to find one. For the most polished and professional pieces, you want to hire someone who can create collateral that will be consistent with and reinforce your organization's image. Take note: Designers usually have connections to printers and other resources. In fact, you may even be able to cut a deal by having the graphic designer give you a discount if he or she receives referral fees for recommending your business to other vendors.

The Details of Decorations

Decoration can enhance your event by taking your proceedings to the next level. You want to make the space as attractive as possible from the standpoint of both aesthetics and comfort. Imagine being invited to an event that takes place in an empty room with a single chalkboard and no refreshments. Now envision that same room with a fabric-covered table, fresh flowers, a pad of paper and highlighter at each seat, a banner announcing the event, and a station with beverages and snacks. Which room would you rather spend two hours in?

That's the mindset you must take when planning. Make your area such that people want to be there and will take away a positive, favorable impression of your company or cause.

Decoration for a Person's Station

When lining up decorations, particularly for a meeting or a space where several people will be seated, think about ways to dress up each seating place. That can be a welcoming gesture for an attendee or participant, putting someone instantly in the mood to simultaneously feel welcome and get down to business. In addition to furnishing supplies such as pens, paper, and ice water at each person's place, put the goods on a paper placemat that has trivia, games, or a map printed on it. Include some treat, such as candy bars with specially designed wrappers, a baseball cap or wristband emblazoned with a logo, or a novelty toy. (Beware though: Whatever you select to welcome each participant shouldn't be noise-emitting or otherwise distracting to the purpose or program of the gathering once it's underway.)

Unique to Your Enterprise

A decoration should brighten the space and have a purpose. Decorations can include such routine elements as floral centerpieces and plants, drapes that cover an unsightly wall, fabric that hides a scratched table or metal table legs, and enlarged color photos or illustrations that tout a company's products or services or show off an enterprise's customers, employees, accomplishments, or publicity clips.

Depending on your business or the nature of the event, decorations can have special twists. You can put up a glass wall filled with colored jellybeans (for a "success is sweet" celebration), shelves set up with rows and rows of cosmetics (for a "company makeover" meeting), or chairs that hold caps with the word "Thinking" stitched on them (for a problem-solving seminar).

Nuts and Bolts

While decorations may be the sizzle, don't forget the wheels of your event or meeting may need simple mechanics. Assess the room or the site. Does everyone know each other, or will nametags be necessary? Do participants need pen and paper? Will anybody need an extension cord for a laptop?

Think about all the items you may need, such as notepads, clipboards, and lanyards. A complete list of event supplies to consider having on hand is in Chapter 12.

Where to Look for Decorations and Supplies

When faced with finding decorations and supplies (and particularly in light of the budgets most organizers must work with), embrace possibilities that may not have occurred to you. Outside of the rental company you may be contracting with and the florist you might be using, supplies and decorations can be found at party goods stores (and similar Web sites), office superstores, discount chains, craft stores, and teacher supply stores. If your event is at an off-site venue, look into their resources; they may use provisioners you hadn't considered. You can find entire Web sites devoted to widely used event and meeting supplies such as *www. justlanyards.com* and *www.1-800-flowers.com*.

Nametags

If you can, steer clear of generic "Hello, My Name Is . . ." nametags. Nametags present another visual opportunity for you to add to your event. Since they're so widely used (and seen) at certain events, they should be taken more seriously. They can run the gamut from adhesive card stock to engraved on metal, on paper placed in plastic holders to laminated on lanyards. Whichever you decide, make sure that the nametags can be placed appropriately and stay where they should. People's names and titles or companies should be clearly legible. Try to include some graphic that represents the meeting or event and why you are all gathered. However, don't include too many graphics such that a name and company logo is lost. To peruse a selection of nametags, check out such Web sites as *www.nametagsource.com* and *www.nametag.com*.

Insurance, Permits, and Related Concerns

No matter where your event is held, check into getting insurance. Discuss the event with your insurance agent. You may be covered, or you may need to investigate add-ons or riders for the event itself. If your event is off company property, find out what coverage that venue carries. Ask about obvious—but hopefully unlikely—scenarios such as if someone were injured, if the event was cancelled, and if damage occurred during your event (if, for instance, there was an electrical fire).

Depending on the type of event, you may also need to include waivers or release forms.

Every event has different needs in this area, so don't avoid or ignore the need for insurance just because it might be another cost to factor in. You'll have more worries if you don't have the necessary insurance if a need for it arises.

Permits represent another component that those planning an event may overlook. Your event may need no permits at all, but more than likely you'll at least have to register the event in the city where it's taking place. In addition, the city may have other aspects that you will need to address regarding fire, emergency, police, parking, or disability concerns. For instance, the city may want to make sure you have enough security or, if your event needs a roadblock, that traffic will be redirected properly. Some cities will have downloadable information on their Web site pertinent to securing the proper permits. To obtain the permit you will have to supply information and possibly even an event plan. Investigate permit procedures with the city during your action-plan writing stage to make sure you'll have all the information you need.

▶▶ Test Drive

Even everyday occurrences can be an "event" you can learn from and take back to your workplace. Going to a movie, attending a church service, having dinner at a restaurant, or participating in a neighborhood watch meeting can all provide an educational experience. At your next such occasion, take a look around, survey the attributes that had to come together, and think of what you need for your next event.

➲ What equipment was needed, such as tables, chairs, or tablecloths? Were they comfortable, in good condition, and appropriate to the setting?

➲ Did anyone use nametags? Were they easy to read?

➲ Was literature used, such as a menu, program, or church bulletin? Was the information it provided worthwhile and professionally presented? Did it help or hinder the cause?

➲ Was the venue suitable for the occasion?

Routine Events:
The Simple Can Be Sublime

PART 2

Recognizing the Need You're Filling

When planning a meeting, you must be focused on its purpose. Too often meetings can devolve into an unorganized mess, but with the right planning beforehand they can be robust, successful, and a boost—rather than a drain—for the participants.

First state the objective of the meeting you're planning. That will inform its direction.

Next decide on the audience. You'd set up a much different atmosphere for investors and shareholders than you would for employees, vendors, or potential hires.

What is the goal of the meeting? What is the reason that you'll be taking your time and energy—and that of your participants—to gather everyone together for a session?

Taking an Approach

Decide the approach the meeting should take. Is a serious matter at hand? Is your venture lacking funding? Is your focus on restructuring a department?

Or can your meeting take a more lighthearted tack? Are you trying to generate fun ideas for a product launch? Are you trying to foster teamwork with group activities?

Consider your answers to these questions in defining and refining your meeting milieu:

- ➲ Why is the meeting necessary?
- ➲ Who will be attending the meeting?
- ➲ Will everyone at the meeting know each other?
- ➲ Are any attendees coming from out of town?
- ➲ Will everyone present be company employees? Affiliated with the company?
- ➲ What problem will the meeting seek to solve, or what decision will be made from the meeting's activities and discussions?
- ➲ What actions do you expect to be taken after the meeting?

Defining the Agenda

Don't have a meeting without an agenda. Agendas are necessary for all events—no matter how big or small. While some event agendas only need a running time with an activity attached, a meeting's agenda needs to be more fleshed out.

Begin the agenda by stating your objective or goal. Then bullet out the headings that you know the meeting will include. Don't stick with generic terms such as "Introduction," "Sales Part," and "Conclusion." Use an outline format (such as that in the example) to list the suggested agenda items. Think of a meeting as a series of important steps that you're gathering toward an achievement.

Further, attach the time each agenda element will last. While you may go over in some parts and under in others, with a schedule you'll have a better chance of keeping your meeting on track. If you are running long, you'll also know beforehand which of your meeting components are of higher priority and, if necessary, those that won't make the cut. That way at the minimum you'll accomplish those of highest priority.

Your initial agenda may not include all components of the sample below, such as location and meeting participants, but make sure you include those in a revised, final version.

A SAMPLE AGENDA:
INTRODUCTION OF SPRING 2009 LINE
Monday, April 11
9:00 AM—10:30 AM
Chi for Three Teahouse/Rock Garden Room

PARTICIPANTS President & CEO
VP, Sales
VP, Creative Services
Marketing Director
Publicity Director
Sales Staff

OBJECTIVE
To showcase the Spring line of necklaces, and discuss strategies for selling to various store chains and boutiques to encourage and influence them to carry the line.

I. Tantrum Necklace Showcase
   A. Sterling
   B. Precious Stone
   C. Costume
II. Other Sales Opportunities for Retail/ Advantages and Disadvantages:
   A. Department Store Chains (e.g. JC Penney)
   B. Trend Store Chains (e.g. Urban Outfitters)
   C. Discount Store Chains (e.g. Target)
III. Specialty Stores and Boutiques
IV. Web Site Store Possibilities
   A. Benefits
   B. Detriments
   C. Web Sites to Consider
V. The Direct Approach
   A. QVC, HSN
   B. Catalog
VI. Free-for-All
   A. Other Possibilities
   B. Questions

Setting up the Time, Place, and Atmosphere

With both your approach and agenda in hand you can decide the time, location, and ambience for the meeting. You should set a time that will encourage the highest attendance of your desired participants and include those whose presence is mandatory. You shouldn't ask every single person beforehand if they can come to a meeting at such-and-such a time, but check the calendars of the most senior attendees. Since their time is considered more valuable, you should start there. As with other events, check other calendars, too. You don't want to send out an e-mail announcing a meeting that falls on Thanksgiving or coincides with a company seminar.

As far as the place for your meeting, it's okay to think outside the box. You don't always have to have a meeting in the office conference room. Maybe just going into an atrium or heading outdoors to a nearby park are options. **Getting away from the expected is invigorating.** Granted, your meeting may be drawing so many attendees that some locations are off limits, or the logistics involved in an off-site meeting might be too time-consuming for the meeting's parameters. However, if holding the meeting in an unusual location is viable, the benefits can be substantial.

The atmosphere—or environment—for the meeting is the biggest area up for grabs and the one in which you have the most latitude. You should have an ambience that matches up with the tenor of the discussion. Don't have balloons floating around if layoffs are being discussed; don't drape the walls in black if you're planning to mull over the new color scheme for packaging.

The Room Setup

Make sure tables and chairs in your meeting space are properly set up to allow participants face-to-face conversation and to give the meeting moderator a commanding view. Roundtable, horseshoe or U-shaped, classroom style, and rectangular are all common meeting room setups. Figure out which layout will best suit the meeting. Make sure there are enough chairs for participants and that the participants will have a clear view of flip charts, television monitors, or computer screens. Before the

Meeting at a Pizza Place

At a national public relations agency, I was assigned to the team for a chain of pizza restaurants. The chain was suffering from sluggish sales in a particular region and needed a quick turnaround in the area as disgruntled franchise owners were threatening to flee.

While everyone on the team loved the company's pizza, we didn't know much about the inner workings of the chain's individual restaurants. And we knew we had much to learn if we were going to help the chain enact swift changes to impact and increase their business. But rather than sit around a conference room table and have a company executive download information, we opted for a far more energetic idea. How about if we held the meeting in one of the chain's local restaurants? The company execs loved the idea, and within twenty-four hours we were in the hearty industrial kitchen of a pizzeria. As part of the meeting we toured the restaurant, sat where customers do, interacted with the wait staff, and read the menus from a customer's vantage point. Then we headed to the kitchen where we all participated in making some pizzas from the restaurant's recipes.

This firsthand knowledge and experience provided us insights and information that could have never come from a PowerPoint presentation, corporate videos, manuals, or handouts. While those materials all supplemented our learning, our real inspiration for devising a strategy to increase sales came from our on-site meeting.

That initial meeting not only laid the groundwork for a very successful publicity campaign and turning franchisees' opinions around, it also fueled a series of ideas that were incorporated in many of the company's future initiatives.

meeting begins, sit in different chairs to get a vantage point of the meeting from several perspectives.

Deal with Distractions

During meetings you may have to contend with outside influences that could interrupt the flow of the meeting or stagnate it outright. Before the meeting's start, circumvent potential problems. Is the room in earshot of a noisy street? Do chimes on a nearby tower clang loudly every quarter hour? Is the room temperature comfortable? Are the lights flickering? If you turned off the lights for a video presentation, would it be dark enough to see screen images and would you be able to find the light switch afterward? In analyzing all the potential room assets and deterrents, think ahead. Make sure one solution doesn't cause another problem. For instance, if you shut the windows, will the room become too hot for comfort? If so, turn up the air conditioning.

Physical space aside, make sure from the outset your meeting participants know what's expected of them. Steer clear of interruptions such as phone calls either on office landlines or cell phones. Ban Blackberries or similar PDAs as well as any text messaging from people's phones. If laptops are being used, establish the ground rules for Web surfing or checking e-mail.

Equipment and Supplies

As discussed in Chapter 5, you may need A/V equipment for your meeting to fulfill its agenda. If that's the case, make arrangements beforehand to have exactly what you will need. And just because it's a meeting and you may know everyone involved, don't shortchange the importance of a run-through beforehand, particularly if you're going to be operating A/V equipment such as with a PowerPoint presentation. Moreover, in a rehearsal of the content you can discern what's working, what's not, what should be added, and what you can leave out.

Take stock of the materials you and your participants will need for the meeting to run smoothly. For instance, does everyone know each other or will you need nametags? Does everyone need copies of a new company handbook or a public relations plan? Do you have the specs or samples of a competitor's product?

Putting Your Agenda in Action

Once your meeting has come to order, make sure that everyone present knows its purpose and the time you expect it to last. While some meetings with very defined purposes could go on for a few hours and up to an entire day, most should last no more than ninety minutes. Once you're edging past an hour with no wrap-up in sight, fidgeting, clock watching, and general restlessness can ensue.

Unless your meeting contains surprises that you want to keep in the dark for your attendees, you should distribute the agenda so everyone can see where the meeting is headed. You can also review the agenda verbally. **Giving your participants a heads-up on the meeting components allows for a unified mission and gives a sense of working toward a common goal, which will be accomplished by the meeting's conclusion.**

Keep on track. Follow the timeline you've created for the meeting. Don't let discussion veer off into unnecessary tangents. Deal with meeting participants in a gentle but firm manner:

➲ Suggest that impertinent questions should be relevant.
➲ Delay off-track comments until their appropriate place in the agenda.
➲ Repeat questions for clarity.
➲ Redirect negative comments into a more positive light.

Keeping Participants Interested

If once all the participants have gathered and the room isn't working, attendees aren't comfortable, sightlines to presentations are impaired, or the air is too warm, make adjustments as soon as possible. Uncomfortable participants make for unproductive meetings.

If enthusiasm is waning, survey the situation. What's not connecting with the attendees? Have you spent too long on the current topic? Has tension invaded the discussion? Does everyone need a five-minute break?

If necessary, don't be afraid to call on a few options to refuel the participants and recharge the atmosphere. It could be as simple as switching around the agenda a bit, introducing a video clip you might have been holding until the meeting's end or injecting a humorous story into the proceedings.

Icebreakers

In fact, if people in the room don't know each other you may consider a few icebreakers to get your meeting going. Often, icebreakers can do wonders to pump up people's energy and, in taking their mind off the challenges of the meeting that faces them, present common ground that will bring more focus to the issue at hand.

The content of the icebreakers should have nothing in common with the meeting's agenda. It should be free and independent and not put anyone's skill set on the spot.

For that Kind of Meeting Break

If you don't have resources to call on for an icebreaker, they're as close as a few mouse clicks. You can find them on Web sites such as the educationally geared *www.eslflow.com*, *www.adulted.about.com*, and *www.wilderdom.com*. Depending on which ones you choose, you may need such props as iPods, balloons, or an amusement park map. Be prepared going into a meeting to have at least one icebreaker ready to go. Research it beforehand so that you know whether you'll need a prop to make it work. Even if that icebreaker is a raging success, don't use one with the same group of people twice. Introduce new ones at future meetings so that they remain a fresh, viable, and effective meeting break.

Take Five

Don't underestimate the importance of a few minutes of downtime. Particularly if the meeting will be lengthy, make sure to build in breaks that allow for people to check messages, use the bathroom, and get water. Your meeting space shouldn't seem so confining that people are looking to break out of it. Let everyone know that you have broken the meeting into chunks with breaks in between, a concept that will seem more manageable to all concerned.

Have Refreshments

Even if the meeting is a short one (and definitely if the meeting is a long one), arrange for refreshments. Food is a wonderful attractor. Depending on the time of day you can offer coffee, tea, bottled water, fresh fruit, cheese and crackers, and the like. While a couple of healthful sweets may be all right, providing heavy and calorie-laden snacks can often lead to low energy after the initial sugar rush.

Meeting with Success

When your meeting runs smoothly, you know it. Participants are interested, dynamic discussion ensues, camaraderie leads to problem solving and creative brainstorming, and participants leave the meeting with a sense that a mission has been accomplished and next steps are clear and assigned.

While that result should always be your goal, it might not always happen. All your components—as structured and well meaning as they might have been—may not have coalesced for maximum benefit.

After a meeting has concluded, immediately ask yourself what went right and what went wrong. Determine if your meeting's objective was met. Did the time run over? Was every item on the agenda addressed? Would handouts or A/V components help get a point across better? Did a piece of A/V equipment malfunction? Was communication among attendees fostered or restrained, and in either case, why? If communication wasn't optimal, what could you have done to correct it?

When you thoroughly analyze a meeting's success you ensure that future meetings will be successful. Occasionally you may also decide to offer surveys to participants at the end of a meeting to determine their thoughts about the meeting's productivity. Sometimes feedback from attendees can provide suggestions for success or point out shortcomings you hadn't realized. In your survey, ask what the participants thought the meeting's purpose was, gauge if the participants thought the meeting took enough (or too much) time, ask how they would describe the meeting's atmosphere; and find out if they have any suggestions for improvement.

When a Meeting Should Be a Retreat

Sometimes companies opt for a retreat: a series of meetings that usually take place off company grounds. Retreats typically last one to three days. Think of a retreat as a company summit. Retreats are necessary when:

- ➲ A series of related meetings need to take place
- ➲ Sensitive issues are in play
- ➲ Too many distractions at the company site have forced it to take place elsewhere to achieve success

While a retreat has an overarching need or theme, you must create an itinerary for the complete retreat, then separate agendas for each meeting that takes place. Don't think of a retreat as one long, extended meeting. That might seem too drawn out (and not very enticing) for the participants.

Particularly where retreats are concerned, schedule breaks and block out time for activities and meals where no business will take place. Those will foster socializing, which will then make the retreat's meetings far more productive.

Regarding Retreats

Retreats typically benefit from out-of-the-way environments, even if they do include modern-day amenities. Popular choices include mountain resorts, quaint beachside locales, and country inns. The act of getting away seems to go far in bringing a group together to concentrate on the tasks at hand. In addition to accomplishing the work before your group, "unity" should be a watchword for the retreat's activities and downtime. During a retreat's multiple meetings, consider icebreakers, team-building and problem-solving exercises, strategy sessions, conflict resolution, and brainstorming for inclusion on the agenda.

The Particulars and Value of Brainstorming Sessions

Brainstorms are meetings that concentrate on generating ideas. Those ideas can be for business plans, marketing strategies, company policies—any number of issues that could benefit from a creative approach. Brainstorms are tremendous for jump-starting ideas and infusing creativity into a strategy or plan. The ideas that are initially tossed out in a brainstorming session shouldn't be restrained or inhibited by budgetary or personnel issues. In other words, let the ideas flow. The opportunity to analyze the veracity of each idea that's drummed up will come into play later.

Brainstorm Event Planning

Don't underestimate the power of brainstorming. If you're trying to get an event off the ground or can't delineate the primary components for a decided-upon event, try brainstorming. You may be so close to your company's goals that an outside, objective perspective will bring you untold advantages and rewards. While you may be inclined to simply invite those you work with most closely, don't shy away from bringing in those you respect from other departments or—if appropriate—even outside the company, as long as they have your best interests at heart. To help with brainstorming meetings for events, bring in newspapers and magazines and printed Web site pages to peruse coverage given to recent business happenings and celebrations.

Follow a Structure

Brainstorming's casual nature doesn't mean the session should flounder in a freewheeling atmosphere, nor is this an excuse to throw out meeting structure and decorum. Set an agenda and a time limit—usually no more than an hour—with your purpose honed for achieving a particular goal or solving a problem.

Invite participants who will be ready and willing to contribute with meaningful concepts and dialogue. Furnish them beforehand with any information that might be valuable for background and as a jumping-off point to generate ideas.

But Make It Conducive to Creativity

As with all meetings, make sure you have a leader in charge of navigating discussion and keeping participants on point. Before the session starts, assign one person to record every idea that is mentioned, elucidated, or expounded upon—preferably on a flip chart (or a Post-it Wall Pad). Filled pages should then be posted around the room so that everyone can see the ideas as they are amassed. Seeing the ideas as they are gathered and posted allows everyone to build upon suggestions and often leads to even better concepts and propositions.

At the end of the brainstorming session, each person should rank his or her top ideas. Those are then handed off to the group leader to prepare a report that will help in using the ideas for the issue at hand.

In a brainstorm session, don't be afraid to "work the room" more than you would in a meeting. Because a brainstorming session is more casual in nature, you have a little more latitude here to provide stimulation than in a regular meeting. Decorate the room with spreads from magazines, posters, or graphics, and supply candy or refreshments. Encourage a relaxed but thought-provoking and energetic atmosphere that fosters imagination, innovation, and inventiveness.

▶▶ Test Drive

Think about a meeting you've recently conducted:

- Did it have an agenda? If so, did the meeting follow it well?
- Was there too much to cover or not enough to warrant the meeting?
- Were all the participants engaged? Did they all have a reason to be there?
- What might have heightened the meeting's success—an A/V component, a break in the action, a more organized approach?
- Would having the meeting in another location have made it more successful?

Routine Events:
The Simple Can Be Sublime

The Event's Vision: Before, During, and After

For businesses starting off or expanding, a grand opening represents a pinnacle event. Often the grand opening is your official statement to the community, city, industry, and potential customers that your business is ready to serve them in totally new ways.

A grand opening that you plan may be targeted to a gathering of community members in celebrating your business' beginning or could be a days-long sale used to attract customers. But to take full advantage of the impact a grand opening can have on your business it should be much, much more.

The "More Than a Party" Approach

Many times business owners, in launching a business or in their excitement over its growth, decide to have a grand opening event. Unfortunately the entire effort sometimes seems to be directed toward having a party. While a party is certainly warranted, particularly given the effort and energy expended in starting an enterprise, a grand opening should be a multilayered event that favorably impacts future sales, initiates valuable contact, sustains relationships, and attracts favorable media coverage. Don't be satisfied with a grand opening that's simply a three-hour wine-and-cheese affair, a ribbon-cutting ceremony, or a one-day sale. Use your grand opening as a platform that extends far beyond a single event.

Beyond Bricks and Mortar

For those engaged in e-commerce, you can still have a grand opening event even though you don't have a brick-and-mortar building. If yours is a Web site-based company, find a suitable place to host an event that jibes with your site's sensibilities. If you're launching a business or service out of your home—and, understandably, that might not be big enough for an event or might not set the right tone—look into venues that will. With some finagling and the right contacts you can arrange for your grand opening to happen in some creative places that will project the right image for your business. Possibilities could include a restaurant banquet room if you're a caterer, a kindergarten classroom if

Ready, Set, G.O. (Grand Opening) | Inside Track |

In my event planning experience I've been in charge of several grand openings. Some very memorable ones involved a mall-based, quick-service food chain. From the company's humble beginnings, grand openings were always treated with fanfare and precision based on a belief that a well-executed grand opening sets the tone for each restaurant's ensuing success. The chain has since moved past its mall roots and now boasts more than 1,200 locations, the majority of them free-standing restaurants.

Each grand opening for the company was planned months in advance and featured a heady slate of activities and components. When I worked for the company we would first extensively research the market in which the restaurant would be opening, checking with the local chamber of commerce for events with which to tie-in, ascertaining demographics, and getting a feel for the community. The grand opening activities began in earnest with a colorful "Ready, Set, G.O." press kit sent to all the local media. For each market we crafted several pitches to garner media interest. Customized letters outlined the various angles.

We also set up promotions with popular local radio stations for restaurant giveaways and—in cooperation with other merchants—shopping sprees at the mall where the new location was based.

At the grand opening itself guests would find the restaurant festooned with balloons in the chain's colors, calendar giveaways that included restaurant coupons for each month, appearances by local celebrities or DJs (from the station we were conducting the promotion with), free samples of some of the company's menu offerings, and strolling appearances by the company mascot.

As you can tell, opening the doors for business wasn't enough. The grand opening took on an integrated approach that reached out to customers, invited the media, and promoted other mall merchants, too.

you're launching a line of kid clothes, after hours at a bank if you're an accountant, or the beautiful grounds of an office complex if you own a lawn service.

Interest the Media

You want your grand opening to attract attention from local newspapers, trade publications, broadcast outlets, Web site blogs, and national magazines—coverage that will enhance business. That being the case, you should plan and design your event so that it not only announces your company's arrival on the business scene but also contains some components that are of news value, prompting positive attention and coverage from the media.

Include in your event plans time and resources to assemble a media contact list, to contact them with news angles for your grand opening, and to follow up with them to make sure they get the information they need to run a story. Getting publicity for an event is discussed at length in Chapter 25.

The Objectives

In most cases grand openings are worthwhile. However, you can't have one just because it sounds like a good idea. To ensure the success of the grand opening—and help your business sustain that impact—you must establish clear-cut reasons for having the grand opening and determine how it will help you accomplish certain objectives for your enterprise. Pinpointing that information will help inform the direction, content, and participation for your grand opening, creating a well-conceived, focused event.

The objectives for your grand opening are comprised of the following six points:

- Purpose
- People
- Timing
- Commerce
- Activities
- Media

Now ask yourself about these areas.

1. **Purpose:** Why have a grand opening? What's its purpose as it pertains specifically to your business?

2. **People:** Whom should you invite? Who will be invaluable to launch and grow your business?

3. **Timing:** Does your grand opening have to be on a certain date? Is this date optimal for your business and prospective attendees?

4. **Commerce:** Will the business benefit from having the grand opening during business hours?

5. **Activities:** What activities at your grand opening will enhance business and add to attendees' enjoyment?

6. **Media:** What aspects of your grand opening can you get the media to cover?

The Must-Haves

As you answer those questions, you'll need to move into planning a budget, building a timeline, settling staffing issues, hiring vendors, determining necessary equipment and rentals, and staging, all of which are discussed in Chapters 1 through 6.

Even if you're planning a grand opening on a shoestring budget, you'll still make a dramatic impact when you plan carefully with key components in mind. For instance, your place of business should be in top form. You don't want to still have construction going on, missing merchandise, or a store with no signage. Individually or collectively, those signify an operation that's not ready for business, casting doubt on the entire notion of a grand opening.

Willing Participants

You've undoubtedly done your research for opening your business, so you know you have an audience for your business or service. Therefore, you shouldn't have any problem attracting a prized demographic to your grand opening. Compile an invitation list that will strengthen your business. Supplement that with advertising and e-mail blasts to ensure that your event attracts the right people: those who will support your business themselves or who will be diligent ambassadors to recruit business on your behalf.

An Agenda

Make sure your grand opening has an agenda. It should include the start and end time of the event and a chronological listing of the activities and happenings you expect to include.

Make sure to give people a reason to show up. Coming by to say hello to the new owners is a nice gesture, but give your attendees more. That could be as simple as a guided tour of the premises or an invitation-only shopping excursion. Some activities (discussed at length in the next section) cost little or nothing to include. For instance, a new clothing store can highlight the current season's in-store offerings with a mini-fashion show, an employee of a frame shop can give a demonstration on framing a piece of art, or a restaurant's chef can show how to make one of the restaurant's signature appetizers and pass out samples of it.

Provide a leave-behind for each guest. This can be a business card or, as discussed later in this chapter, something more substantial. This leave-behind doesn't have to be an elaborate gift or expensive giveaway, but it must be a classy representation of your business, a symbol by which to remember your company.

Will You Be Open for Business?

If you're planning a grand opening that will occur during your business hours—and you expect customers to make purchases during that time—you'll have additional factors to carefully consider and proficiently handle. For instance, if a huge sale is a prime component of your grand opening day, you'll want to advertise it to your target audience. Once the potential customers are there you must do everything in your power to make sure they enjoy such a positive and pleasant shopping experience that they will not only return again and again but will share that experience with others.

Make sure you have:

A store that's ready to shine. Your business should be neat, clean, and well organized. Prices should be affixed to all products, departments should be clearly delineated with professionally printed signage, and you should have a handle on all available inventory.

Employees who are ready to go. Your employees should be exceptionally presentable and well trained, with a firm grasp of all your products' prices and details, answers to common customer queries, and outstanding knowledge of, for example, working the cash register if that's part of their particular job description.

Extended hours. Let your business accommodate customers before and after normal business hours; you'll attract a wider audience and transmit a message that the grand opening is extra special.

Additional employees. Schedule more personnel than usual to ring up sales, answer questions, and provide customer help. Don't let the expense of extra wages dissuade you. The return on investment will be well worth it.

Soft Openings

If you have a restaurant or retail establishment opening for the first time, consider a "soft" opening with friends and family before you have a grand opening with streetwise customers and media. A soft opening allows you to hold a trial run for opening day to ensure that operating systems are up and running smoothly and to address any glitches that could arise. During a soft opening offer those invited a free meal, discounts, or gift merchandise. Act as though they are your first customers: take their orders or help them find items, and ring up sales. This dress rehearsal can save you (and your company's reputation) from embarrassing snafus and lengthy waits that opening day customers might have to endure to fix a problem. It prevents your company from leaving a permanently bad first impression.

The Activities

Grand openings should foster a great deal of enthusiasm for your business. Don't be content with just an arena for conversation when you can make a memorable, lasting impact. Some of the activities you might consider include:

Speaking

Often the activities during a grand opening devote a portion to a brief speech from the company owner. This should not be lengthy. It should contain words of thanks for the community's support, tell your audience that the company is excited to be a part of the community, and mention your expectations that you'll be a valuable part of your particular industry. However, go beyond the routine. Provide a pithy story about how the business got started, graciously recounting how the company is different from its competitors and briefly describing any achievements or media coverage to date. Think about what you like to hear. Everyone loves to hear a story about how someone achieved success through ingenuity or an original or humorous account of how the idea for a company was born.

Sampling

The Chick-fil-A company has a slogan, "There's a 'sale' in every 'sample.'" They often will cut up their famous sandwiches and encourage passersby to try them. When a new Chick-fil-A opens, this practice is also an important component of their grand opening festivities. While Chick-fil-A by no means invented the practice of sampling, they know it can be effective in stimulating interest and generating sales. A grand opening provides the perfect opportunity to offer samples of your company's products or services. If it's not feasible to pass out slices of your product, ask yourself how else might it be sampled: touched, heard, seen, or smelled?

Clinics

Clinics at a grand opening are instructional sessions that tie in with your company's business. For instance, when a new accounting office opened, its grand opening event included several "miniseminars" on such topics as tax return deductions, bookkeeping, and financial planning. While the seminars didn't all include services provided by the business, they created an event through which attendees gleaned helpful advice and remembered the business behind it. A travel agency took a similar approach, offering up sessions on the best locations to honeymoon, the European cities with the best deals, and the hidden jewel getaway spots in the United States. Ask how your grand opening guests can learn more about your product in an interesting way.

Demonstrations

Through demonstrations, the company can provide hands-on experience for attendees. For instance, a scrapbooking store can show guests how to scrapbook and then let them make an art project or scrapbook page they take home. People like to see, learn, and experience, and tackling a new and different project isn't always what they expect out of a grand opening. When you surprise them with such an activity, you create a lasting impression that translates into sales.

If you decide to offer demonstrations, have your demonstrators practice first. You don't want them fumbling around with a demonstration, creating doubt in the audience's mind about the product, service, or process. In addition, showcase new equipment in your demonstration. The demonstration pieces being handled shouldn't look unappealing or used. Put your company's goods in the best light possible.

Co-op Clinics

You might feel that your enterprise doesn't have enough hands-on or visual interaction for many clinics or demonstrations to work. If that's the case, check out possibilities in your area for other noncompeting businesses to set up at your grand opening for entertainment or education. It's best if they add entertainment value, but they shouldn't dilute your company's message. Perhaps the local bakery could set up a cookie-decorating station, the camera shop could host a photography classroom, and the computer store could have a troubleshooting session. Those businesses get exposure in return, and they may then invite your business to appear at an upcoming event they host or sponsor.

Ribbon Cutting

The activity most associated with a grand opening is a ribbon cutting ceremony. Consequently, these have become clichés that generate little interest or photo opportunities. If you are wedded to the idea of a ribbon cutting ceremony, try a different take on it, an outside-the-norm approach that might attract substantial coverage.

For instance, if you're opening a garden nursery have your "ribbon" made of evergreen garland and use tree pruners as your ceremonial scissors. Or if you're opening up a bakery you might string together cupcakes so that your guests get to eat through the edible ribbon. Either of those would create a photo opportunity presenting a fun, never-seen-it-before strategy that would give you an advantage in getting the picture placed in the press.

Creating the Scene

For a stylish grand opening that will enthuse your invitees and impress press and potential customers, think of a high-energy forum to highlight your business. Consider both visual and audio stimuli in dressing up your place of business. First draw up a diagram of the space you'll be using for the grand opening. Make sure it's to scale and includes any fixtures such as poles and racks. Use that to map out the area, dividing it into appropriate areas for activities you're planning, to make sure you have ample staffing for the different areas and to make arrangements for any staging those areas will need.

A Sparkling Environment

Make sure you're welcoming guests into a clean, well-presented place. The business should look its best. Hire professional cleaners the day before or day of the event if necessary. Take a complete survey of the surroundings, inside and out:

- Is construction completed?
- Are window coverings/blinds/curtains in place?
- Are the walls freshly painted?
- Are the bathrooms fully stocked and in working order?
- If an area is off limits, is it tastefully cordoned off?
- Is the furniture in good shape?
- Are boxes put up or concealed?
- Is signage professionally presented?
- Is parking available? (If not, consider hiring a valet service.)

Working with a place of business as your base that's in tip-top shape, you can dress up areas for various activities or for food stations. In that environment consider such festive additions as floral or balloon arrangements, strolling entertainment, food servers passing hors d'oeuvres, and fabric backdrops for picture taking.

Creating a More Energetic Atmosphere for Less

While you may not have a large budget for entertainment, you do have lower-cost options with which to charge up your surroundings. If you know kids will be at your grand opening, you might find strolling entertainment in the form of mascots from other local (noncompeting) businesses. Some city's attractions and colleges have costumed characters they gladly send to events around town for the exposure. If your company places advertising on a local radio station, you may be able to arrange for one of their DJs to set up a live remote at your celebration for a nominal fee. Players from farm teams for professional ball clubs may also be willing to come sign autographs to promote their team's schedule. And a nonprofit organization with a visual media component, such as a bookmobile or a roving museum exhibit, may be available to make a stop at your event.

Employees

Have your employees there to welcome guests. Make sure that they are in uniform or appropriate dress. They are ambassadors for your enterprise. Let them know they are a valuable part of your company's success, and hold a meeting with them in advance of the grand opening to apprise them of your goals for the event and their clearly delineated responsibilities that fit within those goals. It should go without saying that since they will be working at the event you should make sure they're fairly compensated, particularly if having them at the grand opening means paying them overtime.

Audio and Visual Considerations

Think of a comfortable arena for your guests. If the event is after hours, you won't want them to hear the whir of machines or a cacophony of ringing phones. If possible, use a sound system to play upbeat but appropriate music. If necessary, put all phones on voice mail.

Audio cues aside, what visual images might be appropriate to include? Has a promotional reel for your business been produced that you could put on a continuous loop in one area of the room? Are there digital images—representative of your business' people, products, and services—that can be enlarged to poster size and put around the space? Do you have a PowerPoint presentation or slide show that could run?

Food and Refreshments

A grand opening usually features food and refreshments, which not only make the atmosphere more festive but also foster conversation and encourage people to stay and join the festivities. You don't have to have a full catered lunch or a dinner buffet and a full bar; you can stick with simple appetizers or sweets, and coffee, water, and soft drinks. However, you must have ample for those attending and present the menu tastefully. For instance, don't serve food out of store-bought food containers, and don't set all the food out at once. Secure nice trays or dishes, and have someone assigned to replenishing menu items as they run low.

If you're not using a caterer, visit a warehouse store or restaurant supply company to buy serving pieces, napkins, and paper goods. Rent china, utensils, and other necessary supplies from a party goods company. Even if you're not serving liquor, hire a bartender to pour drinks. That's a modest investment, and taking away a self-serve element makes a better impression for your event.

Giveaways

These are considered your party favors, but—like the grand opening itself—they should have a lasting effect. Giveaways, also known as advertising premiums, serve as a token to remember your business. Popular giveaways—and often inexpensive—include key chains, refrigerator magnets, and highlighter markers and should be emblazoned with your company's name, phone number, and Web site.

While these are popular choices, think inventively. Think of a product that will represent your company well, has a logical tie-in with your enterprise, will be used again by the recipient, and isn't something the attendee will have gotten several times before from other businesses. For instance, a high-end gift store's grand opening giveaway was a small, beautiful leather-bound book: a gift log for registering people's names and gift ideas for them throughout the year. It fit in women's handbags and was a constant reminder that the store could fulfill whatever gift needs they might have.

Being a Gracious Host or Hostess

To maintain a jovial atmosphere during the grand opening you must consider yourself the host or hostess of the event. Be outgoing and greet all guests. Remember as many names as possible. If the event has many needs to tend to, delegate those or hire others to handle aspects that might take you away from the matter at hand: promoting your business with this audience. If you're behind the scenes arranging flowers and carting out food, you're missing prime opportunities for meeting future customers and thanking supporters.

Providing Incentives for Future Business

Here's where you can make sure your grand opening has lasting power. Use the opportunities it affords you to influence your guests so they make a return visit. Give them a desire to do business with you in the future. Collect guests' e-mail addresses so that you can, with their permission, send them e-mails about sales, new product launches, and other promotions.

If the grand opening wasn't invitation only, gather business cards by putting them in a drawing for a shopping spree or a prize. In addition, have plenty of business cards of your own, as well as company handouts or brochures about your business' services and products. **Make it easy for anyone who expresses interest to obtain information about your company and how it can help an individual or business.** Finally, offer coupons—with an expiration date—to give guests a reason to return to your business or support your products or services.

Gauging the Event's Success

Since this will likely be the first of many events for your business, use what you learned from your grand opening to make your future events more successful. Talk to trusted colleagues, associates, or friends in attendance who can report back to you on how they thought the grand opening unfolded. From their experiences at the event they can let you know of both happy occurrences to celebrate and disappointments to correct.

A few days after the grand opening, gather your associates to conduct a thorough debriefing. If your business was open during the grand opening, determine if any of your operating systems are faulty. Follow up on contacts who indicated the potential for business.

On the media front, track coverage of the event. Follow up with media who attended to determine if stories ran or will run, and procure copies of the coverage.

Finally, coupons also provide a valuable assist. If they're redeemed within their expiration window, you can quickly find out if the grand opening made enough of an impression for attendees to come back.

Grand Reopening

Has the opportunity for a grand opening passed you by? Or have you been around for a while and would like to reintroduce your business to the community? Consider the value of a grand reopening to establish a stronger market position, celebrate a remodel, or herald the addition of a new product line. Take the same tack as you would with a grand opening, and make sure you invite those who have contributed to your success along the way—loyal customers, community leaders, and other business owners.

▶▶ Test Drive

Make it a point to attend a grand opening celebration in your area— a restaurant, a national store chain that's new to town, or even a civic event such as a new library or post office. In your assessment:

- ➲ What makes this event special? What detracts from it?
- ➲ Is there a feature or highlight you wish you'd thought of or that could be repurposed for your business?
- ➲ How did the enterprise's employees and operations fare? Were the employees trained? Did systems work flawlessly?
- ➲ How were you treated as a customer or guest at the grand opening? Was it a positive or negative experience?
- ➲ Based on the grand opening alone, how likely are you to return to the business for repeat business? Why did you answer as you did?

Routine Events:
The Simple Can Be Sublime

Reasons for Participating

No matter what industry you're in or what your company does, chances are that the opportunity will arise for you to participate in a trade show. A trade show is an organized exhibition of products, based on a central theme, at which manufacturers of a common or related industry meet to show their wares. Generally conducted in a bustling environment where companies or organizations rent display space or a booth, trade shows allow these enterprises to promote their business through exhibiting their goods and services. **Trade shows can consist of manufacturers simply displaying their products, offering those products or services for sale to visiting wholesales and retailers, or a mix of the two.**

While participating will cost time, money, and resources (all of which will be explained later in this chapter), establishing a presence at a trade show can create untold benefits, which include:

- Providing face-to-face contact with buyers and competitors
- Allowing you to gauge the competition in a compact arena
- Giving the opportunity to generate sales leads, as well as sales, to a vast audience
- Reaching targeted audiences
- Prospecting for new customers
- Introducing new products and services
- Enhancing your image and visibility

What Are Your Company's Marketing Objectives?

In determining the feasibility and effectiveness of your participating in a trade show you must analyze your company's current marketing objectives. Just because you've been approached by a trade show or find out about one that sounds interesting doesn't mean you should sign on. Before registering with a particular trade show, research the show.

Answer this ten-point questionnaire:

1. Does the timing fit in with your needs?
2. How convenient is the location?
3. Have you attended the show before?

4. If so, did you consider your participation successful?

5. What have your competitors said about this show?

6. How will the show be promoted?

7. What is the show's track record?

8. Is the show a prime venue to reach your targeted audience?

9. Will it allow you to achieve a stated goal?

10. If you don't attend, what will be the downside?

Know Your Reasons; Check Out the Possibilities

Your industry may have many trade shows that want your participation. But many are expensive, so choose wisely from your options.

After considering both the benefits of trade shows and your specific needs, determine which trade show is the best fit for your organization. A trade-show presence may allow you to break into a new market, gather new customers, and make profitable sales. But you must state your goals clearly before embarking on the work a trade show will entail. Particularly if you haven't been involved with a specific show before, don't be afraid to ask questions before you make your decision. Make sure it's a good fit for your enterprise. Organizers want to make sure they host a show that will have happy participants and attendees.

Then Comes the Paperwork

In all likelihood you'll be able to peruse an exhibitor prospectus and application form that will include such information as an overview of the show and why it's worthwhile to participate in it, fees associated with the booth and deadlines for deposit and full payment, the location, and dates for the exhibition itself as well as move-in and move-out dates. In filling out the application you'll have to provide information about your company and its products or services, booth location preferences, who's attending from your company, and a liability waiver.

The Timetable for Involvement

While the show's management provides you with a crucial breakdown of days (for show dates, setup, break down), the particulars of your timing and deadlines must involve far more. Once you've signed up for the show you'll receive an exhibition bible, a manual covering every aspect of the show that you need to know. Commit to learning as much about the show as possible and your responsibilities therein by reading the manual, which is usually chock full of guidelines, rules, and regulations. Your familiarity with what's to come will be a huge factor in successful planning—both for your timetable and for your budget (which will be discussed in the next section).

For now, consider these other vital factors for your timetable for trade-show involvement:

Design: Preparing for the design of your booth and the actual execution in having it up and running at the show

Travel: Planning travel and hotel accommodations for employees attending the show

Promotion: Conducting ample promotion via e-mail blasts or direct mail to encourage attendance at your booth during the show

Collateral: Creating collateral material, such as press kits or sales sheets, to hand out at the show or to mail immediately afterward

Giveaways: Producing giveaways that you plan to have at the show to add excitement to your booth and leave a lasting reminder

Taking Costs into Account

Having a booth at a trade show will cost, both the fee to have a booth and building, organizing, staging, and staffing that presence. As you lay out your timetable, you'll need to attach costs to each of those line items.

Paper, Paper Everywhere

Whatever you hand out to attendees shouldn't be expensive. Much of the paper (nearly 70 percent of it by some estimates) does not go home with the attendees. While you don't want to be exclusionary in handing out the collateral, try to be selective if possible. For instance, don't have stacks of all your promotional materials out for the taking. Have some material that can be perused. During conversations with people who visit your booth, you can ascertain if their questions and interest level warrants giving them additional information. Though you should make some information available to everyone, you might consider taking down attendees' mailing information and sending materials to prospects or interested parties immediately after the show.

Make sure you have current press kits for media attending the show. In addition to having hard copies, have them available in e-mail, CD, or DVD formats so they can be quickly downloaded and distributed. Because of the news value of a trade show, you should supply information about your company and its products or services at the show itself—not afterward when the media has moved on to their next story.

Smart Thinking about Giveaways

Select promotional giveaways that directly tie in with your brand. Sure, everyone likes the fun of a novel tchotchke (also known as swag)—a knickknack or trinket usually emblazoned with a company's logo—at an event. But is that giveaway likely to be kept or remembered after the show? Too often giveaways end up in a trash can, a goodwill pile, or a toddler's toy trunk. **What kind of promotional item can you give out at your booth that says something about your company, has some use for its intended audience, and may even be considered a must-have?** Brainstorm the possibilities. Think about a simple item you see and use everyday, something that could be useful to your target audience. Before you talk to a representative who specializes in mass producing these kinds of objects, have a list of ideas you think would be appropriate. While salespeople certainly have a great idea of what's hot on the market and what's available that can be created quickly or cheaply, don't let those details be your only guide to the best giveaway you can have.

You might also consider a piece of literature as a giveaway, such as a thoroughly researched report or a listing of services for a particular industry. Again—even if nicely bound—it must have value for the recipient. So many companies hand out the ubiquitous sticky notes, paper clip containers, and bouncy balls that your thoughtful, creative approach to a giveaway will be a true standout that will make you remembered in a trade show.

Sponsorship Opportunities

Depending on the size and importance of the show, you may also want to sponsor an event such as a breakfast, a cocktail hour, a speaker, a panel discussion, or a seminar. You may have an idea, or the show may have options they're offering for sponsorship. In either case, you'll need to discuss the details—when, where, and whom to invite—with show management. While the endeavor will take time, money, energy, and commitment, it may be well worth the effort.

Aesthetic Planning for Your Booth

In all likelihood, the show has contracted with an exhibition services company that will be laying out the exhibition hall with booths. These may be tables surrounded by partitions, or they could be more elaborate. Make sure you're apprised of this information in your exhibitor manual. If you don't see the details you need, ask for them.

The exhibition services company has been contracted by show management to provide the booth, signs, setup, and other services for a set price to each of the show participants. However, if you have additional needs—such as special wiring or more electricity, additional furniture, or even plumbing—you will pay separately for those.

The exhibition services company is just providing the basics that they've prearranged with show management. Even with that help, you'll have to figure out how big you want the booth to be, how it will look within that space, and how you'll design your exhibit to draw in traffic.

To make those decisions, decide what's of top priority to feature in your booth. What are your goals for the show? Is there a particular product that should be highlighted? What visuals would be stimulating for people to see and speak volumes about your company?

Booth Location

You may be able to request your booth location, though your request might not necessarily be fulfilled. Most trade-show participants opt for the center or right-hand aisles of an exhibition hall because that's usually where attendees begin their trek. Request a diagram of the entire space so that you can get a sense of where the "hot" places are.

Fair Comparison

Remember the project you had to do for your high school science fair? Or perhaps you've recently observed a niece or son work at putting one together. Those science fair projects were in many ways a microcosm of trade-show exhibits. They needed to attract judges (their intended target audience) with a colorful, well-thought-out exhibit and then sell their project by touting well-researched information (their product or service). A good science fair project is organized, interesting, and worthy of a stop-look-and-listen visit. These same attributes are necessary for a company's much bigger and more expensive trade-show exhibit. In fact, mapping yours out on a smaller scale may enable you to notice what's instantly alluring for a passerby and can help refine components that may be lacking.

A few tips to consider:

1. **Pay close attention to the floor plan you receive.** Make sure your space won't be blocked by columns, poles, corners, or other architectural deterrents.
2. **Try to steer clear of being close to bathrooms.** While that's a heavily traveled path, attendees have a higher priority on that pathway than stopping at your booth.
3. **Avoid a position close to high-tech exhibits that incorporate heavy use of motion, electronics, or video screens.** While you may get residual traffic from such a booth, yours may also—unfortunately—pale in comparison to the sheer noise and color of the other one.

The Space You'll Need

Booths tend to be mapped out in multiples of ten feet, beginning with a ten-foot-by-ten-foot square. If you've got a major demonstration planned in your exhibit, will feature expansive equipment, or expect to staff the booth with twelve employees, that would be too small a space. As a general guideline, plan on sixty square feet per person, then add space required for equipment and staging as well as for the all-important visitors.

The Display

As you factor in space, you need to focus on displaying your product or service—the reason you're at the show. You have many options to choose from: modular, tabletop, and popup displays; panels; literature and banner stands; shelving; bridges; and possibly a combination of several of them. Your displays may be graphically intense—with large, looming images—or very product focused with merchandise lined up on them. If you don't feel as if you have the design sensibility to map out your exhibit, consider hiring a trade-show consultant who can help you with both focus and features. Additionally, exhibit companies that sell trade-show equipment such as panel displays can be of service in selecting the system that will work best and most successfully for your company. Check out the Web site *www.buyerzone.com*, and jump to the trade-show display link under marketing. Answer a dozen questions about the event you're preparing for, and you'll receive trade-show exhibit display quotes from multiple vendors. Those vendors can help you identify and narrow down needs.

The Extras

Once you're squared away on the display, think about how else you can make your space instantly inviting so that attendees will want to visit it and spend time there. Consider these attributes in making your booth appealing:

- Live plants and floral arrangements
- Offering tea, coffee, or water
- Vibrant use of color

➲ An inviting aroma

➲ A comfortable area to sit and meet, take down information, answer extended questions, or write up an order

What Should You Bring?

In the confines of a booth, be prepared for just about any situation that pops up so that you—or a designate—don't have to fetch an item, taking away valuable time from being in front of customers and making sales. Be prepared to make a handy repair or stave off a headache. To handle any situation that may arise, have on hand such necessities as packing tape, scissors, a stapler and staples, a staple remover, an extension cord, a screwdriver, pen, paper, highlighters, business cards, an office contact list, shipping labels and instructions, rubber bands, a disposable camera, glass cleaner, paper towels, breath mints, pain reliever, facial tissues, Band-Aids, and a sewing kit.

Making Your Booth Effective

Even if your space is the apex of aesthetic appeal, if it's not generating business, the look does nothing for you or your product. Returning to your company's goals and objectives, make sure your exhibit is consistent with your company's image. The show marks a golden opportunity to embolden or establish your presence; don't detour from that mission. If your company sells custom electric guitars, don't outfit your booth with soft pastels and play music featuring pianists. Make sure your booth projects a positive image consistent with your company and its goals.

Consider introducing an element of fun in your exhibit through a demonstration or projected images. That tack, which could even turn out to be a conversation starting point, can be alluring for visitors and easier for discussions to be initiated.

Additionally, take a look at the space's flow. Can visitors make their way in easily? Are they dissuaded from coming in because they'll feel "trapped" once they enter? Create an open atmosphere that eliminates any physical or psychological barriers. Make your employees easily identifiable, dressed in a professional, similar fashion with nametags that

---

| Inside Track | Harmony Art Organic Design |

Recently at an enormous textiles trade show in Southern California you could find suites, booths, and tables overflowing with fabrics, notions, and designs. While many of the areas were well-designed and enticed visitors with structure and purpose, one booth stood out.

A new company, launched by a husband-and-wife team in northern California, had set up their first-ever booth to showcase their new organic fabric line, Harmony Art, and take orders. The booth had an open layout and, what was essential to making an impact at this particular show and in this industry, Harmony Art took advantage of the company's beautiful fabric patterns and styles. They hung many yards of their fabrics, allowing them to both decorate the booth and highlight their offerings.

Harmony Art went further: They carpeted their booth with natural fiber coverings, filled it with decorative lamps emitting soft lighting that flattered and welcomed visitors, and company personnel offered all those who stopped by warm mugs of organic tea. The company's materials matched the tone, tenor, look, and style of their booth perfectly; everything meshed together to create a cohesive message.

For the buyers they were courting it was a perfect pitch, prompting a bushel of orders and encouraging other companies to attend upcoming trade shows and outfit their booths in a similar vein.

For your next trade show, explore how you can carry your message throughout your booth's look, materials, and approach to send an inviting signal to potential buyers and give a clear indication of what your company sells, what it stands for, and how it can help its target audience.

clearly feature your organization's logo. You don't want them lost in the crowd that you're aiming for. Instead, they should be easily pinpointed for potential customers to approach.

Drawing in Customers

Once you've got an exhibit that's attractive and consistent with your company's message and goals, make sure your booth's staff is ready for customers. Prior to the show, give your staff the information they need to be effective ambassadors for the company. Make sure they're also apprised of the company's overall vision and goals for the show. Maintain constant contact with them throughout the show, including daily debriefings, to monitor successes and to pinpoint and ward off potential problems.

The employees should provide a continual welcoming environment. You should prohibit eating, smoking, drinking, or reading on duty. They shouldn't be talking on the phone, clustering in conversation groups with each other, or leaning against the exhibit walls. They should always look as if they're raring to go, eager to engage in conversation with prospects, supply information, take orders, and answer questions.

In addition, make sure that your booth's staff knows how to record leads. Many shows have technology and equipment that allow you to scan information off an attendee's name badge. Then you'll get a print-out—which can obviously be a boon to your business—that you can input into your database.

Direct Mail and E-blasts

As mentioned before, your timetable should include an alert to potential customers that you'll have a booth at the upcoming show. A postcard announcing your presence at the show followed by an e-mail reminder keeps you in the participant's mind. You may also want to offer an incentive that makes your booth a "must" stop at the show. (This is in addition to giveaways at the booth.) You can offer a free gift, a discount on orders written to the first twenty-five visitors, or some similar draw. If the giveaway you've decided upon is a limited edition or expensive, you can use that as an enticement, too, by stressing its exclusivity.

Ringing Up Sales

When a sale is made, make sure to show appreciation and thank your customer. Don't rush off to the next sale. If you don't typically make sales away from your business premises, make sure that you get down all the necessary information. Further, have a remote credit card station set up that can approve and process the orders quickly, or—if you're using your office as a satellite to process the orders—make sure you've got someone on call who is well versed in completing sales. Have someone available back at your office during trade-show hours to conduct any necessary follow-up, provide shipping details, or to check stock.

Check Out the Competition

You'd be remiss if you didn't find out how other companies are competing with your business. What do their booths look like? Are they professional and polished or slapped together? Are their booths crowded with show participants? If so, how are they drawing in customers? And are those customers buying or merely lured in by a gimmick? In the same spirit of research, take notes about any booth, display, or suite that captures your interest. Pick up brochures that look attractive, and use ideas that you gather as a springboard for your own company's future endeavors.

After the Show: Conducting Follow-up

Be timely and responsive in following up with customers after the show. You may also want to send a thank-you e-mail for making your booth one of their stops. If you say you're going to send out a package, more information, or supplemental material to them, do it promptly. Once you've made a valuable contact, you want to keep it. Even if that particular contact doesn't result in a sale, your impressive response may lead them to refer your company to others.

Also conduct a thorough internal evaluation. Immediately after the show hold an extensive debriefing. Your honest assessment and analysis of this trade show will not only influence whether you'll participate in it again, but it will help determine how you'll prepare and present at others. Questions that should be considered during that meeting include:

- ➲ Were you prepared for the show? What weren't you prepared for?
- ➲ What product or service garnered the most attention? The least?
- ➲ Did you reach your pre-set goals both in sales and in image and impression?

- Would you participate in this show again? Why or why not?
- What did your competitors do better than you did?
- What changes would you make to your exhibit in the future?
- Were advance direct-mail pieces or in-booth promotions successful?
- What leads did you procure? What follow-up action is being taken with those leads?
- How will you monitor if/when/how that follow-up results in a sale?

▶▶ Test Drive

Analyze your trade-show potential. Think about an area that's easier for you to excel in and another that will require more effort. For instance:

- Does your business—by its product, service, or environment—lend itself to furnishing your booth or exhibit in a special or extraordinary way?
- Do you have ideas for giveaways that would be particularly memorable?
- Does your staff excel in customer relations and sales?
- Can you think of incentives for visiting the booth and ways to conduct follow-up afterward?
- Should you hire consultants who can guide you in better showcasing and spotlighting your company at a trade show?

Conventions, Conferences, and Expos

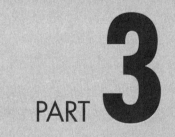

PART 3

Laying Out the Who, What, Where, When, Why, and How

You may have decided to take on a much bigger initiative than planning a meeting or participating in a trade show. As part of your enterprise's overall objectives you may have chosen to host an event that takes on grander proportions and incorporates more elements: the conference, convention, or exposition.

A *conference* generally refers to a series of meetings that begins with a keynote address and includes seminars and workshops. *Conventions* take on a bigger tone with a greater number of participants and include meetings and possibly voting. They also can feature opportunities for buying and selling with exhibition space. While conferences and conventions are often industry or group specific, *expositions* are large gatherings with exhibition space related to a certain industry or cause and are typically open to the public. Consider a few examples:

A small publisher of a new home magazine may hold a remodeling conference that would feature speakers on the ins and outs of contracting, do-it-yourself tips, as well as exhibits sponsored by major home improvement chains.

The owner of a fantasy collectibles store might have a sci-fi convention for fans, featuring booths that sell collectibles from popular and cult TV shows and autograph signing sessions or panel discussions with show celebrities.

The purveyor of a small chain of cake decorating supply stores could sponsor a cake celebration with workshops on baking and decorating cakes and many items such as coloring gels, cake toppers, and wedding stands for sale from companies.

The developer of a new medical device geared toward helping kidney patients wanting to cultivate relationships with doctors, nurses, and hospital personnel could sponsor a conference that highlights new research in the field.

In any of these cases you've moved from being a trade-show participant to being an organizer. Organizing such an endeavor can be expensive from the outset, though you may be able to break even or make a small profit through collecting admission or registration fees and renting exhibit space. In taking on an event of this magnitude you'll be spearheading the organization of an entire conference or convention, booking the hall, arranging for host accommodations, planning entertainment, procuring a contractor for exhibitor services, and—perhaps most importantly—attracting participants and ensuring that they have an enriching, fulfilling experience.

Even if you don't plan to take on the responsibility for organizing a conference, convention, or exposition in the near future, you'll undoubtedly glean helpful information for your next event from learning the details that go into such an event. Because these events are done on a grand scale, the thought and planning ratchet up in intensity. Dissecting how they're put together actually makes smaller events seem more manageable. Assessing the responsibilities and duties that are wrapped up in planning a conference or convention will make you more aware of the methods and necessities to make smaller events that much more successful.

In addition, your company may be asked to participate in some way in organizing one of these bigger events, so getting a handle on the varied aspects integral to it will be essential in your involvement.

The Initial Analysis

For the planning of a convention, conference, or expo, it all starts in a breakdown that assesses the reasons behind the event and how it will be held. In this analysis you must consider:

The who—How many people do you plan to invite? Whom do you plan to invite? Why are they being invited? What will they specifically get out of attending? What will you get out of having them there?

The what—What is the actual event? How is it being positioned? What are the activities within the event?

The where—Where will it be held? Depending on how many you're expecting, do you need a convention hall, a ballroom, or a series of meeting rooms?

The when—When will the convention or conference be held? How long should it last?

The why—Why are you having the event? What is its purpose? What are the theoretical and measurable goals for having the event?

The how—How will you carry it out? How will you plan it? How much money is in the budget for it?

The Bigger Why

After you conduct the initial analysis, you have to delve deeper to make sure that this undertaking will be worth the time, money, and effort you put into it. Ask yourself:

- ➲ Why are you doing it?
- ➲ How will hosting or sponsoring this event impact your bottom line?
- ➲ Will this elevate your standing in the community, industry, or nation?
- ➲ Will this help you to position your company as a brand leader?
- ➲ What will be the benefits or advantages of your planning/sponsoring/executing this conference or convention?
- ➲ Does it have the potential for significant media coverage and exposure?
- ➲ What would be the possible disadvantages?

The Entire Collection

Keep in mind that planning a convention, conference, or exposition is taking charge of several smaller events, such as meetings, exhibits, meals, and seminars. Therefore, while this chapter, as well as Chapters 11, 12, and 13, gives extensive overviews of and insights into the process, consult other chapters as well that can give you further information. For instance, if your event includes a luncheon, check out details,

Christmas in September

One of the most accessible themes revolves around Christmas. In one metro area a few hundred companies that specialize in advertising premiums—apparel, housewares, sporting goods, office supplies, and novelty toys that can have a company logo screened, printed, or embossed—come together annually to host Christmas in September.

These companies invite thousands of current and potential customers from a variety of industries to see and sample their wares. Among other benefits, the customers who arrive to shop at Christmas in September have the opportunity to find the perfect holiday gift to distribute to their own customers, clients, or patients. For the companies hosting the event, they also renew and initiate ties with customers who may need advertising specialties at other times of the year as well.

The Christmas in September theme instantly puts everyone in a shopping mood. In addition, attendees are treated to an array of small gifts, as well as free meals to encourage them to shop longer.

Taking the concept a step further, the Christmas in September organizers also use a theme-within-a-theme to keep each year fresh. For instance, one year's "Have a Winning Season" took on a baseball tone, and exhibits were encouraged to incorporate a World Series–type flair and flavor with such paraphernalia as pennants, baseball caps, and team jerseys in full force. Food served included such ballpark fare as hot dogs, popcorn, sodas, and cotton candy.

tips, theories, and suggestions offered in Chapter 15, which deals with banquets.

Determining a Theme

Once you've decided to move forward, you must then give the initiative an overall theme. This theme should resonate with your intended audience and present a unifying component for attendees.

What is the overarching reason that you're bringing these people together? To educate them on corporate ethics? To promote being a green company? To market better to ethnic audiences? To see silkscreen applications on numerous different products? To showcase the latest advancements in Web design?

Even if your gathering is held annually (or seasonally) and has a punchy name, commit to establishing a theme for each year. Adopting a theme will inform the event's direction, a particularly helpful component when an event lasts for more than a day.

In coming up with a theme, think of a particular issue you want to emphasize. Consider a theme that is action oriented and will pull in participants and get them involved, that can translate well to an image (that could serve as a logo), and that's catchy and easy to remember.

Giving the Event Structure

To give the event structure you'll need to make decisions regarding how long you want the event to last, how many sessions you'll include, whether you'll have workshops, if there will be exhibits and—if so—how many, and how much space you'll allow for them. In addition, you'll need to decide how all the event's components adhere to and expound upon the conference or convention's theme.

A Template to Draw Upon

Even if you're a professional event planner, coming up with an entire game plan from scratch for a three-day conference that will gather remarkable attendance and present an inestimable program can seem daunting. To that end, do your homework. More than likely you or your colleagues have attended an event that contained elements you would like to include in your conference or convention. The Internet also brims with ideas to consider.

By no means should you copy another organization's agendas, itineraries, and programs word-for-word or hire the same speakers, present the same seminars, or employ the same theme or entertainment. Your research should turn up the kinds of interesting suggestions that will fit into your program's format. Your options may include a mix of business, educational, or social endeavors or slant more toward one particular area. Consider this breakdown of those three areas (and realize that there may well be crossover in the activities you design for your specific program):

➲ Business—meetings, general sessions
➲ Educational—seminars, workshops, clinics, panel discussions
➲ Social—receptions, cocktail hours, themed parties, banquets, dinners, galas

Simultaneous Tracks

If you're attracting several audiences in a common industry for your conference or convention, consider dividing your educational sessions into different tracks or groupings. For instance, a conference geared toward the gaming community separates their sessions into subject disciplines, as in the game design track, business and management track, production track, and audio track. With the conference's presentations assigned accordingly, professionals in each discipline can quickly tell which sessions are more in line with their priorities.

Logistical Concerns

In this section you've learned about some of the theoretical concerns in setting your program for a multiday event. You also must take into account physical concerns regarding the location of it and consider how to make your attendees comfortable in that venue. Later in this chapter you'll delve into securing a venue for a larger event. For now, in giving form and function to a conference and convention you have to examine the venue from different perspectives: Does the setting have or is it near ample hotel rooms for attendees (if the event is longer than a day)? Does the venue have all the services you need, or will you need some furnished by outside contractors? Does the venue have the space you'll need for meetings, big and small, and exhibits, if they're part of the program?

Meeting Space Calculators

If you're trying to find a locale that can hold several different meetings simultaneously for several different audiences, take advantage of meeting space calculators you can find on numerous Web sites, such as those for national hotel chains Marriott and Hilton. Plug in the number of attendees you're expecting for a meeting or event into these online calculators, and they'll instantly determine how many people will fit in the room or what size room you'll need.

The For-Profit Possibility

Some enterprises decide to host an event not only for exposure but also for profit. If this is an area that interests you, realize that while the potential for a financial upside may be exciting or promising, the downside is also significantly riskier. If you decide to take the for-profit plunge, begin by determining what the moneymaking ventures involved in the event might be. For instance, consider the following:

Activity	Upside	Downside
Lease exhibition space	Take in fees for leased space	May be countered by fees the hotel or convention center charge
Procure sponsors	Paying sponsors may want to reach a target audience commensurate with your potential attendees	Your message may get muddled with multiple sponsors
Sell tickets	Charging attendees for breakout events	May be a turnoff to attendees unless the offerings are significant

Some enterprises host events that are highly profitable. If you go this route, carefully weigh your options. **Unless you're an accountant or financial advisor, hire a professional who can help you brainstorm all the possible moneymaking ideas specific to your event.** That person should also be able to offer assistance charting out deficit, break-even, and surplus scenarios to establish the financial goals you'll need for success.

Identifying the Prime Components

In reviewing the program elements you want to feature, determine what will be the star attractions for your event. Do you plan on attracting a top professional in your field to speak or have a celebrity give a keynote presentation? Will there be panels brimming with trusted professionals? Will someone present groundbreaking research?

Next assess the type of venue you're going after and the city it's in. Is the location enticing? Does the city present other entertaining, educational, or business networking possibilities for participants? Is the time of year for your event particularly attractive, or does it tie in especially well with your theme? All of these components combine to present a stellar array of selling points for your event, which will foster buzz, attract attendees, and set up a healthy platform for a successful convention, conference, or expo. As you identify those prime attributes, continue building upon your event's structure to put together a blueprint that describes your intentions, gives estimates of attendees, provides an outline of the meetings, seminars, clinics, and—if applicable—offers details for exhibition elements.

Finding the Venue

With that game plan in hand you can take an informed approach to securing a location for the convention or conference. In approaching a location for a bigger event, such as a conference, convention, or expo, you'll have far greater needs and concerns than in planning a one-day retreat for twenty or a one-evening reception for 100. The site you lock in must have several connected spaces for meetings and exhibitions, capabilities for using A/V equipment in many rooms simultaneously, possibly room for a bigger gathering, catering abilities or connections, and—hopefully—experience in routinely hosting grand-scale events.

Fam (Familiarization) Trips

If you're visiting several venues to make your decision, you may be invited to make a familiarization or "fam" trip to a property. On such a venture you'll be treated to a hospitable trip and wined and dined to convince you that the venue you're visiting will make the perfect locale for your event. Make the most of your time by compiling and asking all the questions you have, taking complete tours to check out meeting and exhibit space, conducting food tastings, and meeting all the on-site contacts. However, understand that your accommodations and experience may be somewhat better than your conference attendees as the venue will want to impress you to procure your business. Only accept an offer for a fam trip if you're truly interested in the venue.

Before setting out to find the perfect venue, make sure your game plan includes all the details you can possibly include at this point. The more information you've accumulated, the more informed you'll be in approaching venues and, in all likelihood, that also means you'll save time and money. Your search will be more fine-tuned, so from the start you can weed out places that won't fit your needs and you won't ask for unnecessary space and equipment from ones that might be suitable.

Putting Your Needs in Writing: The RFP (Request for Proposal)

That blueprint you've devised will assist both you and the vendor in developing the RFP, the request for proposal, your next step in attracting and securing the perfect venue for your event. An RFP is a document you put together and distribute to the conference sites you are considering for your event. In the RFP you lay out the specific needs of your conference or convention and solicit bids from prospective venues. An RFP must include such details as the event's dates, expected attendance, meeting room needs, equipment needs, and catering requests.

For help with your RFP, you can go through a city's convention and visitor's bureau. They most likely have a stock form that you can use. Fill out details pertinent to your event then route it to the potential sites.

You should give those sites ten business days to complete the RFP, then, you can review them and see which most closely fulfill your event's needs. Once the site is selected, work closely with the designated contact to fill out paperwork and set deadlines for your deposit and subsequent payments.

This contact should also become part of your team. You'll be working closely together to get guest rooms booked, procure A/V equipment, line up the catering, and all the other facilities that will have to come together to produce your event. While you shouldn't plan on needling that person mercilessly, keep him or her abreast of significant changes that impact costs, numbers, and stated needs. Regularly check in with your contact via phone or e-mail. As the contact is probably in charge of other events happening sooner (and thus having a more immediate priority), all of your requests or questions may not be answered immediately, but they should be dealt with in a timely manner to ensure that you all are contending with any potential crisis responsibly and avoiding any minor problems that could become major flare-ups.

Setting the Itineraries

Nailing down the venue puts you considerably closer to fleshing out your event's other components. In so doing, you should detail itineraries for:

- ➲ You, as the event planner, listing all the responsibilities involved
- ➲ The event's lineup, which gives a time, day, and location breakdown of all the event's activities
- ➲ The attendees, with an arrive-to-depart, start-to-finish schedule

These might not be the definitive, finished itineraries, but they should start out with a general outlook that will alert you to any holes or missing elements you should consider, repair, and fill in.

As the event planner, your itinerary must factor in many of the considerations outlined in Chapter 3 regarding timelines. As the event nears, it will alert you to moving equipment in and out, providing final numbers to catering, and holding rehearsals.

For the event itself, pinpoint each element—from opening session to closing ceremony—of the entire program, including the start and end time for each one, where it takes place, who attends, and what each of those components consists of (a Q&A session, a featured speaker, a dance).

With the venue selected and the program more defined you can begin alerting potential participants to the dates and location. For their itinerary you'll craft a schedule that takes their viewpoint into consideration: What's attractive about attending this convention or conference regarding program content and networking? When and how should they make travel and accommodations arrangements? How much time overall do they have to allot for attending?

Travel and Transportation

If you are expecting attendees to travel from many other cities, establish a relationship with a travel agency that can handle the details. While attendees may make their own arrangements, ideally they should have the option of contacting an agent to book a flight or set up other transportation.

As with any other vendor arrangement, do your homework in finding a reputable travel agent to work with. A good one will have access to various package deals, solid relationships with the airlines, and can deftly handle any scheduling mishap that occurs. For instance, the agency may be able to secure a better rate for travelers on a particular airline. In addition to airline bookings, the agency may also help out with rental cars for attendees and ground transportation in the city hosting the event.

Enticing Participation and Mailing Information

Once you've lined up the venue, confirmed your dates and your star attractions, and have a sound, solid account for what the event experience will entail for all concerned you're ready to start lining up attendees.

An Event Web Site

Create a Web site for your event as soon as possible. You can begin with just a memorable URL and a banner page announcing the event, saying that details are forthcoming. But don't leave it in that state for long. Commit to providing well-written, timely text and visual content about the event itinerary, program elements, the speakers and their bios, scheduled entertainment, travel and accommodations, and other pertinent information. Update the material frequently with announcements and information that will create excitement and provide a contact point for potential participants' questions.

Save the Date

First approach potential attendees with a save-the-date announcement. You can do this through direct mail or less expensively in an e-mail blast format. For the save-the-date, you don't necessarily have to have your entire program plotted out. But your save-the-date announcement must have a date, the location, and the event's name and theme. You should also provide a contact with e-mail address and phone number and provide a Web site for potential attendees to gather more information as it becomes available.

The sooner you can release a save-the-date announcement the better. People's calendars get busy, and they appreciate plenty of notice, particularly when you have a event they'd like to be at. In addition to announcements, release save-the-dates to newsletters, industry publications, Web sites, and other relevant media that your potential participants read.

The Invitation and Direct-Mail Pieces

At a predetermined time, send an invitation to the event. The timing can vary, but give as much time as possible. **Have your invitation and all direct-mail pieces prominently display a logo and event masthead that are easily identifiable.** Make sure the pieces are professionally produced, demand attention, and motivate subsequent participation in your event. If the invitation doesn't look inviting, your event will suffer.

Incentives for Invitations

Whichever mode you decide on to distribute invitations, consider an incentive for attending—particularly if this is your first event—which you describe in the invitation. A premium, a coupon, and a credit for a college course have all been used to encourage attendance. Of course the popular preregistration—with a cutoff date for signing up and sending in attendees' money—entices people to commit to the event early and receive a discount or reduced fees for doing so.

Include relevant copy and all pertinent details about the event. Be succinct and don't overwhelm the reader. For instance, if you're mailing an invitation packet, keep it organized with a purpose for every piece of paper. Alternately you might send out a simple invitation and then follow up by snail or e-mail for those who respond with all the necessary registration materials. In fact, an increasingly popular alternative is going the e-mail route in soliciting, organizing, and registering attendees. You can't deny the effect of someone receiving an impressive invitation by postal mail; there are still effects and embellishments that can't be transmitted electronically. However, for confirmations, registrations, and the like, e-mail is undeniably a cost-effective alternative.

Include a respond-by date in all the materials. People need deadlines, and you need to keep a head count for all your activities.

The E-Mail Effect

Going electronic with your attendees pre- and postevent for inviting, confirming, collecting fees, and following up has become increasingly popular. You can design your own Web site to invite would-be participants to register online and receive information, or you can work with an online event registration company. If you opt for a completely paperless route, find ways for your event to cut through the e-mail clutter. For instance, have any e-mail you send regarding the event outfitted with an event logo jpeg. If you go electronic, try not to sacrifice the flavor and excitement that hard copies can sometimes convey.

Follow Up for Attendance

If response is slow, you'll want to conduct follow-up with potential participants at select intervals leading up to the conference or convention. While you can send e-mail messages, you may have a better response rate by assigning or hiring people to make follow-up phone calls.

▶▶ **Test Drive**

Consider the advantages and disadvantages in taking on the organization of a conference, convention, or expo:

- ⮕ Could your company benefit from hosting a large-scale event?
- ⮕ Brainstorm possibilities that might attract a big audience and suit your company's mission statement and goals.
- ⮕ What would be the biggest deterrent to holding such an event: the budget, the time involved, or the personnel required?
- ⮕ Is it possible that the upside would outweigh the downside?

Coordinating Food and Beverages

When you're in charge of scheduling and planning a conference or convention, one of your most important responsibilities is feeding the participants. If you're interested in keeping your attendees in good spirits with unwavering attention spans and committed to staying involved, you need to keep them fed and therefore happy.

Some conferences may not feature a luncheon, breakfast, or even meetings. However, with those you still need to have food catered for VIPs, speakers, or sponsors involved with the event.

Additional catering needs are further discussed in Chapters 15, 16, 17, and 18, which explore social-intensive events such as banquets, black-tie galas, open houses, and cocktail parties that include food and beverages as a focal component.

Food Considerations

Assessing food for a big-scale event requires careful thought about several questions:

- ⮑ Which items on the itinerary need food?
- ⮑ What will food add to those activities?
- ⮑ Will food be a necessary feature of particular parts of the event, such as a banquet or a snack that will help break up meeting times?
- ⮑ If you need a meal break, should you send attendees out to restaurants or should the meal be a gathering of attendees to spotlight an agenda item such as a speaker or awards presentation?
- ⮑ What money can be allocated for a food budget? (With a multiday conference or convention, a significant portion of funds must be allocated for food and beverages.) Can the event site accommodate the catering?
- ⮑ Should you contract with an outside vendor for food service?
- ⮑ How many people will need to be served?
- ⮑ How will you handle special requests, such as vegetarian, low-sodium, and kosher meals?

Pinpointing the Occasions

Having a blueprint of your event will allow you to ascertain the points at which food and beverages should be served.

- Breakfast, the most popular choices being buffet or continental
- Lunch, with such options as sit-down, buffet style, or box lunch
- Dinner, which can be served sit-down or buffet style or could be an event in itself as in a barbecue, pool party, or luau
- Breaks in between meeting times, which can include snacks such as granola bars and chips, popsicles or an ice cream sundae bar, fresh fruit, sodas, coffee, and tea
- Cocktails, which may be a hosted (paid by the event's host) or a cash bar (paid by attendees), as well as light hors d'oeuvres

Devising the Menu

Working with the caterer, catering department, or food contractor, fine-tune your menus for each of the occasions that food and beverage will be offered. You may also take this time to taste some of the food options and explore meal and snack possibilities for the venue. A few tips to consider:

- Go for healthy—but tasty—choices. You want your attendees energized by meal breaks, not loaded down from them.
- Ask for fresh instead of canned or frozen foods.
- Make sure you have several options for those with dietary restrictions.
- Request variety. People don't want to see their plates with the same foods at dinner that they had yesterday at lunch.
- Don't be afraid to consider themes, such as a chopsticks lunch, or different locations, such as a picnic supper at a nearby park, to break up meal monotony. These different takes on meals also foster new discussions from participants and rev up enthusiasm.

Drafting the Order

Having decided when food and beverages will be offered, work with a catering manager for the hotel or a representative of the food contractor you're using to hammer out an agreement that will include a wide range of specifics. This document is also known as the banquet event order (or BEO in event parlance), your definitive take on what's expected from both parties. It will include the guaranteed numbers for the meal, the menu selection, the room setup, service requirements, and other details pertinent to food and beverage.

You should take the time to read the BEO carefully and make sure you understand every element listed before signing. **In all likelihood, you will have a separate BEO for each mealtime, snack time, or cocktail event.** This document is often used by all personnel involved with the event, so double-check it thoroughly before signing. If you need any changes, get them in as soon as possible so that they can be accommodated.

Though this document may guarantee a specific number of people to be served, you won't need to turn in the actual number of attendees for the meal until—typically—seventy-two hours before it's served.

Event Publications

Event planners rely on several trade publications to keep up on industry trends and tips. These publications contain a wealth of articles ranging from tabletop décor and the latest in room dividers to newly opened venues, the hottest speakers, and recent themes that are all the rage. As soon as you see an event rising on your horizon, read up! Soak up all the possible ideas, current know-how, and relevant knowledge that will benefit your event. Visit the Web sites for *Expo* magazine at *www.expoweb.com*, *Special Events* magazine at *www.specialevents.com*, and *Event Solutions* magazine at *www.event-solutions.com*. Peruse the latest issues, review archived articles, and sign up for subscriptions.

Taking Care of Décor

Depending on where your large-scale event takes place, you may be responsible for a wide range of decorations or none at all. If your venue is a historical facility or artistic setting, you'd be wise to leave the current surroundings as decorations enough, save for perhaps centerpieces on tables needed for meals or registrations. If on the other hand your site is a massive, empty fellowship hall, the atmosphere may seem too drab on its own to create any excitement.

Survey the surroundings of the site at least six months (a year if possible) before a large-scale event takes place.

- ➲ How empty does it look?
- ➲ Do you think it's boring?
- ➲ What will an attendee first focus upon when entering the setting?
- ➲ What decorations will be striking and complement the event but not detract from it?
- ➲ What visual elements will motivate and stimulate participants?
- ➲ Are some decorations such as logo screens or backdrops necessary to keep attendees focused and as staging for media that are covering the event?
- ➲ Does any current architecture (structures, panels, partitions, unsightly cracks) need to be repaired or temporarily removed?

While you don't have to go overboard in your decorating regimen, you do want to present a welcoming environment, strike a jubilant mood that will put participants in the spirit of the event, and design surroundings that contribute to its success.

Not every space will need a massive redo. Remember some basic decorating choices that enliven a space: flowers, plants, balloons, and draped fabric. In addition, depending on the tenor and activities of the particular program component or activity, some decorations are really part of the entertainment category and can also be interactive. These include photo booths, bubble-making machines, chocolate fountains, and—if you're outside—fire pits and water features.

Procuring Speakers

Speakers are often an integral part of a conference or convention, and because of their time commitment, cost, arrangements, and the preplanning involved they must be selected well in advance. If speakers are a primary component of your overall program, they will set the tone for the proceedings. Depending on your budget, you can go with an expert in your field, a celebrity, a news commentator, a politician, a comedian . . . you name it. But spend some time brainstorming on what speaker will have the greatest impact on your event. Keep the tenor, scope, and focus of your event in mind to narrow down the wish list.

Fortunately you have a wealth of options where speakers are concerned. You can begin with Web sites such as the National Speakers Association (*www.nsaspeakers.org*), Premiere Speakers Bureau *www.premierespeakers.com*) or International Speakers Bureau (*www.international speakers.com*). While many of the choices from those sites may be out of your price range, you can brainstorm on who might be a good idea. Check with other professionals or others who have planned events with speakers to get a sense of who's out there. Referrals provide an exceptional resource for who can and can't add to the warmth, spirit, education, and enthusiasm of an event.

In finding a speaker you need to pinpoint these four considerations:

1. What topics will fit in with the program itself?
2. What are the hot topics your audience would appreciate most?
3. Who would be the ideal speaker?
4. What is your budget?

Having answered these questions, you can set about finding a speaker. In your research, gather up as much relevant information as possible about him or her, including a biography, references (that you check on!), available topics, and even books, articles, clips, or video that the speaker or the speakers' bureau can provide.

Don't assume a speaker is excellent just because he or she is well known. Everyone has his or her own strengths. **A person's celebrity status doesn't guarantee that he can deliver on a topic that's important to your group.** Similarly, a speaker who doesn't necessarily have name recognition could provide your event with a dynamite presentation that has everyone awestruck.

Look at Video, Get References

Do your research. Obviously the best reference is you. If you've heard the speaker—or she has an upcoming engagement you can attend—you're a leg up on whether she'd be suitable for your current needs. Even if you can't see the person you're thinking about hiring, look at any video, DVD, or mp3 file that she can provide.

While a keynote address will be your most expensive speaking engagement for which to budget, you may be able to find other valuable, enriching speakers at less cost. Many times they will be just as memorable—as long as they're compatible with your event and audience needs, you're familiar with their credentials and experience, and you've gathered sufficient and excellent references for them.

Get the Details in Writing

Put together a contract for the speaker that includes in writing all your expectations, including the day he's expected to arrive; the time, day, and length of his talk; a general description of his content; and any amenities you will be providing, such as hotel accommodations, airplane fare, and transportation to and from the airport. In addition, you may be asked to provide certain special foods and fulfill special requests. If the speaker is a celebrity, you may also need to have additional security on hand.

Get the speaker's biography that he would like used in collateral such as the conference program and your organization's Web site announcing the event. You should also use his official biography in composing an appropriate introduction at the event.

A Speaker's Program Confirmation Form

A helpful tool for both you and the speaker is a form that tells her the number of people you're expecting to attend and the size of the room, the title of the speech the speaker is giving, and the length of the program (segmenting out the speech as well as the other activities that may be involved). On the form, also ask for such particulars as handouts the speaker may be submitting that need to be copied (and give a deadline for such) and A/V equipment she expects in the room. Finally, make sure you include a contact name, phone number, and e-mail address for any questions that she may have when filling out the form.

Selecting Other Entertainment

Aside from speakers, you may decide to enliven your event with other, far different kinds of entertainment. Jugglers, strolling musicians, costumed characters, clowns, crepe makers, storytellers, fortunetellers, face painters—all can make a great contribution depending on what's appropriate for your event.

Here again, brainstorm what might work for your event and what money you can allocate to it. These kinds of entertainment can bring excitement because of the variety they offer. Often they cost less than you might expect, so they're well worth researching.

To book this kind of entertainment check with a convention and visitors bureau office. Or if you've seen an act featured at another event, check in with that event's organizer to see if they have information on how you can contact the entertainment professional. Additionally check the Internet for listings about entertainment-for-hire in the area of your event. You can also take a look at parenting magazines, which often contain ads highlighting entertainment for parties.

Staffing

Depending on where and how big your event is, it may require an inordinate amount of staffing. The next chapter discusses the places at your event that need staffing, but take a look at this sampling to get an idea:

- ➲ Attendants for registration tables
- ➲ Ushers for checking badges
- ➲ Personnel for setup and cleanup
- ➲ Floaters for answering questions and troubleshooting
- ➲ Chaperones for VIPs
- ➲ Security

Considering Volunteers

Depending on the breadth, scope, and cause of your event, you may want to recruit volunteers. This notion, however, depends fully on your

Filling Out the Program

In programming an event of this magnitude, I—and the team I'm working with—always strive to make the biggest impression on attendees (no matter the budget). I realize that for many that might seem a trying task, but I've developed a few tactics that have been helpful in formulating a superior program for conference or convention participants.

First off, what is relevant to the attendees? Even though it might not be a focus of the show, what program components will be remembered as helpful and worthy? When consulting with organizers for a gift show that was exhibiting a multitude of lines and designers' work for various retailers, we decided to hold a series of workshops that offered real-life strategies for marketing, budgeting, and tracking inventory.

What is the competition doing? For conferences and conventions that target the same audience, we do our research to determine how we can go above and beyond the competition and to make sure we're not missing anything. In planning an educational conference that concentrated on strengthening parent-teacher-student communication, we investigated a wide range of similarly themed gatherings to see if we were in line with the hot-button topics and to gauge our slant on the offerings.

Finally, look at a completely different industry's approach. For instance, I like to review information and schedules for conventions and conferences that showcase cutting-edge occupations such as video game developers and software designers. As I started a consulting job for a medical convention, I looked at those materials from a completely different industry and asked: "What are they offering their attendees? How are they appealing to their core audience? What strikes me as particularly interesting? Is it something that could work for us?"

enterprise. For instance, if your event is linked to a nonprofit or educational cause, people will see a need and be likely to help out. If, however, you're an entrepreneur who's simply looking to cut corners by using volunteers instead of paid employees, you might not have much luck.

Still, if your for-profit enterprise interests them, college students may be willing to help out for real-life experience. In other words, make sure your volunteers are getting something out of their help—philanthropic, experiential, or otherwise.

Informing Staff and Volunteers

For both staff and volunteers, take the time before the event starts to calmly, patiently, and completely describe their duties and what's expected of them. Carve out definitive, structured meeting times for this download to occur. Include them in on all updates and, if possible, in the debriefing you'll conduct after the event is over. **You'll get a much better performance out of both staff and volunteers if they have a complete understanding of their duties and can appreciate how their responsibilities fit into the bigger picture and its resultant success.** In addition, make sure staff and volunteers are familiar with other aspects of the conference that will be helpful to attendees, such as directions inside the venue, nearby facilities and restaurants, and times and locations of major event happenings.

Make sure they understand—and hear—how much you appreciate their time and willingness to contribute. Emotions can run high during events; avoid becoming overheated or upset. You always want to present a smoothly running, well-oiled machine. You can't do everything by yourself; your staff and volunteers will undoubtedly do all they can to give you the help you need to assure success.

Taking Care of Staff and Volunteers

Even though you expect everyone to fulfill their responsibilities competently, don't expect them to work hours on end with no breaks. Treat them well by instituting predetermined break times and mealtimes. During those times, make food and beverages plentiful and easily available. Food is one of the simplest ways to make and keep people happy.

In addition, if your budget allows you may want to have all staff and volunteers in uniform so that they're easily identifiable. Uniforms present another opportunity to bring cohesion to the event. If uniforms are cost prohibitive, encourage staff and volunteers to wear similar clothing, such as white button-downs and khakis, or red golf shirts and black pants.

Signage

More than likely, you'll never have enough signs: signs for meetings, directional signs to locations, signs for registration tables, signs for schedules, signs for panel members . . . the list goes on. However, you don't want them to be a gaudy assemblage of posters. Thoughtfully review your itinerary components—and all the places connected to your event at the site itself—to ascertain when and where you need signage.

Have your signs professionally printed beforehand. If that's not possible, use design software on a computer, such as PowerPoint, to create good-looking signs that can be laminated or placed in sign holders.

If there is a program or location change that needs a sign, be prepared to print a new one off your computer. Do not simply handwrite a sign on legal paper. It won't look professional or credible and will reflect poorly on the event.

Don't forget easels, tripods, or tabletop holders to place the signs. Hotels and other conference-savvy sites will often have these available, but double-check beforehand. They usually are a separate breakout budget item, so they will cost to rent. If the cost to rent them seems unreasonable because you need a hefty supply, you may want to buy them in bulk from an office supply chain.

Handouts, Leave-Behinds, and Packets

For the initial mailing to attract your attendees you should include the following in registration packets, which can be mailed out or can be available on your event Web site:

- A registration form including information regarding registration, meal, and workshop fees; the dates; the site; the keynote speaker; and other top-billing details
- Information regarding special rates and reservations for hotels, airlines, and rental cars
- Details regarding shuttling or traveling to and from the hotel
- A conference or convention overview
- Specific workshop, seminar, and meeting information

Even if this information is e-mailed or downloaded, have hard copies available just in case it needs to be snail mailed or faxed.

Establish all the handouts you'll need for different sessions prior to the event. Using your itinerary, compile a list of the handouts for each event, including ones that speakers have sent or e-mailed you to be copied for their presentations. Some conferences and conventions post their handouts on the event's Web site so the handouts can be downloaded by participants to bring on their own or just have available on laptops they'll have with them. Even if that's the case, plan on having hard copies available for any participants who forgot to bring necessary materials.

Once they arrive, participants are usually given welcome packets, which can be compact or extensive. Depending on the theme, tone, tenor, number of attendees, and the program you're offering, decide what attendees must have when they check in to the conference or convention. Dissect your itinerary and the entire event to determine the necessary attributes for your welcome packet, which might include such suggested elements as:

- A comprehensive itinerary
- A name badge
- Tickets to events they've paid for
- Flyers about special events
- Information about the conference site and amenities
- Information about the surrounding area

They're Not Just Handouts

Handouts give you another opportunity to spotlight your event. Don't ever hand out literature, information, or details that have simply been copied on a plain piece of white paper. Use available space to include your organization's logo, the event's title, and sponsors' logos, or have the copies made on your company's letterhead. In a best-case scenario, every piece of written material that's distributed—though different in content—will have the same, consistent, cohesive, and attractive look and feel to it. That approach is also helpful to attendees for them to keep similar materials together.

▶▶ Test Drive

The time will come for you to hire a speaker for a large or small event. In preparation for that, begin to recognize areas of interest, concern, education, or entertainment that would make a significant contribution to an event if it were presented as a topic. Think about the following:

- ⮑ What are you most interested in as a current or aspiring business owner, entrepreneur, or company executive?
- ⮑ What's most important to your customers as it relates to your business?
- ⮑ Who do you think are the foremost experts on these topics?

Your Final Checklists

Having taken on the details, duties, and responsibilities of a tremendous event like a conference or convention, you must take the final steps to ensure your hard work will not be wasted. While each event is unique, checklists will help you get a sense of the tasks that should be fulfilled, pinpoint specific concerns, and serve as a starting point from which to expound upon initiatives tied to your event. They are divided into three categories: foundation, filling, and physical plant.

The Foundation Checklists

Unsurprisingly, you as the event planner and your staff form the event's foundation, having given structure for all to follow. At the core of the event you need to address some general points:

➲ Is staff (or volunteers) informed of their responsibilities?
➲ Have signs been made, and are they designated for and placed in the right locations?
➲ Have fire alarms, exits, and fire extinguishers been located?
➲ Is a contact list ready and in place? Does it contain emergency information?

Before the Kickoff

Before your event officially launches, hold a final meeting to review all the checklists with your team, reconfirm each individual's responsibilities, and restate troubleshooting procedures so that everyone is clear on how to handle any crisis that arises. Further, take this opportunity to restate the reasons the event is taking place: the purpose of the conference or convention, the goals you are trying to achieve, and the expectations you hope to fulfill for those attending. Despite the looming tasks swirling around, this meeting will help keep everyone focused on the overall vision and committed to the event's success.

There are a plethora of materials that you'll need at your disposal, particularly when planning an event of this magnitude. Being away from the office, a toolbox, sewing kit, or fishing tackle box (all with handles) comes in handy and makes a sturdy home for essential supplies. These include:

- Tape—transparent, double-stick, electrical, light tack, and masking
- Scissors—big and small
- Label maker
- White copy paper
- Three-hole punch paper (in case of scripts)
- Ink cartridges for a portable printer/copier
- Staplers and staples
- Paper clips
- Brads (for scripts)
- Permanent markers
- Ballpoint pens
- Scratch pads
- Safety pins, pushpins, and straight pins
- Rulers
- Extension cords
- Small alarm clock

The Filling Checklists

In this arena, double-check details pertaining to specifics for all content, which may involve meals, programs, seminars, entertainment, and speakers. For instance, for meals, your checklists will involve menus, food and beverage quantities, and meal numbers. For speakers and entertainment reconfirm program times, arrival information, and necessary equipment.

Food and Beverages
- Have you reconfirmed times and menus for all food-related events?
- Were final tallies of expected attendance for each food-related event delivered promptly?
- Have any changes been submitted to the banquet event orders? If so, have you double-checked that the changes were incorporated?

Speakers and Entertainment

⮑ Has the time the speakers are to arrive and speak been reconfirmed with them?

⮑ If necessary, has someone been assigned to pick up speakers from the airport and escort them to the site?

⮑ Has any special A/V equipment been arranged for any speaker who requested it?

⮑ If other entertainment has been scheduled, have arrival times and durations of appearances been reconfirmed?

⮑ Have any special equipment requests been prearranged?

⮑ Have the checks been cut to be delivered immediately after the engagement, or have other payment procedures been arranged?

The Physical Plant Checklists

These checklists pertain largely to setup and inherent materials, supplies, and equipment. Your checklists should include such details as:

Registration

⮑ Are registration packets complete and ready to be handed out?

⮑ Have registration tables been set up?

⮑ Has adequate staffing been arranged for registration?

Meeting Rooms

⮑ Is there sufficient seating, and is it properly arranged?

⮑ Are place cards in place, if needed?

⮑ Are water pitchers, note pads, and other supplies in place?

⮑ Have the lights and electrical needs been checked?

⮑ Is the microphone and lectern ready?

⮑ Has special A/V equipment been arranged for and installed?

⮑ If technicians are to be present to work equipment, has their time and presence been reconfirmed?

Exhibits

⮑ Have exhibitors been reconfirmed regarding exhibition hours?

⮑ Have you maintained contact with the exhibition contractor to ensure that exhibitors' needs are being met?

> ## Walk in a Participant's Shoes
>
> As part of ensuring that you've tended to all the details, come into your event before it starts as if you were an attendee. Walk through the entire experience, from checking into the hotel (if applicable) to registering at the event, picking up your packet, and putting on your name badge. Visit each area involved in the program: meeting rooms, ballroom, exhibition space, banquet hall. Look at it from the perspective of an attendee to confirm that your event is coming off as welcoming, inviting, professional, and exciting.

Receiving the Attendees

Even before you and your staff start greeting participants for a convention or conference, make sure they feel welcome by setting an inviting tone and enthusiastic attitude. If you've got many participants who traveled from far away, you want them to know that their time and money is well worth the effort they've taken to be here.

In so doing, you're getting your program off to a positive start. Attendees will remember the hospitality that's being extended. You can build up much goodwill from the initial impressions attendees have, particularly if they've already endured a delayed flight or missing luggage.

Registration

Often the registration table is the first impression a participant has of the entire event experience to follow. Make it count. If problems arise with the registrations—and most likely they will—let the attendees know you're working diligently to check on and fix the problem. Be attentive. **Have your staff and volunteers apprised of procedures and ready to handle any troubleshooting.** Don't be the only one who has the game plan or the answer or you'll be torn in a thousand directions.

Make sure that the tables are staffed with knowledgeable personnel and that the tables themselves are sharp with pressed tablecloths and subtle decorations. Further, make sure the tables are organized under appropriate headings so that registration will flow smoothly. For instance, one table could be for attendees A–H, another I–N, another

O–Z, another for VIPs and guests, and one more for press. If you are issuing parking validations, whether it's stamping the parking passes or handing out cards to be given to parking attendants upon leaving, have your system ready to go.

If you will be collecting money for late registrations, have all monetary systems set up. If you're taking credit cards, have a remote system that's been tested and is up and running. Wireless systems can be costly, but they give you nearly instant approval. If you're handling cash, have enough for change.

While you may have a set time for initial registration, such as 9:00 A.M.–1:00 P.M., consider a soft opening. There will undoubtedly be early birds who will appreciate being accommodated, and they will offer you the chance to work out any kinks that occur.

Presenting a Well-Oiled Machine

No matter how sprawling or all-encompassing your event may be, remain supremely confident at all times. Staff, volunteers, and attendees take their cues from you. If you're running around wild-eyed, frantic, or otherwise in a panic, those around you will suspect the event is in trouble. Even if the subsequent experiences go off without a hitch, they'll spend the next hours or days wondering when the other shoe will drop.

To help your situation, take care of whatever can be crossed off your own final checklist and do so before attendees arrive. You can project a calm image if you know you've got a handle on the event's myriad tasks.

Intermittently during the event, check with staff, volunteers, and attendees to gauge their experiences. You're not asking for approval or evaluation. You just want a general sense of how things are going and, if necessary, to deal with issues that might be popping up and can be easily remedied.

If possible, take walk-throughs before each event's session or meal to check and double-check room setup, table and chair arrangements, that supplies are in order and A/V equipment is up and running and tended to, and that the meal about to be served is the one on the banquet event order.

Do your best to be as proactive as possible before the event begins, then be promptly reactive once your event starts. If you find a problem in a room beforehand, take care of it as soon as possible. When a room is filled with participants waiting for a presentation to begin, that isn't the most opportune time to ask for their patience while you or a designate rummages around the room trying to find an electrical outlet that works, runs off to exchange a malfunctioning microphone, or deals with hotel staff to adjust the thermostat.

As sessions or meals conclude, make the time to inspect bills as they are presented to prevent being charged for extraneous items. On an audio-visual equipment invoice be sure the equipment used and services rendered match up to the accounting on the bill.

Keeping the Program Flowing

Stick to your itinerary. Pay close attention to start and end times. Float among the happenings to check on attendance at meetings, exhibits, and the like. Since you can't be everywhere at once, assign similar responsibilities to designates and have them report back to you.

While you monitor the itinerary, keep constant check on what's ahead, noting meeting rooms that should be available for certain times, equipment that should be arriving, speakers that should be present, and so on. Your best bet for keeping your event from stopping dead in its tracks is fending off the culprits that will cause program pieces to stall, such as late arrivals, no-shows, nonworking equipment, and ill-prepared meeting spaces.

From the Beginning, Assess on the Spot

If your first attendees are encountering problems checking in to the event or getting into their rooms at a hotel, find out why as soon as possible. They shouldn't be your guinea pigs, but learn from any entanglements they experience to prevent other participants from having the same snafus.

If you are repeating certain sessions on successive days, you have a terrific opportunity to ward off problems and make those sessions even more successful. Assess the first session, and take stock of any areas that can be improved on subsequent days.

In a similar vein, if an initial meal doesn't go well, take the matter up with the hotel's catering department or your contracted caterer to make sure other meals don't follow suit.

Treat Site Staff Well

You can particularly help your cause by treating the hotel or site staff with consideration and respect. Most of them will strive to help you, but you'll find that they will take even greater care if you reciprocate their efforts with kindness.

Plus, always be ready to tip. You don't have to be extravagant, just remember to do so with a reasonable amount. Many times you might be able to add their tip to a bill you're signing. If the situation is such that you would typically give them cash—and find yourself without any—take their name down and let them know you will make amends shortly. Then do so as soon as possible.

Befriend the Venue's Staff

Work professionally and courteously with the staff at the hotel or other venue hosting the event and you'll be rewarded. For instance, take the time to talk with them before a session or meal starts to make sure that they are aware of information regarding BEOs, A/V equipment, room setup and the like. More often than not they will go out of their way to help you keep the event running smoothly. Most likely they will appreciate that you took the time to fill them in and check in on their knowledge of the event. Now made to feel part of your team, they will want to contribute even more to ensure the event's success.

Evaluating the Event

As soon as possible after the event, preferably within forty-eight hours and not more than a week after, hold a committee meeting to analyze each of the event's components. You should address specific challenges—expected and unexpected—that the event posed. Further, you should delve into whether you and the staff were prepared to meet those challenges. Break your evaluation into categories, with questions and analysis focused on the venue, program content, food, speakers, equipment, lodging, conveniences, inconveniences, and the attendees' overall impressions. Don't try to lump everything into one general "How did everything go?" **For an evaluation to have its greatest impact it must be specific in its agenda and resultant content.** With each evaluation comes even more discerning knowledge about how to make all the events you undertake go more smoothly and more successfully.

Evaluating the Site

During your debriefing, consider responses to such questions as:

➲ Would you use this site again? Why or why not?
➲ Was the site's staff responsive to your needs?
➲ Was the venue easily accessible?
➲ Were there attractive elements about the site beyond the event, such as amenities, resort activities, or nearby attractions?
➲ Which rooms worked, and which ones didn't for their sessions or activities?

Break out the food category. If catering was provided by an outside contractor, evaluate their performance:

➲ Was the food served as agreed?
➲ Were there extra, unexplained charges on the bills?
➲ Did participants seem happy with the food?
➲ Was it average and just passable, or was it memorable?
➲ Meal by meal, were there any positive or negative surprises?

Evaluating the Program Content

This evaluation will be enhanced by distributing surveys to program participants to determine their interest in the sessions they attended and the value they attached to them. Hand out questionnaires at the end of each session to attendees, or include a portion in the event's overall surveys that you ask attendees to fill out at the end of the conference or convention. If at all possible, you or a designate should try to be present at sessions, at least for part of the time, to experience them firsthand, determine what works and what doesn't, and to find out if your observations jibe with what paying attendees thought. As part of your assessment of the program content, you and your team should ask:

➲ Were speakers effective overall? Which ones were more effective? Less effective?
➲ Would you hire the speaker again?
➲ Was A/V equipment for the speaker in working order?
➲ Did the equipment facilitate the presentations, or was it more for show?

Evaluating Transportation

To determine whether you'll again depend on the transportation companies you used—airlines, rental cars, limousines—ask the following:

➲ Did special fares with airlines and rental car companies work out to everyone's satisfaction?
➲ Did car services deliver speakers on time?
➲ If problems arose, did the companies handle them justly, promptly, and considerately?

Evaluating the Exhibits

If exhibits were part of your mix, discuss how they added or subtracted to the atmosphere and the participants' experiences:

➲ Did the exhibits add to the overall value of the convention or conference for participants?
➲ Was the work worth the time and effort?
➲ Which exhibits would be must-haves at a future conference or convention?
➲ Which exhibits would you not invite back?

Overall Evaluation

To make the most accurate assessment you should include the attendees in your evaluation. For ease in scoring, set up questions that can be

Evaluations Off the Page

Make your convention or conference evaluations as comprehensive as possible. While written evaluations are ultraimportant, don't let them be your only measure of success or the only method you use to gauge your attendees' satisfaction. Before, during, and after the event, make it a point to have at least one person check in with participants. And above all, be mindful not to operate in a vacuum as you plan, design, and execute an event.

For a few years I was integrally involved with an automotive company's dealers' convention. One of my responsibilities during the convention was to check in and talk with dealers about their convention experiences. I got as much as I could from a multitude of one-on-one conversations and group discussions with them. In doing so year after year I was able to build upon sessions we had for them, tailoring meetings and panel discussions to be more meaningful for them and adding components they said they considered valuable. In those face-to-face discussions at each convention I was able to follow up and ask additional questions on the spot—a convenience and enhancement that written surveys don't immediately afford.

In making those kinds of contacts and connections during the convention itself I could check in afterward with dealers who had been particularly helpful in their input or whom I deemed to be representative of several others in asking for help in future plans. In a sense they afforded me an instant response team. I could go to them and run ideas for an upcoming convention by them as we began putting plans into motion. In addition, after several years I realized I—luckily—had a surplus of ideas for program elements. I was never at a loss for filling the convention days with enjoyable and well-received sessions.

answered on a 1–5 scale (with 5 being the best and 1 being the worst). Make sure to include all relevant categories. Ask for their input on the sessions they attended, their attitude regarding the food and lodging, what they thought about the event's theme, and what they're taking back to their business. In addition to numeric answers, give them an area where they can give in fuller detail any comments—positive or negative—that may provide you even more insightful information.

You can offer the survey to attendees before they leave. Or you may choose to e-mail one. However, your best recourse may be to get evaluations for attendees before they leave, with memories fresh and a desire to fulfill an obligation present. Those you don't get responses from you can follow up with in an e-mail and a questionnaire attached.

Whether you get the survey from them in person or via e-mail, let them know their feedback helps your efforts in planning future events that will serve them even better. If possible, offer them an incentive for filling out the questionnaire. For example, each questionnaire can be numbered and the winning number turned in wins a cash prize, a gift certificate, or a product or service particular to your company. To complete your overall evaluation of the event, ask your own staff the following:

- ⮞ What comments, compliments, and criticism did you receive?
- ⮞ Did you feel that there was a general sense of happiness or unhappiness among the attendees and at the event?
- ⮞ What was the event's greatest accomplishment?
- ⮞ What was the event's weakest moment?
- ⮞ Did anyone or any company renege on a contract?
- ⮞ Did anyone or any company not show up? If so, why?
- ⮞ Which vendors would you use again? Why?
- ⮞ Which vendors would you not use again? Why?

▶▶ Test Drive

Delve more deeply into a conference or convention you have recently attended. Learn from that experience to craft and inform your own. Examine your thoughts on the following:

- ⮞ Do you think the event organizers looked at the event from an attendee's perspective? Why or why not?
- ⮞ What did you draw from the experience? If it's an annual event, do you plan to attend it again? Why or why not?
- ⮞ What program components would you have eliminated? Which ones would you have added?
- ⮞ What was your most positive experience about the event? How could more of those kinds of experiences be incorporated?

PART **3**
Conventions, Conferences, and Expos

Have a Master Plan

When planning events on a large scale you have to make arrangements for grander venues, lots of attendees, travel considerations, exhibition space, and food. But you have opportunities to make an even bigger statement with your event. You can take those extra steps that will bring a more favorable response from participants, prompt return attendance, and add luster to your enterprise. **When taking on events such as these you must have a master plan.** Because of the time and resources involved, conferences and conventions aren't simply just a good idea or a possible moneymaker. They take much time, thought, and advance planning—and specific, stated goals—to ensure their success.

A Convention Glossary

The Atlantic City Convention Center, one of the nation's most popular destinations for meetings and events, offers a helpful glossary of convention and conference terms on their Web site at *www.accenter.com*. They've deemed these terms the "most commonly used words and phrases, as defined by the International Association of Assembly Managers (IAAM)." Perusing that glossary and the site's FAQ page (both accessible at "About the Center" on the navigation bar) before you put your master plan in motion can be a fail-safe measure. The information on those pages may help you ascertain whether you've unintentionally omitted any important component from your planning.

For Exposure, Profit, or Both?

As discussed in Chapter 10, your goals for the event have to include whether you intend to make money on the event or are simply holding it to provide exposure for your company, goods, and services. If you're trying to make a profit on the event, understand that will ratchet up the pressure on it. Ideally your registration and exhibition fees will cover the costs of your enterprise.

Sponsorships

One way to generate additional funding is through sponsorships. Calling on companies to sponsor different portions of your event helps defray costs, and it could raise visibility. The downside is that you may cede some control over your program, and the sponsoring company could steal some of the spotlight.

Particularly if you're in a cash crunch, sponsorships can fund several attention-grabbing events that could enhance your event, including the following:

- ⤵ Hospitality suites
- ⤵ Evenings at local attractions
- ⤵ Luncheons, dinners, and cocktail hours
- ⤵ Entertainment such as bands or recording artists
- ⤵ Ice cream socials
- ⤵ Themed parties such as a 1980s night
- ⤵ Featured speakers
- ⤵ Educational seminars
- ⤵ A spouses outing

The Importance of a Theme

Too often enterprises and organizations forsake the idea of a theme for an event because it seems too difficult or unnecessary. But deciding on and selecting a theme must rise above that sentiment. A theme gives form to your stated goals, as the event's theme should encompass both those goals and why your participants will be attending. For more information on determining a theme that's right for your event, check out details in Chapter 10.

Carrying Out the Theme

Once you've got a theme, it should be visible on all printed and electronic materials. The theme gives you a chance to reinforce your message with participants at every turn. A recognizable theme with correspondingly catchy graphics provides a visual representation for your event. That means that with each piece of literature or e-mail you send you're putting your recipient in the frame of mind to receive what you're saying about the upcoming event. Don't waste that opportunity.

Another Kind of Theme

Theme can also relate to the design for an event within an event. For instance, you may have a red carpet soiree or a casino night for the final event. Try to make those events parallel or correlate to the entire event's overall theme. If, say, your conference theme is "Technology for Tomorrow," and you want to hold a sock hop as a special event for attendees, fashion the dance as a "Sock Hop in the Year 2020." Taking this tack elevates the inner workings of elements within your event, fosters enthusiasm, and makes participants feel special. It also allows you to mirror and reinforce the conference or convention's overarching theme.

Organize with a Vengeance

Being organized saves time and money. Take advantage of the resources offered in other parts of this book regarding budgeting, setting timelines, staffing, finding venues, and securing speakers and other entertainment to draft a series of comprehensive to-do lists.

Being unorganized can cost you. For instance, if you're late turning in the number of people who will be eating at a banquet, you'll either be charged for more people than were initially promised to the catering department or you'll have banquet attendees who won't get a meal. Either way, you'll lose money and credibility.

Being unorganized is a magnet for all kinds of problems: late fees, packets missing information, meeting rooms that are too small or too large, speakers showing up at the wrong time, long lines for registration. Don't let any of these happen to you.

Keep tabs on designates who have been assigned responsibilities, and keep your appointments for weekly meetings to check the status on the myriad components of a large event.

Be Diligent in the Details

Complementing organization is attention to details. You've no doubt heard the saying, "It's the little things that count." Be mindful that little things add up to a big, impressive presentation.

When Murphy's Law Is in Play

Because you can never anticipate every disaster that may befall an event, everyone's ruthless organization must be constantly in play.

I was on a team of four that was in charge of a large hospitality industry conference. The outdoor ceremony alone involved several celebrities, a world-renowned CEO, and one of the biggest painted renderings of a map of the United States ever created.

We on the event team were based in Atlanta, but the event was taking place in Chicago. Just two days before the event was to begin, an artist—weeks past his promised deadline—finally finished the map. However, the overnight delivery of the map to Chicago was waylaid and redirected to Alaska. As one of us tried to reroute the map to Chicago, another opened boxes of giveaways (that had already been reordered because of a previous mistake the manufacturer made) only to find that the event's name had now been misspelled on hundreds of duffle bags.

Fortunately we had struck up friendships with Chicago hospitality professionals and were able to procure premium giveaways quickly (though they, understandably, couldn't be printed in time with the event logo). And by constantly tracking the map painting we ensured it showed up in time to be installed for the ceremony.

Right after the ceremony, however, rain fell. Fortunately—just in case of inclement weather—we had planned for tents to be erected for the reception that followed, so we directed everyone into the waiting shelter for cocktails and appetizers.

Since you never know what will happen, think ahead, devise as many reasonable worst-case scenarios as possible, and prepare for what you can.

For instance, would a flyer you're handing out look better in a four-color format? If that's too expensive, could it be reproduced digitally or color Xeroxed? Should the folding chairs at the banquet be covered? Are the tablecloths big enough to cover up scratched table legs? Does the lectern have a graphic of your company logo on it that everyone can see?

Granted, some of these details will cost you. But not all of them will, and often there will be less expensive solutions you can consider, particularly if time is on your side (check the organization section above!).

Don't Put Off Until Tomorrow

The most necessary tasks for an event are often those that get put off until the last minute. While it's advisable to have these done earlier than later, complete these regardless. They include compiling an emergency contact list for your team, outlining steps in the case of an on-site medical emergency, devising a contingency plan in case of inclement weather, having a company or event spokesperson designated in case of a crisis that is covered by the news media, and having a company team—including a media relations specialist and a lawyer—on call in case a situation warrants it. Finally, creating a Web site for an event sometimes gets put on the back burner. It shouldn't. This Web site is your event's calling card and a prospective attendee's initial impression of how seriously you take the event and whether it should command their attention. Until you have set up a fully functioning site, at least have a URL address and a static image that announces that details are coming soon.

The Particulars of an Audit

Canvass each aspect of your event. Conduct an audit. Think about the following:

- What would make this aspect even better?
- Is it professional? Is it polished?
- Would you be impressed if it wasn't a part of your own event?
- Does the event reflect well on your company, organization, or enterprise?

An Absolute Must

In addition—and very importantly—are there details that can make the sponsoring company or organization look better (or worse)? For instance, if that company makes coffee, the coffee served should be impeccably fresh and tasteful; if that organization distributes chalkboards to schools, all the chalkboards in use at the conference should be new. Consider the details that will make your organization look like one that other companies and individuals want to hire, refer business to, and otherwise be associated with.

Have a Contingency Plan

Now more than ever you have to have a contingency plan. Think about the unfortunate natural disasters and serious security threats that have happened in the past few years, prompting cities such as New York and New Orleans to dramatically reconstruct convention plans for visiting companies and organizations.

A contingency plan doesn't mean that you schedule two events and cancel one at the last minute. Sometimes a cancellation of an entire event will be unavoidable. (Fortunately that rarely happens). Still, you can usually expect at least one thing to go wrong. Your conference or convention plans should have a series of preplanned solutions and resolutions should minor inconveniences pop up or outright disasters emerge.

Your contingency plan should canvass such instances as a speaker backing out at the last minute, a caterer falling through, and A/V equipment malfunctioning. **To avert these minor and major crises, begin by reviewing your program components.** Just having a sense that something could go wrong means you won't be hampered if it does.

If possible, have backup vendors lined up for any need that could arise. One way to make such arrangements is to stipulate in your signed contracts a backup plan for each vendor should it be unable to fulfill its duties due to an emergency or sickness. For instance, speakers can usually come up with a fill-in. While that won't be the person you researched, you may have little choice if it's the last minute, and at least you won't have a room full of people staring at an empty podium.

If you have outdoor events scheduled, check with the site to see what arrangements they typically make should rain or inclement weather occur. Tents are a possibility, or if the event is at a hotel you may be able to move into an available ballroom or restaurant.

The Contact Sheet

Once the event begins, have a contact sheet on your person at all times that includes your immediate staff members' and vendors' home phone numbers, cell phone numbers, and e-mail addresses. When you book the site, ask the owners how they've dealt with last-minute problems in previous events. For instance, if your contracted vendor doesn't arrive, they may have a preferred list of vendors they work with who might be able to fill your needs.

Once you know of a looming problematic situation, rally the troops. While you don't want to spend hours discussing a solution for a minor problem, someone may have an immediate response that could work.

Befriend the Convention and Visitors Bureau

Get to know your convention and visitors bureau before you visit a city. If you've established contacts there, they probably have a thick file of people and places who can fill a variety of needs should you require their help. Establish a relationship before you arrive, and check in with them once you arrive, particularly if you need some assistance. They want to make sure that you have a stellar experience so that you'll plan other events in the city, so more than likely they'll be glad to help.

The Particulars of Protocol and Etiquette

Your event must have a kind and appropriate tenor at all times that is respectful toward all attendees. Thoroughly analyze your agenda to ensure that all program elements are considerate and inclusive of all cultures. Don't bring in any activity or program that would be considered gender or race biased. Take an all-inclusive approach.

You must also make sure that your venue is accessible and complies with government regulations regarding anyone with special needs, which may include wheelchair-bound, visually impaired, and hearing-impaired participants.

If political figures are part of your program, make sure that references to them in the conference literature and introductions for events accurately give their title. If you have visiting dignitaries from other countries, check with their office on the appropriate greetings, responses, and expectations. In addition, determine if a foreign language interpreter or sign language specialist will be necessary at any juncture during your program. Figure out these needs beforehand; locating and hiring an interpreter at the last minute is no easy feat.

Message Continuity

You should also review all program components to ensure they relate back to your theme and stay on message. Do the following analysis:

Content—Does each and every aspect of the program relate to why all these people are gathered together? Does any element seem extraneous, unnecessary, or unimpressive?

Graphics—Scrutinize each piece of event literature, including programs, itineraries, handouts, sales materials, and even your Web site and giveaways. Are all your graphics on point and consistent with your program? Do they advertise your theme? Are they professionally presented?

Audience—Will each program component, individually and taken together, be valuable to the conference's audience? Why?

Don't be afraid to let some content go if it's not valuable to the program. You will probably be liable for a cancellation fee, but that sum will be worth it to present a unified program that reflects your program goals and rewards and makes sense to all attendees.

Similarly revise or get rid of graphics or materials that are inconsistent with or not representative of the messages you're trying to bring across and the impressions you want to leave.

Compelling Programs

Commit to having all your written elements be well-presented materials with articulate language. For instance, for your attendees to grasp each session presented and understand what he or she will get out of it, have a program booklet that outlines each one, including a few lines of description; a brief bio about the presenter; the time, length, and place of it; and an "Instant Download" or "Idea Takeaway" that conveys the session in a quick, pithy sentence.

Making Participants Comfortable

Treat your participants like customers. They have paid to be at the conference. They want something out of their attendance, and you want them to leave with an impression that they got something in return, whether they were educated, motivated, inspired, informed, or positively influenced. You want them to leave with a banner impression of your company or enterprise as the responsible organization behind that.

From the moment the attendees arrive to the moment they depart, you're "on." For all intents and purposes, you won't even have a break. That's a daunting prospect, but stay the course and be committed to making your participants' time worth every minute. Be constantly courteous and proactive. Quickly solve problems that arise.

While checking in with attendees is important, you may want to tap a few trusted participants at the beginning of the conference to routinely survey them to get their impressions of how the conference is running, presentations they enjoyed, problems they encountered, and so forth.

Giveaways

Typically, participants are crazy for giveaways. That being the case, come up with one—if your budget allows—that will be useful and have a life beyond the conference or convention's timeframe.

Find one that will be a constant, positive reminder of the event and your enterprise. Tote bags are a top choice for conferences as they present a handy carryall for conference literature and notes. Brainstorm beforehand to determine if specific products are unique to and would be coveted by your particular industry professionals. These are different in that you're not necessarily trying to drive traffic to your exhibit like a giveaway at a trade show booth. In this case you've got your attendees already there; you want to give something out that creates buzz and becomes a lasting reminder of your company. Gravitate toward one-size-fits-all options rather than items like polo shirts or other clothing items that will require you to stock several sizes (and most likely will leave you with the picked-over sizes). Other possibilities include:

⮑ Laptop bags, duffle bags, or backpacks

⮑ Water bottles or insulated tumblers with nylon fabric cases

⮑ iPod covers (which are particularly effective if each one contains a number for an iPod raffle held during the event)

⮑ A special edition of a book that is pertinent to your industry and would be especially appreciated by attendees

⮑ An item made that has cachet, such as stationery from a designer's line or a cap or scarf created by a fashion mogul

Generally speaking, the higher quantity of an order, the less cost per piece. You might find a product that—besides having a longer life for the participant—also is an item you can use for future gatherings, customers, and events. However, you'll most likely want to specialize the piece, emblazoning it with the conference title and date. Also, the more time you can allow to plan the piece, the less you'll run into rush fees. This gives you time to check final artwork and perhaps receive a product prototype.

▶▶ Test Drive

What is your first priority in making an event special? In each instance, write down ideas for how you can make it unique to your enterprise.

⮑ **Giveaways**—Are there ones that you immediately think of? Check out some advertising specialty Web sites to get ideas.

⮑ **Emergency plan**—Do you already have one intact for your company in the event of a crisis? Would it be adaptable for an event-related emergency?

⮑ **Graphics**—Is this already a priority for your company, or is it an element that finds you feeling out of your depth? Are there graphic designers you could call on when a need arises?

⮑ **Web site**—Are you happy with your company's current Web site? Could you add a site within the site for an event? Do you have the resources—Web designer, Web master, and so forth—to launch a separate site if an event warrants it?

Special and Social Events

PART

Getting Started

Executives at and owners of many companies realize that fundraising events—which can embrace a variety of formats—can raise the profile of their business. Getting involved in these initiatives can cast them in a positive spotlight as they garner attention for giving back to their community or contributing to a worthy cause. Involvement generally takes on two forms:

1. Being a sponsor or participant in a nonprofit organization's initiative
2. Conducting your own event that benefits the nonprofit of your choice

You may consider donating funds because of an immediate need and, as a responsible corporate citizen, decide to give money, time, products, or services with no ties to your enterprise's marketing efforts. For instance, devastating events such as the 2004 Indian Ocean tsunami and Hurricane Katrina in 2006 presented widespread, urgent opportunities for companies to devise and conduct fundraising initiatives.

You may also elect to implement specific fundraising events as part of your company's overall marketing plan. In those cases, and as with other events that you consider for your company, you have to decide to participate because it can help you reach goals you've set for your business and, obviously, for the good of reaching out to others and the community. Where fundraising is concerned, if you make it a part of your marketing, promotion and publicity activities, you shouldn't jump into an event because it sounds like a good idea. Nor should you take an exploitative tack: becoming involved with an initiative because it's popular or appears to have a good hook. Doing so detracts from your goodwill and creates questions as to why your company got involved in the first place.

In the case of philanthropic events, your company could be spurred to action on two fronts: You could be regularly approached for involvement or sponsorship, or you could research and identify a nonprofit partner that logically fits in with your company's mindset, plans, marketing, and goals. Pinpointing the perfect partner is discussed later in this chapter.

Most of the discussion in this chapter pertains to hosting your own event to benefit a charitable organization. You will also find details for participating, such as contributing your presence or products at a philanthropic event.

Community Service and Its Value to Your Company

Fundraising events can generate plentiful goodwill and coverage for your business in whatever community you're in (and beyond). **While you must always have genuine interest in and concern for the charity, your involvement can bring a significant impact to your bottom line.** The more excited about and vested in the philanthropy you are, the better the results will be.

Events linked to charities almost immediately conjure up positive associations. When consumers know that an event is related to a cause, an emotional attachment ensues and—whether your company's attachment encompasses participation, organization, or both—your business also benefits from that good feeling and support.

Where to Give?

If you would like your company to become involved in a charity but want more information on the many that may need your time and resources, you can start at *www.give.org*. That Web site—from the BBB (Better Business Bureau) Wise Giving Alliance—lists hundreds of charitable organizations alphabetically. For those philanthropies listed, the alliance offers a brief description of it as well as charity reports that give a snapshot of the organization. This information may at least provide you with a baseline for a cause's focus and direction. From there you can check out the philanthropy's Web site to get further details about it.

Further, you can also extend your involvement and burnish your company's image by spreading the word that you have hosted, sponsored, or participated in an event that resulted in significant funds to, for example, find a cure for a disease or begin research; the launch or completion of a project, site, or building; or continue the good works of an organization.

Why Do It?

If you decide to orchestrate a charitable event, you must have a game plan to determine why this event will be of value to your company. You may know of a cause that has personal meaning to you. Many companies become involved for that very reason, becoming good corporate citizens in the process. The cause may be specific to your business as well, such as an environmentally friendly dry cleaner that sponsors an Earth Day initiative.

If you don't have a particular philanthropy in mind, you may want to pinpoint one that draws the support of clients or customers that you're already in business with and who, therefore, makes an ideal association.

Give Serious Consideration

Depending on your type of business, you may be routinely bombarded with charitable requests. While you may not be able to fulfill them, you (or a delegate) should review the information that is sent to you. Even if providing the charity with financial resources or a large commitment of time would be difficult for your company, you may be able to offer a limited service or auction item that still helps them out and gives you the opportunity to engender goodwill. If you can't help out the charity but know of another business that could, give the philanthropy that information; they will no doubt appreciate your time and consideration.

In another direction, you may decide to find one that has the backing of similar, like-minded people as your target audience. By being in league with them you create a natural link to your business, and in doing so it will probably benefit that entity further because of an association that is organic and makes sense. Nonprofit organizations have to operate like businesses too. They want to attract companies that will provide them with mutually beneficial exposure and support. Philanthropies will want to point out how they can help meet your company's marketing goals through events with them. So be ready to ask: Who are you targeting? Why is that particular audience important to your company? How will this event reach that intended audience?

Extending the Success

Your goal in becoming involved or sponsoring a philanthropic event is to help that charity meet its goal of fundraising or recruiting. Afterward, any mention or publicity for it must be done in good taste. You never want your involvement to seem one-sided, disingenuous, or exploitative. Take care that your wording and presentation put the charity, its cause, and mission, front and center and how your business is supporting—not instigating—their good work. Some ways to extend your association include:

➲ A press release that announces results and includes quotes from the benefiting organization
➲ Information about the event on the benefiting organization's Web site that points to your involvement
➲ Postings on your company's Web site that include pictures from the event
➲ Media coverage—print and broadcast—of the event

Picking and Tying in with Charities

There is no shortage of charitable organizations that would gratefully benefit from your company's association. In assessing your approach to take on fundraising events, consider one that is logical, that is a cause you are personally interested in or that has the interest of many of your company's employees or clients, and one you'd like to be involved with for a long time. For instance, if you have a gardening service you might consider a series of beautification projects in your city, or if you have a product that's pink you might consider a breast cancer philanthropy.

"Mutually beneficial" should be the catchphrase you embrace. You want the charity to have a wildly successful event that reaps the funds they need, and you want your company to engender goodwill through its support and generosity. It should be an association that reinforces your brand. When it does, you have a better chance of reaping more recognition and support for the cause you're trying to better.

While many organizations may be appealing to you, you should focus your initiative on a single one. Rarely do two charitable organizations complement one another in terms of efforts or messages that can be dovetailed. Further, it's easier for participants to rally behind one cause that your company is behind rather than two or three. You run the risk of diluting your message and paring down potential giving when more than one charity is involved.

Communicating with the Organization

Don't take the tack that your company will be solely in charge of putting together the event, supplying all the manpower, creating all the ideas, and executing the entire plan. You must work in concert with the charity. For some partnerships this practice may require a delicate balance and diplomatic maneuvering. From the outset, establish communication channels. This means:

- ⮩ Designating a single point person for both your company and the charitable organization
- ⮩ Delineating who is copied on which memos, letters, and e-mails
- ⮩ Deciding what the committees will be and who will comprise them
- ⮩ Selecting regular meeting times

Types of Philanthropic Events

Philanthropic events can take on many shapes and forms: a fair, a conference, a fiesta, a marketplace. Having selected the charity you're supporting, next you need to craft an event that is meaningful to both your company and the charity's mission. In so doing, brainstorm ideas that will best attract participation and attention.

Speaking of Communication

Everyone involved with the fundraising effort—both from within your company and within the philanthropic organization—must be clear about your involvement. Decide, and write down in concise language, what you've agreed upon. Make sure that it makes sense, that everyone understands it, and that it's not cumbersome if you wanted to explain the method of contribution to someone else. That agreement will provide the talking points for a presentation, a program, and perhaps more.

A few years ago I was asked to consult on the future of a company's cause-related marketing program for a national telethon. While the company had the philanthropy's best interests in mind and had made a large financial commitment to the telethon, no one had crafted the right language for the commitment. During certain times throughout the telethon, representatives of the company would make check presentations. Upon viewing the tape of each presentation, I realized that confusion was rampant. The company spokespeople struggled with the right language to convey how the donations were being made. For instance, one would say that the company was contributing "proceeds from the profits of particular products," and another would explain "For every purchase made on certain days, we'll donate the profit on the net profit on certain items toward the cause." Not only were the representatives' interpretations each a mouthful, but the viewing audience had a vague, scattershot understanding of exactly what the commitment was (which was actually quite substantial) or how their purchases might actually benefit the telethon's cause.

While we agreed that the company should move forward the next year with their commitment, we restructured the agreement (and wording) such that it was easier to understand but still brought the philanthropy a comparable contribution.

Event Possibilities

Following are some common (and a few not-so-common) ideas that have been successful.

Auctions, which come in the form of both live and silent; these are so popular I discuss them on their own later in this chapter.

Tasting events, which encourage audience participation as you corral attendees to sample foods of different cuisines.

Bake sales or cook-offs, which feature food front and center and can generate great returns since you can usually arrange for all the food to be donated.

Bazaars or fairs, also known as marketplaces, which feature an array of vendors, all of which are invited to sell their products or services then donate a prearranged percentage of the sales for that day.

Athletic events, such as walks or runs (and even tug-of-wars), which require stringent registration procedures for optimal organization but in most communities can generate significant participation, particularly by securing advance publicity and placement in community and media calendars.

Pageants or fashion shows, which can be a huge draw in showcasing talent and trends, particularly if in addition to ticket sales another component is featured, such as auctioning couture or props, or featuring a marketplace to buy accessories.

Screenings or film festivals, which can be held in conjunction with a studio or network for an upcoming feature or television project and gives the audience an exclusive first look. These could also attract audiences with celebrities involved. A days-long festival will also give your company repeated exposure with audiences.

Live entertainment, which can include bands, standup comics, and dance troupes; while this can require a substantial cash outlay upfront, it can reap great returns.

Entire meals, such as luncheons or banquets (see Chapter 15) and galas (see Chapter 17).

Newsworthy Ways

One of your event's goals will be to draw media attention so that the philanthropy your company is supporting will gain exposure that may increase funding or donations from other sources. In that vein, think of events that will be inviting and interesting for the media to cover. The press may not write stores on an ordinary bake sale. They're more likely to want to do a story on an organization's "Cake Walk" that features towering, incredible, edible creations that have been baked for charity, or a contest that invites hundreds of children to come up with original icing designs on cookies. A television station will be more apt to send a crew to a fashion show that includes local or national celebrities modeling clothes rather than neighbors or students.

Take Note

As an individual, you probably have ample opportunities to take part in a philanthropy or cause. The next time you participate in one, look around. How many companies have decided to partake in the event? What activities are particularly striking? Has any "regular" activity been given a twist that makes it more enticing or exciting? Was there an activity you'd never seen before at a similar event? How is the turnout? What brought you there? What would you have done differently to encourage more involvement? Is there a company you've gained new exposure to? Did any company involved impress you? Why or why not?

Creating and Producing the Actual Event

Consult Chapters 1 through 6 to break down the event into a list of responsibilities, and be ready to allocate the necessary staff and resources. However, events that are held as charitable endeavors often have aspects unique to them. For instance, as your company has employees involved, and the nonprofit organization does too, realize that volunteers are likely to be part of the mix of carrying out and completing duties.

Committees

Like other large-scale events, fundraising events need to have their tasks and responsibilities broken down under specific headings. Those headings become committees devoted to carrying out those particular duties. Further, within the committees—each spearheaded by a person or committee chair—committee members are assigned specific responsibilities.

The number and kind of committees can vary widely according to the event that is underway. Some possible committees include:

➲ Leadership or steering—comprised of a chairman of the event, as well as committee heads, who will advise, direct, and coordinate the efforts

➲ Volunteers—organizing the volunteers into various committees

➲ Graphics—responsible for such elements as the invitations, programs, and signage

➲ Procurement—soliciting corporations and individuals for items to be donated, such as for a live auction

➲ Publicity—coordinating media efforts, press releases, and interviews

➲ Decorations—lining up and implementing the staging needs for the event

Finances

Where fundraising is concerned, don't intermingle the event's costs and income with your company's daily financial activities. Set up a separate account to track expenses and contributions.

Time

Even more than other events (save for conventions that are attended by thousands), fundraising initiatives need a cushion of time, particularly in deciding upon and working with the benefiting charity, putting the event on calendars and setting up other publicity, possibly lining up a host committee of community stalwarts, collecting items for an auction component, coordinating ticket sales, and assembling necessary support.

Combinations to Consider

In laying out your action plan, realize that you may also be in the position to include several facets within one fundraising event. For instance, your event may include a meal and a fashion show for which attendees bought tickets, a silent or live auction for which attendees bid for items that have been procured for the event, and a marketplace that offers up goods for sale. Obviously the more events within the event you have the more separate committees and manpower you may need to dedicate to those initiatives.

Focus on the Fundraising

Sometimes, in the thick of getting an event off and running, you lose sight of why you're conducting it in the first place. A gentle reminder: Your efforts must always be front and center directed to raising funds for the benefiting charity. Certainly you want everyone involved to have fun, to remember the event fondly, to present the goings-on with polish and professionalism. Unfortunately all those endeavors—even though they're well intentioned—will be for naught if little or no money results, and you'll have no positive news to report afterward. Such an outcome will mean that a fundraising event brought more harm than good to your company's reputation, and you may even have a looming crisis to deal with.

To augment your efforts and to assure that you'll at least have some proceeds from the event, consider building in a ceremony to present a check to the organization as part of the festivities. Ideally a representative will present the check on your company's behalf. You could even build this into your fundraising event budget. However, it's also perfectly understandable if organizing the event is taking its toll on the budget. And you certainly don't want to draw attention to your company in the spirit of "look at this great thing we're doing; it's costing us a fortune!"

The Popularity of Silent and Live Auctions and How to Conduct Them

Auctions are an immensely popular component of—and sometimes sole activity of—fundraising events. Call it the eBay effect. The online auction site has made the activity a national pastime, and people who were never comfortable before bidding on items now do so with regular fervor. Take advantage of the national trend and your attendees' interest in it by instituting an auction that will be an event within an event and stimulate excitement, particularly if you're offering one-of-a-kind items.

Find Unique Objects

Your auction will benefit from items that auction participants can't find or buy easily: limited-edition clothes, an experience such as a walk-on role in a movie or a lesson with a famous chef, a signed first edition of a classic book, or a pitching session with a Major League Baseball player. If possible, give your auction a theme that fits in with your event's theme. Taking that tack will give your efforts focus in brainstorming what items you'd like to see as part of the auction.

Above all, know the audience that will be attending. What interests them? What are they likely to find interesting to bid on? Brainstorm with fellow employees or committee members and devise a wish list.

In letters that you send to solicit auction items, find the names of contacts and their correct addresses. You can e-mail your written request, but a letter on letterhead will make more of an impact.

Keep the letter to one page. In the letter briefly state the event's title, theme, and purpose, the particulars of the auction, and a specific request for a contribution to the auction. Let the recipient know what kind of exposure she or he will get from participation. Offer the opportunity to publicize their business and to include them in an auction program. Let them know if the item is tax deductible and, if so, offer a tax ID number. Give them a deadline by which the items must arrive in your office and say you'll be calling or e-mailing them to follow up. If applicable, you may also want to include an auction commitment form with the letter that has them fill in donor and item information. Finally, follow up with all your contacts either by phone or e-mail.

The Pros and Cons of Live Versus Silent

A live auction can be a centerpiece of an event. You need to have a start and end time, and encourage everyone to enter the auction area as an auctioneer corrals the audience to bid on the items. Once the bidding ends on one item, a new item is introduced.

A silent auction can play a less conspicuous—but still important—role in your fundraising effort. You still set up an area devoted to the items, but participants can come and go throughout the event to bid on items. With a live auction, since you're offering a procession of items one at a time, you need to hire a professional auctioneer to conduct it. The auctioneer starts with a bid and draws the crowd into bidding. You need to have paddles or fans available for participants to use in making their bids.

With a silent auction, place the items on sturdy, well-decorated tables that attractively feature the objects. Set up the tables in a place that is easily accessible, and position the objects in plain view so that they're easy for potential bidders to see and appreciate. In front of each item place a bidding sheet that describes the item in exciting language. Beneath the description include blank lines for names and amounts that bidders can fill in. Also let bidders know the bid increments expected in the bidding as rounds continue. (For instance, increments of $5 are typical for items under $50, $10 for items $51 to $150, and so on). To keep the bidding continuing and rising, assign people to track the bids and approach those who may need to bid again to win an item.

Organizing the Auction

The auction may have its own committee or, if it's a large one, may need several subcommittees. **In gearing up for an auction give yourself plenty of time, and give your potential donors a firm deadline.** Remember, some donors will back out, and some items won't arrive on time.

Be diligent in cataloging the items as they come in, and make sure to ask the donor for an accurate description and value of the donation. Once you know the items you will be showcasing, figure out how they will be laid out on tables if they're for a silent auction, how they can be displayed beforehand for a live auction, and how they will be brought to the auctioneer in the case of a live auction.

Make sure to have arrangements for collecting the money from the winning bidders at the end of the auction. Have clear instructions on when payment is expected. If you can, make it possible for bidders to pay by credit card or PayPal. Have staff prepared to, if necessary, wrap the items (in bubble wrap or their original packaging).

Encouraging Involvement

Make sure that your staff, volunteers, and vendors know the vision of the event and how it will benefit the charity. When people know where all their hard work is going, they get more excited about their participation and involvement and become more dedicated to doing a good job. Their enthusiasm is infectious, and that good attitude prompts others to get involved.

Have the charity provide as much information as appropriate about the cause and their organization and where the proceeds from the fundraising will go. The more people know about what they're supporting, the more thrilled they are to spread the word.

Participating in an Event

Aside from planning a charity fundraising event, your company may be invited to participate in a large-scale event that will also feature several other businesses. For instance, a hospital may hold a holiday bazaar and ask local businesses to set up booths to sell merchandise. Your company's participation will most likely be contingent on donating a portion of your sales to the hospital.

Be Ready

Your presence at the event will show how you do business, especially to those who have never visited your store (or Web site). Be prepared to set up shop as if you're inviting people into your brick-and-mortar establishment.

Usually in these cases the organization hosting the event sets up a sales area to sell merchandise. Know as much as possible before the day of the event and ask your contact to answer the following:

- How big will the booth or sales area be? What are the dimensions of the tables that will be supplied?
- Are you in charge of decorating the space, or is the sales area divided into uniform spaces?
- How long do you need to have your area staffed?
- What percentage of sales is expected to go to the charity?

If you're putting your product on tables, have the following:

⮑ Tablecloths that will cover your table and extend all the way to the floor (which will not only cover unattractive table legs but also any boxes of merchandise and other supplies you may be storing underneath)

⮑ Plenty of merchandise

⮑ Sales flyers or post cards that are professional looking and descriptive of your business

⮑ Business cards so that new and prospective customers know where to find you to patronize your business after the event

After the Event

As always, take the time to consider the worthiness of your participation. While you undoubtedly have helped out a charity, was this event the best one to contribute your time and presence to? Was it mutually beneficial? Did this event draw an audience that is consistent with your target demographic? What products sold or didn't sell? Did you tap into a undiscovered sales sector? Would you be open to participating again?

▶▶ Test Drive

What is a philanthropy that you already support or a charitable cause you feel strongly about supporting? Consider the following:

⮑ Review your marketing plan or goals, including your commitment to community service. Could a fundraising event for a cause help you accomplish any of those?

⮑ Regarding an organization you might support, could efforts dovetail with your company's for the good of both?

⮑ Place a call to the philanthropy and hold an initial conversation to investigate how your company might fit in with its overall mission and specific needs.

⮑ If you work for a nonprofit, try this the other way: Make a wish list of companies you'd like to have involved with your efforts, and research ways that your goals could mesh with theirs.

PART **4**

Special and Social Events

The Reason Behind It

While luncheons are often part of bigger events, such as conferences and conventions, you don't need a colossal approach to plan them. While they should always take on a professional mien, luncheons don't have to be extravagant affairs or include hundreds of people.

Luncheons can serve a variety of purposes and lend a convivial atmosphere to those attending. They can also provide an economical lesson when you're leaning toward a meeting or gathering that needs to be centered on a meal. In the case of lunches—which are typically less expensive than dinners—you also can count on less time involved. With a luncheon in the middle of the day—when you know your attendees have to get back to work—you must stick to a schedule. Besides saving time and money, luncheons also tend to take on a more businesslike atmosphere, since they occur during the workday.

The guidelines set out in this chapter for luncheons can be adapted for banquets, which can occur at breakfast, lunch, or dinner. Keep in mind that these luncheons (and banquets in general) take on a more business tone than the dinner and cocktail parties covered in Chapter 16.

Luncheon Opportunities

You can organize a luncheon for:

- Making a presentation to a prospective client
- Generating company publicity by giving out community awards
- Positioning your company as a leader or expert by hosting a question-and-answer session with area business leaders
- Fostering goodwill by showing gratitude to employees or vendors
- Tying in with an already scheduled conference or convention
- Building brand recognition by sponsoring an appreciation luncheon for volunteers or professionals in an associated organization or industry

Matching the Tenor to the Event

Make sure that a luncheon or banquet is the appropriate forum for your event. With that, pinpoint the attitude of the event, its focus, the impression you're trying to have your company make, and the mood you're trying to convey. If you're looking for a more familiar arena, or one that will be more conducive to lengthy conversation, you may want to opt for a hosted dinner instead. Or, if you don't want to have a restricted schedule, you may consider a cocktail party or open house.

Return to your reasons for hosting the luncheon or banquet to ascertain exactly what your goals for it are. Then ask yourself the following questions:

1. Why will the event work better as a luncheon than as a dinner or cocktail party (which typically fosters more conversation)?
2. If you don't hold the luncheon, what will happen?
3. How will the luncheon benefit your business?
4. Do you need to take a more informal approach?
5. Should the event be held at a person's home or in a smaller venue to reach the goals you've set for the event?

The Program

A luncheon you're planning isn't just for eating, but it shouldn't be so jam-packed with activities that no one has time to eat and your program doesn't finish. You want a well-paced schedule that allows time for those attending to enjoy a meal while also presenting content that will be educational or informative and entertaining.

In most cases you want the program after the meal, and it should culminate in a memorable focal point that will be the takeaway for those attending. You need to decide what that program will be and how it can fulfill your purpose. For instance, which of the following might be appropriate:

- ➲ A speaker
- ➲ A panel discussion
- ➲ A PowerPoint presentation
- ➲ A video or digital display
- ➲ An interactive exhibit

Inside Track — A Topical Luncheon

When I was handling publicity for one of CNN's news programs, we were trying to raise the profile of one of the show's anchors. When she told us she was pregnant, we decided to hold an event that would tie in with this. It was a current issue as a spate of other female newscasters and actresses had recently made announcements in the press that they were expecting too.

We planned a luncheon featuring a panel of working women in similar fields to the CNN anchor and had them discuss how they juggled work and family. Their experiences would benefit others in similar situations—even in different careers. The panel included news anchors, news directors, a producer, and actresses, all of whom either were expecting or had recently had a baby and returned to work. One of the panel members had actually encountered controversy when the TV series she was working on had publicly denounced her needs upon returning to filming.

Those invited to the luncheon and panel discussion included several working mothers as well as members of the media such as fellow news talent and producers. Another CNN anchor worked as moderator, fielding questions from the audience and handing them off to the most appropriate panel members.

The luncheon was an unqualified success and drew more coverage than we expected. While the anchor herself definitely brought attention, the issues the panel canvassed and addressed were considered newsworthy and, subsequently, that high opinion also elevated the anchor's show.

A Sample Schedule

Consider this schedule as a rough guideline for a luncheon that has a noon start time:

12:00	*Guests arrive; refreshments are offered*
12:20	*Guests are encouraged to take their seats*
12:30	*Host welcomes attendees*
12:35	*Lunch is served*
12:55	*Dessert is served with coffee and tea service*
12:55–1:25	*Speaker and program*
1:30	*Luncheon adjourns*

A Program to Hold

Even if its not printed on a heavy cardstock and passed out to all the attendees, you must have a schedule for the luncheon. If it's only for your reference, have a finely detailed breakdown of activities to keep yourself on track. If you're designing an additional program to be passed out for everyone, you should include a brief schedule of the events and information about your company. Then have details regarding your program's prime component, such as a seminar, speakers, or award presentations. Include necessary bios of those being feted or serving as panelists.

The Venue

The next section discusses the different sizes of luncheon audiences your company may be hosting, but prior to that assessment you need to realize that different arenas provide distinct, valuable venues for your luncheon. A luncheon through which you're trying to attract attention or generate interest in your business will not work if you hold it in a company conference room. Unless you have amazing scenery in and around your office location or on its grounds, find a suitable location that will make the event special.

In addition, particularly since a luncheon is during the day, it doesn't always have to occur indoors. Think about sheltered areas or outdoor locales. Of course when considering such a location, make sure the facility can serve meals on site or works with a caterer who can provide the necessary equipment and accoutrements for preparing and serving the meal.

Nice Touches

Wherever your luncheon or banquet occurs, the space should be top-notch. If you've got a head table at a banquet, make sure you have a floral centerpiece with complementary arrangements at the other tables. Would it be appropriate to have soft music playing before your luncheon starts? Is there a favor or company memento you'd like to put in each attendee's seat? As you consider places to hold your event, keep in mind ways you might add to the event. Ask your venue or facility contact for suggestions as well. That person's experience could give you many insights into ways to make your event more memorable.

Potential Places

Whether you opt for your luncheon or banquet to be indoors or outside, consider both the typical and the different:

- ➲ Hotel conference or meeting room
- ➲ Civic auditorium
- ➲ Fellowship hall
- ➲ Restaurant
- ➲ Facility overlooking a theme park, botanical garden, or lake
- ➲ Golf course clubhouse
- ➲ Museum's dining room
- ➲ Tourist attraction's conference center

Other Considerations

When you're considering the perfect venue for your luncheon, make sure you have ample room for those invited and space for the presentation or program you're expecting to have. Look at the room from all of those vantage points.

Will you have space for the panel or a proper place for a speaker? Will the room be conducive for all the attendees to view a PowerPoint presentation that's shown on a large screen? Does the facility have technical services, or do you have to acquire those elsewhere?

Catering to a Specific Audience

Once you've ascertained why you've brought everyone together for this meal and where you want to host them, you can get down to serving them food. Typically the larger the gathering the less impressive the food tends to be, but don't follow that rule of thumb. People have become more selective about the kinds of foods they eat. There are vegetarians or vegans, Zone or Atkins dieters, people lowering their sodium or cholesterol intake, and many more people on special diets. You can get ahead in your planning by being cognizant of just two concerns: avoiding substandard fare and tending to dietary needs.

Particularly if the meal will be at a hotel or banquet facility, do your best to get out of the rubber chicken rut. Figure out ways for the meal to be particularly enticing. While chicken is a safe bet for most luncheon attendees, perhaps you could spice up the meal with a selection of sauces to be served with it. Investigate a few sizzling side dishes to accompany it. At the very least, order a memorable dessert.

The food doesn't have to be whipped up by a celebrity chef, but it is a luncheon and people remember bad food. **Lend some pizzazz to your event by focusing some of your efforts on a menu that will spark positive interest and conversation.** In the end that also works in your company's favor, no doubt one of the reasons you wanted to plan a luncheon in the first place.

Try to ascertain from the outset the possible dietary needs of some of your attendees. For instance, when you send out the invitation for a luncheon, include a box that can be checked for special food consider-ations and space for attendees to write their food preferences. Usually (unless someone has a medical cause for food restrictions) you'll find that people tend to go along with a luncheon's menu. But be responsible and ward off any potential problems. You don't want to be scrambling to find a meal for the guest of honor because you didn't find out until five minutes before the event started that she was allergic to every item on the menu.

Proper Place Settings

Without fail, once a meal starts you'll hear someone say, "Which bread plate is mine?" or "What am I supposed to use this fork for?" Particularly if you're the host, be familiar with a complete place setting so you can gently guide your guests. Generally the utensils are placed in the order you use them, starting from the outside. Forks are on the left and knives and spoons are on the right; the bread plate is to your left, and stemware and coffee cups are to your right. For illustrations of the types of table settings, go to *www.emilypost.com* and click on etiquette tips.

Small Affairs

In the event of a smaller, more intimate, gathering of less than eight you'll most likely opt for a restaurant setting and let everyone select from the restaurant's menu. If possible check with attendees to determine if any food allergies need to be taken into account. It's up to you to gauge the best menu that will appeal to your specific group. A steakhouse (no matter how upscale) won't go over well with a group of vegetarians, and your best efforts for an impressive luncheon will be derailed.

No matter how small the size of your party, make reservations beforehand, and be familiar with the restaurant's layout, even suggesting a table that you'd like to be seated at.

Consider checking into restaurants that have separate areas or sectioned-off booths to accommodate your group. Many restaurants have spaces that offer a more private ambiance.

As you have invited those attending, take your role as host seriously. For instance, be the key point person with the wait staff to make sure that all the guests have what they need. **Don't begin eating until everyone has been served, and take the lead to establish when business will be discussed.** Typically you'll want to reserve the most serious of business topics for after the meal has finished.

In the case of more intimate gatherings, consider a setting conducive to conversation and getting business done. If you're trying to woo a potential client, take into account how noisy or, preferably, quiet the surroundings will be. Chapter 16—which focuses more on dinners and cocktail parties—also has more useful information about this type of setting.

Preplanning the Menu for Bigger Banquets

For larger gatherings—which could be in a restaurant's dining room, a hotel conference room, or a banquet hall—come up with preplanned menu. You can design the menu to have options for entrées or to be completely fixed. If the luncheon is being held at a hotel you may have the choice of a seated meal or a buffet. At a restaurant you'll most likely work with a private dining director to make all the necessary arrangements. At a hotel or banquet hall or similar large facility you'll most likely deal with a CSM, or catering sales manager.

In addition to giving them responses when they inquire about your needs, ask to see successful menus they've prepared in the past to get a sense of meals that might work for your event. Ask them about specialty or signature dishes they prepare that may be particularly memorable for your event.

Taking Care of Other Details

Whether you have many attending or just a few, keep in mind that you want to have enough food—if you're ordering meals beforehand— and yet not too much to waste money. Ask for guidance from your contact at the facility you're working with for his or her policy on setting up the order, overages, and last-minute additions. Remember, you're likely to have a few no-shows, but you don't want to commit to dozens of extra meals that won't be eaten yet you have to pay for.

Make sure the luncheon or banquet area fits the proceedings. You don't want your event swallowed by too much room or, conversely, too cramped to eat or conduct conversations comfortably.

Table Configurations

How will your banquet best work? How will the audience be most comfortable? If there is a presentation, how close should the tables be to the head table? Depending on the number attending, you may want round tables of eight or ten, two or three long tables, or one long table. What will work best for the program you're planning? Work with your facility contact to configure tables in the best way to conduct and foster conversation, enable ease in viewing a presentation, fete a guest of honor, or otherwise enhance activities particular to your luncheon or banquet.

The Follow-Through

Once all your planning is in place, take a proactive approach and conduct the follow-through to make sure that all your parts are in place. For instance, send confirmation notes to those attending, particularly guests of honor and speakers. If the luncheon is low key or small, you can send an e-mail or place a phone call. However, if the luncheon will be larger, send confirmation letters to your guests of honor and panelists once all the details are set. As a courtesy, remind them by phone call or e-mail or both a few days before the event. Further, distribute an e-mail a few days before the event to all the attendees reaffirming all the particulars of time and place. Have guests reconfirm their attendance as well. You may also want to include a map in the e-mail address or a link to Google maps (*www.maps.google.com*) so that they can get directions on their own.

The day before the luncheon, take the time to review all the necessary components.

If the luncheon is taking place at a restaurant, reconfirm reservations. Determine who will be the point person while you are at the restaurant. Verify that choices exist for anyone with dietary concerns.

If the luncheon is bigger, review the BEO (banquet event order) to be certain that what you are expecting is what will be served. Reconfirm numbers, the menu, options that are involved, and the room setup. Double-check that your site contact will be there or, if not, that a substitute will be on hand to answer questions and contend with any problems. If A/V equipment is part of your mix, reconfirm the expected equipment will be on hand and the time it will arrive.

Making the Event Count

Once the luncheon is over, assess its importance for your company. Did it accomplish what you had wanted it to? Did it meet the goals you set forth? Was it well received? Could any aspect have gone better? How about the food: Did people comment favorably? Is this luncheon worthy of consideration as an annual event? Why or why not? Can you use the experience of this luncheon to host a corollary event that will also benefit your business?

Luncheons are events that routinely occur in business. Because of that, plan to keep notes about aspects you think went particularly well or components you would change in the future. Refer to your hits and misses notes for the next luncheon you plan. Keep tabs on such features as the restaurant or facility's key attributes, point people who were especially competent and paid attention to details, your audience's reaction to the food and place, and your assessment if the pricing was fair and reasonable.

▶▶ Test Drive

Think about how a luncheon might work for your company.

➲ Might hosting a luncheon be a new or rarely explored way to meet with and entice new business prospects?

➲ Are you in an industry that ever or often is in the news? Could a luncheon be a way to get more coverage or position your company as a leader?

➲ Have you attended luncheons that particularly stand out as appealing or memorable? Why did they strike you that way?

➲ Could a luncheon that your company hosts be a less-expensive—but still worthwhile and positive and possibly more effective—alternative for an annual event you have?

Accomplishing a Mission

Sometimes the best way to conduct business is to take everyone out of the business setting and skew the event toward a social scene. When you do that, you make a conscious decision to cast the event in an entertaining light. While business may be accomplished at the party, it is not your sole goal. **In fact, be mindful that you are more concerned with creating a memorably exquisite evening than in getting a deal signed.** With these kinds of parties the context may be business, but the content is typically more entertainment focused and presented with style and class.

For some, hosting a cocktail or dinner party is anathema: They're unsure of where to begin, what to serve, and worse, why it could make a difference for their enterprise. But rest assured you have many options—several that are easy and affordable—in creating a memorable experience that enhances your image and positively affects your bottom line.

What Is the Mission?

In organizing this type of event consider the purpose. This will segue into how many people to plan for.

A cocktail or dinner party that's linked to business has a different purpose and origin than one that's purely social. A social one might center on a holiday or a birthday. But such an event must tie in to your organization's goals. Even a cocktail or dinner party falls under event marketing when your company is hosting it. Reasons for such an event may include:

- ➲ To woo potential customers or clients
- ➲ To celebrate an award the company has received
- ➲ To informally bring together organizations in a way that might benefit their interests and those of your company
- ➲ To determine if candidates for hire are a good fit for your company
- ➲ To gather information from those who have a genuine concern for your company
- ➲ To form bonds with those who have the same professional interests

➲ To procure leads for new business

➲ To show appreciation for employees or vendors

➲ To express gratitude to community members whose support helped your business flourish

In all these instances you're bringing attention to your company in a way that will have positive ramifications for your future business dealings.

Investing in a Party?

If you're trying to attract investors you may also consider a cocktail or dinner party. But make sure that your pitch stays on track. Too often in this kind of setting you face too many distractions, and amid the lighter tone of the event convincing investors of your company's worth is sidelined. While you may have heard of substantial deals being signed after a cocktail party or at a dinner hosted at someone's home, that's unusual and could be a high-stakes gamble for your enterprise. It's possible this setting will be your best approach to closing a deal, but give it careful consideration and seek trusted advisors' opinions.

The Process

In planning the dinner party or cocktail party, keep in mind all the facets of planning any event: determining the budget, making the guest list, picking a location, and setting a date and time.

Size Matters

Dinner and cocktail parties can vary widely. For instance, is it a party for eight at your home or a supper for sixty at a nice restaurant? Is it a Saturday evening cocktail party poolside for twelve, or an after-work networking cocktail reception for seventy-five? Do you want your guest list to be strictly for invitees, or are they encouraged to bring a spouse or a date?

In outlining your purpose for the party you'll get a feel for and ascertain the appropriate number of people to expect. Do you need a more informal tone? Will discussion possibly turn serious? Are you celebrating, in which you can take a more-the-merrier approach, or are you on more of a fact-gathering mission, in which case you may want a more exclusive, serious tone and smaller group.

Will some kind of presentation be part of the festivities, and what will the content or format of it be? That may also play a role in how many people you invite.

Pinpointing the Atmosphere

With your mission established, lay down further specifics. Are you looking to have a stand-around crowd that convenes at tables dotting an atrium, or do you want a more formal sit-down dinner at your home? Will you be gathering people for a couple of hours or for a full evening?

What do you think will work best for the purpose at hand? Cocktail parties generally take on a lighter tone than dinner parties, which tend to be a lengthier, richer experience. Both can vary in size.

Cocktail parties:
- Offer drinks and light appetizers
- Concentrate more on meet-and-greet and networking
- Attire ranges from business to casual
- Tend to be less formal than dinner parties
- Are a better choice for a more confined space
- Can be the precursor to another event

Dinner parties:
- Present full-course meals
- Focus on initiating and continuing conversations
- Are appropriate for hosting a presentation or feting someone
- Usually suggest more formal attire
- Usually have a more formal approach than cocktail parties
- Are typically stand-alone events

Who's Coming and Why?

Once you've determined the purpose and decided upon how small or large you'd like the event to be, the next task, sometimes daunting, is compiling a guest list. In some cases those you wish to invite will be clear cut: vendors and their significant others, the contacts on a new business list you've been compiling, or civic leaders who had a hand in bringing your company to town. Assemble a list that is comprehensive and will foster conversation and enthusiasm. Think about those outside your immediate sphere of business but who may add to or enliven the goings on and who have a relevant link to your business. Don't invite good friends just because you think they'll make good company unless they have a tie-in with your organization.

As you've analyzed your mission for the party, you've been nailing down a notion of how big or small the event will be. That will lead you to consideration of the venue (discussed later in this chapter). At this point assess whether your goal is to have those invited sit around at one table together or do you expect to have a reserved room at a restaurant that will hold a few dozen. Consider your reasons for inviting each person and what you hope their presence adds to the proceedings.

The Particulars of Timing and Budget

After you identify the purpose, tenor, and kind of event you need to set the date and length of the event and determine your company's financial commitment to it. The traditional time frame for a cocktail party is two to three hours, and it is usually held somewhere between 6:00–10:00 P.M., which means it's either prior to dinner or after dinner. If prior to dinner, you can offer light appetizers or heavy hors d'oeuvres. If the party is being held later, consider making the cocktail party one that features coffee drinks and has a dessert buffet instead of appetizers. Dinners usually begin between 7:00–8:00 P.M., with cocktails served for a half hour to an hour beforehand and coffee service and dessert afterward.

As you consider venues, determine costs and decide which is the best fit for your budget. While some venues such as restaurants and hotels may seem more expensive than hosting an event at your home, there are costs such as staffing and rentals that you won't need to bother with at an arena set up for serving. It all comes down to the tenor and atmosphere you want to establish for your event.

Invitations

Undoubtedly in this technological age electronic invitations make inviting others a breeze. However, unless your intended invitees or the theme of your event are heavily into technology, a printed invitation makes a tremendous statement and immediately sets the tone for the event. Crane & Co. (*www.crane.com*) offers a nice selection for business purposes. If you're interested in pursuing a more casual tack, try Kate's Paperie (*www.katespaperie.com*) or the national store Papyrus (*www.papyrusonline.com*). Also online, *www.paperstyle.com* offers an outstanding array of choices, a separate corporate link on the navigation bar under Invitations, and exceptional service.

Make sure the wording on your invitation makes expectations clear about what the party will be (cocktails and dinner from 6–9 P.M., dress casual, for instance). Include an RSVP line with a contact phone number or e-mail address to respond and the date by which you want to receive an RSVP.

For dinner parties, make sure the food is offered to all diners at the same time, and avoid straggling guests and latecomers who will interrupt your flow. On the invitation you also may want to politely inform guests when dinner will be served.

Money for Food and Drink

If the event is at a hotel or other facility with food service, you can work out the details for cocktails and menu choices with them. But if you're hosting the event at your home or a place that doesn't typically serve food, find a caterer who will make your event shine (unless you run a catering business or consider yourself to be a chef with skills that many appreciate).

The skills, experience, and specialties of caterers are quite different. You can identify possible caterers several ways. If you have a favorite restaurant, ask the manager if he can provide you with any leads for caterers. The manager may indicate interest in having the restaurant itself cater the event. In addition, talk to a manager of a cooking store in your area to see if he or she can refer anyone. The increase in personal chefs has created an entire category of people who might be available to cater your event. Whichever route you go, work with a service that is licensed to prepare and serve food. Ask those you're considering for references you can call to determine how previous events they catered turned out.

A few other caterer considerations to keep in mind:

- ➲ Obtain a sample menu or two of what they intend to serve.
- ➲ If you're not familiar with their food and services, see if you can arrange to sample their food or visit their cooking site before the event starts so you can see them in action.
- ➲ If you're hosting a larger party, determine how many servers they will bring. Make sure you have enough for the number of guests on hand. In addition, discuss the catering staff's attire for the event.
- ➲ Find out exactly what their fee entails. You'll want it to include, for example, setup and cleanup, preparation and serving, and garbage disposal.
- ➲ Part of their service to you may be extras to them. Will they supply linens and utensils, for example? If so, find out what they look like to make sure they match the tone you expect to set.

Budget for Help

Those events that aren't held at facilities that normally serve food—such as your home—need to take additional staffing into account. **Even if a cocktail or dinner party has a small guest list, don't try to handle every detail during the night of the event.** If you're head of the company or an entrepreneur currying favor or interest from those you've invited, you want to be available to them. If you're washing dishes, serving food, restocking the bar, and taking coats, your attention will be diverted.

Depending on the crowd you're expecting, you might do with just a server and a bartender. However, if you're expecting dozens of people for a sit-down dinner, plan on one server per eight to ten people to make sure everyone eats at the same time.

Rentals

If you're not having the event at a hotel or restaurant, take an inventory of items you'll need for cocktails, supper, or both, such as dinnerware, glasses, platters, and linens. Party rental companies offer a large supply of all of these items at a reasonable cost. For instance, you can browse *www.classicpartyrentals.com* to ascertain what products, such as china and chairs, you might need for your event.

If you are hosting a series of cocktail or dinner parties for your business ventures, consider buying sets at a restaurant supply company or at large chains such as IKEA or Pier One. Such stores offer a wide range of stylish but affordable settings.

You want to leave a favorable impression on your party guests. Because of that, don't consider plastic glasses and cutlery and paper plates for this kind of event. Your whole event will be raised another notch by renting china and other niceties.

Affordable Entertaining

If you're committed to hosting several events on your own turf and all of them will be on a tight budget, purchasing supplies in bulk may be a less expensive move—and you get to keep what you've bought. Check out plates, glasses, cutlery, platters, and linens from Crate & Barrel outlet stores, as well as such chains as Big Lots and Tuesday Morning. Additionally you may find what you need at *www.cb2.com*, *www.overstock.com*, and *www.welldressedhome.com*. Some sites offer free shipping, so you can buy what you need and not have to transport it yourself, a boon to the harried event planner.

Selecting a Venue and Setting the Scene

The venue can be a substantial part of your costs if you're renting a site. With hotels and restaurants though, your room fee can often be reduced or eliminated depending upon the amount of food and drink you order. Keeping your focus on where the event will be best, your choices include:

- ➲ Your home
- ➲ A restaurant's private dining room
- ➲ A hotel meeting room
- ➲ An outdoor area such as a courtyard, poolside, a private beach, or a country club dining room

Survey the Site

If you're scouting locations for a cocktail or dinner party that is prepared to serve food and won't require that you contract with a caterer, make sure you have answers to the following:

- ➲ By what date do you have to reserve the site and submit a deposit?
- ➲ Can you get an estimate of the average cost per head?
- ➲ When is the balance due and what is the cancellation policy?
- ➲ When do you need to give the final guest tally?
- ➲ For a presentation or entertainment component, does the facility have the equipment and electricity you need or will you need to procure that separately?
- ➲ Does the site have ample parking? Do you need to hire or make arrangements for valet service?
- ➲ What time can you arrive to set up? By what time must everyone leave?
- ➲ How many servers, bartenders, and attendants are guaranteed?

On the Home Front

Often business owners wish to use their own home to host such an event. If this is clearly the best choice, do so. But if you're just trying to save money and may sacrifice a good impression, weigh other options.

Hosting an event in your home gives you the chance to create a warm setting that can foster conversation and be hugely inviting. But if your current home doesn't show well, could present parking problems, or is in the midst of a remodeling project, search for another venue to give your cocktail or dinner party the top-notch atmosphere it deserves.

If the event is at your home, first make sure that the house can comfortably accommodate the number of people you are inviting. Then tend to these details:

The room—How much space do you have or can you make? Will furniture need to be moved? Will tables or chairs need to be added?

The flow—Where will chairs, table, and the bar be placed such that areas don't become clogged?

The diagram—Take a picture of the space beforehand and create a diagram. Map out exactly where you expect tables and chairs to go, people to sit and stand, and the bar to be placed. In addition, consider outside areas for milling around and conversation. For instance, is there an outdoor area that could be transformed for entertaining or overflow?

Entertaining Books

While they're more dedicated to the social realm than the business arena, *Occasions* by Kate Spade, *Essentially Lilly* by Lilly Pulitzer and Jay Mulvaney, and *The Swell Dressed Party* by Cynthia Rowley and Ilene Rosenzweig all offer a litany of wonderful ideas for party themes, ideas, and menus. You can easily tailor some of their suggestions for business parties you have on the horizon.

Atmosphere's Starring Role

Particularly when the event is in your home, you have the opportunity to create a welcoming, even luxurious environment. Even when the venue is not your home, you can still add touches that make your atmosphere more sumptuous.

Candlelight—Candles or light controlled by dimmers is typically flattering, but don't have the light so low that people are in the dark.

Music—If possible (and depending on the venue), select CDs that will be suitable for the evening. Cocktails generally feature more upbeat music, such as jazz, swing, or lounge classics, while dinner is set off nicely by classical or instrumental music.

Table décor—Consider floral arrangements that accent but don't dominate and, for a seated dinner, place cards. For a buffet table, attractively feature platters at different heights and include smaller floral arrangements (preferably ones that are not highly scented) to dot the tablescape with color. (For different heights, turn boxes or bowls upside down to create a sturdy, flat surface, then cover with fabric or a tablecloth. Place the platter on top of the covered surface.)

Fleming's Prime Steakhouse & Wine Bar Inside Track

This restaurant provides an exquisite experience and an excellent example of how to host a dinner party with class and style. At each of its locations, Fleming's has a private dining director who can help guide the course of a dinner party you'd like to host. The director will sit down with you and interview you about your needs and expectations. His or her questions about your upcoming event will help you fine-tune your goals and prospects for it.

In helping you shape the evening, you'll pick from preplanned menus the restaurant offers, but it can also customize one precisely for your event. The restaurant also anticipates any food requests by offering the choice of a red protein, a white protein, and a fish on every menu. Everything is made from scratch, and the meats are cut by hand.

If you're running short on time to scout locations, you can take a 360 degree virtual tour of the meeting rooms in a location near you at *www.flemingssteakhouse.com*. The beautifully appointed areas exude posh comfort and privacy.

If you need your event to include a visual component or presentation, all the restaurant's private dining rooms are outfitted with a drop-down screen and LCD projector. The chain is also a pioneer in video-conferencing capabilities, which can blend video, PowerPoint, and Q&A elements for a real-time conversation, bringing people together audibly and visually from other Fleming's private dining rooms in cities across the country.

What to Serve

If you're working with a facility that caters, it can help you select the menu or appetizers to serve. However, if you're planning the event from scratch and hosting the event at home, you have several decisions to make regarding the foods and cocktails to offer. The guidelines presented here for serving styles and quantities will help you in your budgetary and planning decisions for other venues as well.

Serving Styles

If your event is a cocktail party, you can either have servers present appetizers or serve them on a buffet table. Appetizers should always be bite-sized, easy to hold in the hand, nongreasy, and easy to serve. Served appetizers require personnel versus buffet style where guests can help themselves.

Dinner can be served buffet style or as a seated meal. With a seated meal, the food is either plated beforehand and served by wait staff or presented by French or Russian service, where a server doles portions to guests from a platter or assembles the plate from ingredients on a cart.

Appetizers and Cocktails: How Much to Serve

The following information demystifies the process of figuring out how much food and drinks need to be available for your guests for both cocktail and dinner parties.

MEAL	APPETIZERS	DRINKS
Dinner	4–8 per guest	2–3 per guest
Appetizers Only	6–12 per guest	2–3 per guest
KINDS OF APPETIZERS	NUMBER OF GUESTS	
3	8–10	
4	11–16	
6	17–39	
8	40-plus	

Mix up the appetizer flavor and appeal by having an equal number of hot and cold ones and a variety of salty, sweet, and spicy ones. Also vary the appetizers' ingredients, such as cheeses, meats, seafood, nuts, and vegetables to add depth to your offerings.

ALCOHOL	YIELD
750 milliliter liquor bottle	16 cocktails
1 liter liquor bottle	22 cocktails
1.5 liter liquor bottle	39 cocktails
750 milliliter wine bottle	5 servings

Stocking the Bar

The following represents a fully stocked bar, but stick to the mentioned guidelines concerning servings to allow for the number of people you're expecting:

Liquor—vodka, rum, gin, scotch, bourbon, blended whiskey, tequila

Beer and wine—include light beer as well as red and white wines

Beverages—club soda, tonic water, bottled water, cola, lemon-lime soda, ginger ale

Flavorings—freshly ground pepper, kosher salt, grenadine, simple syrup, cream of coconut, horseradish, angostura bitters

Juices—freshly squeezed lemon juice, lime juice, orange juice, grapefruit juice, tomato juice, pineapple juice

Extras—dry and sweet vermouth, half-and-half

Garnishes—lemon and lime wedges, lemon peels, cherries, olives, celery stalks

Entertaining Accents

You can sometimes take your party to an entirely different realm with a few touches that won't cost that much. For instance, you might make a cocktail party a Coffees & Cocktails soiree that could include some alcohol-based coffee drinks. This requires that you stock the bar with such extras as Kahlúa and crème de menthe. Or you may decide to feature a selection of after-dinner drinks, for which you might want to include brandy, cognac, or Grand Marnier.

Also, if appropriate, devise a cocktail that is particular to your event, perhaps named after your company or the person you're honoring. Plan on offering a selection of nonalcoholic drinks that is also special, such as flavored iced and hot teas.

Finally, if the event calls for it, you may want to have a favor for each guest. Favors for event parties are discussed further in the next chapter, but—and particularly if your cocktail or dinner party is taking on a celebratory tone—this touch can create a more lasting impact for the evening and be a nice reminder of your company as well.

▶▶ **Test Drive**

While hosting a cocktail or dinner party can seem overwhelming, its social nature and intimacy has its rewards. Think about the last dinner or cocktail party you attended.

- ⤶ Was it for business or pleasure?
- ⤶ What was your relationship to the host?
- ⤶ Did any business referrals or networking with any of those who attended result from it? If so, how could you tell?
- ⤶ Did you leave with a favorable impression of those gathered?
- ⤶ Would you have done anything differently?

Why So Formal?

Events can sometimes ratchet up to this level where the dress, atmosphere, and goings-on are extravagant. Black-tie affairs and galas represent the pinnacle of celebration for a company and can be the most time-intensive and expensive to organize. Much of the discussion and explanations in this chapter build on the information in Chapters 1–6, as well as Chapters 15 and 16 and, if a fundraising component is involved, Chapter 14.

There are several reasons to hold this type of gala, which immediately signifies a celebration of the highest order. If your company is fashion or entertainment oriented, you may find that you have more than a few occasions that can adopt a black-tie format to befit your business. Whatever your enterprise, a black-tie event could be a fitting way to:

- Commemorate a business' anniversary
- Honor an individual for years of service
- Conduct a fundraising endeavor
- Reward a company milestone
- Cap off a longer event (such as a grand opening week or convention)
- Tie in with a holiday

This kind of event takes the cocktail party and dinner party into an entirely new realm. Black-tie affairs usually involve more people, a number of tables and seating assignments to organize, invitations that specify appropriate dress and the reasons for the soiree, entertainment that is on par with the event, and many times extras in the form of ornate decorations and lavish favors. If fundraising is part of the initiative, you also may have to incorporate such activities as auctions into your plans (discussed in detail in Chapter 14). In many ways, orchestrating all these elements is akin to planning several dinner and cocktail parties that are all happening at the same time. However, you also have other tasks that must be prepared for, sorted out, and executed.

With all the work these events can produce great rewards in the form of generous sums raised for a cause, extensive positive publicity for your company, and goodwill among employees, investors, colleagues, vendors, and the like.

Generally speaking, more extravagant events are commensurate with their importance. Black-tie events tend to conjure up images of high-society weddings and glitzy red-carpet award ceremonies. While your company most likely won't be planning that sort of event in the course of your business, taking on an event of this magnitude attaches a significant measure of distinction to the business. So if you want to make a statement about your company, a black-tie event is certainly an option if you designate a worthy cause for celebration, ruthlessly prepare for it, and flawlessly execute it.

Black-tie events rarely take place in a person's home. Locations are discussed later in this chapter. Bear in mind that the guidelines suggested here target a venue that specializes in catering to a large audience.

The Focal Point of the Affair

Why will your company be hosting this high-class affair? Answering that question helps you lay out some of the themes you want to carry through the entire evening. **The focal point guides your food selections, activities, and entertainment.** In most cases that focal point gives structure to your event's theme. Concentrating on the focal point assists with the order and events of the program and the timing of your duties and responsibilities leading up to the gala.

For instance, if your gala is a fundraiser, you have to work with the benefiting organization, mapping out a timeline that charts both your efforts and taps into possible activities that will draw in additional funds such as an auction or a bazaar.

Or if your company is honoring an individual, you need to consider ways to celebrate him or her. That might include a video presentation or a roast with colleagues, whose schedules must be coordinated. If your event is the conclusion to a few days of activities surrounding a convention or a grand opening, the program should feature highlights of the previous events and suitable celebratory elements such as an awards presentation.

Steering Committees

Having decided on the focus, realize that you're more apt to get a large job—such as organizing the entire gala—completed more efficiently and effectively by assigning tasks to committees for the program, food and beverage, publicity, and so forth. Each committee should have a committee head, and those leaders should routinely meet with the person who is in charge of the entire event.

Black-tie events often have an honorary or advisory committee or board comprised of civic leaders, local or national celebrities, company heads, and other dignitaries. While these people may not have day-to-day responsibilities for the event, they are happy to lend their name to help spur ticket sales, give credence to your cause, or support the event financially depending on its goal and mission. Determine whether your event will benefit from and be suitable for such a committee.

Timing Is Everything

Because of the importance of such an event, you need to take your responsibilities even more seriously when it comes to the timing for deciding upon a location, sending out invitations, gathering RSVPs, initiating publicity efforts, and coordinating graphics and collateral. And because your event's guest list may include local celebrities, be sure and check your community's event calendar, local and state holidays, and even school schedules to make sure that the evening of your gala isn't conflicting with the date of another high-profile event.

Securing the Location

Pinpoint a location that is a logical fit for your event in terms of both size and atmosphere. Assess the number of likely attendees, and steer clear of venues that will dwarf your festivities or be too boisterous for them. Because black-tie events tend to imbue the same feelings of pomp and class across the board, there are fewer choices where locations are concerned. Again, rarely will a black-tie event be held at your place of business or inside your home.

Typical settings include:

➲ Hotel ballroom
➲ Museum
➲ Country Club
➲ Historical attraction

Don't be afraid to think outside the box if a potential venue is a good fit. Consider these possibilities:

➲ Underneath white tents on an expansive lawn
➲ On a yacht
➲ In a park or pavilion within a zoo
➲ In a casino
➲ At a winery

Looking for Just the Right Place?

Although your company won't be hosting a wedding as its business event, places that wedding receptions and dinners are held often provide the perfect setting. In California, *Here Comes the Guide* by Lynn Broadwell and Jan Brenner and its companion Web site offer an extensive list of places that are conducive to black-tie events. Check out similarly compiled sources in your area for ideas and possibilities.

Particulars to Note

Give yourself plenty of time to find the right place, especially where a gala event is concerned and particularly if your timing is tied to a holiday. For instance, a Christmas-themed event limits you to only a few weekends, and places are often booked months in advance. If you go off the beaten path—onto a yacht or in a remote location—be prepared to pay additional transportation fees for bringing in outside services.

Be open to possibilities outside of the traditional Saturday night fete, especially if you're looking for ways to rein in costs. However, make sure the tenor of your event matches your decision. A Sunday afternoon or Tuesday evening black-tie event doesn't have the same cachet as a Saturday night one does.

Black-Tie Excellence: Four Seasons Hotels

When planning a gala event, you want to make sure that you're preparing and selecting a venue that is commensurate with your affair. In so doing, look for a property that exudes the tenets you want your event to command.

For instance, one of my favorite hotels to work with has been Four Seasons. When an invitee knows that an event is taking place at a Four Seasons Hotel, you have automatically communicated that this is a special affair. Four Seasons' reputation for service and style gives your gala built-in credence.

In addition, they have set a standard for unparalleled service and attention to details. Even if you don't choose a Four Seasons property for your event, you can be guided by their commitment to excellence. Consider a venue that is upgraded, that has been particularly well cared for, and that—even if it's historic—has new amenities. Look for a setting that is stunning and welcoming with, if possible, scenic or otherwise attractive views.

In addition, make sure the menu is outstanding, expertly prepared, and impeccably served.

The Four Seasons has also given me excellent examples of well-trained staff that are eager and willing to answer questions and accommodate; and a facility or hotel contact who helps brainstorm ideas and lends creative suggestions keeping the success of your event top of mind.

Especially when you're planning an event that makes a statement and impresses, select a place like the Four Seasons that will from the get-go match the impression you're trying to make for your company.

Give the Location a Double-Check

Often the person you make initial contact with to scout the site will be your primary contact, but he or she might not be. Find out for certain who is going to be the CSM (catering sales manager) or similar representative responsible for your event. If he or she is working with someone else who can also tend to your needs, find out. Planning for a gala can take twists and turns, and the timeline can fly by. You want to build the foundation for a solid relationship in which you have a banner event and they have a happy customer. Meanwhile, before you commit to the site, make sure it can accommodate every element you plan to incorporate into it. For a black-tie gala you may need to consider such unique components as:

⊃ Separate areas for a cocktail reception and dinner

⊃ Additional areas for a silent auction

⊃ A green room for celebrities, speakers, or guests of honor to wait before they are introduced

⊃ Setup for entertainment, such as a band, and a dance floor

⊃ Attractively staged space for such functions as check-in and gift bag or favor distribution

In addition, don't forget to check on site capabilities for other aspects (covered later in this chapter) such as:

⊃ Adequate parking and valet service

⊃ The ratio of wait staff to people to serve

⊃ The number of bars and bartenders

Invitations

Use your invitations to set the tone. While you don't want to allocate a disproportionate amount of money to produce them, don't skimp on them either. For a black-tie affair, you wouldn't, for instance, print them on neon color cardstock on an inkjet printer. Plan to have them professionally printed. If your gala is a fundraiser, your invitation should include tickets for purchase and a return envelope for payment. See Appendix B for a list of Web sites you can turn to for your printing and invitation needs.

Invitations Don't Have to Be Paper

A favorite invitation of mine for a studio black-tie event was engraved on a piece of an orange mirror. Dramatic? Yes, and attendance and buzz were significant. Classy invitations for black-tie events don't always have to be exorbitantly expensive and don't always have to be black-and-white. If the occasion fits, take liberties with the invitation as long as it's in good taste. Consider printing on something unusual: painted wood, bejeweled fabric, a message in a wine bottle, presented in a silver frame. I've even received one imprinted on the outside of a candle. See if there's an alternative that is cost efficient, in the spirit of your festivities, and perfect for sparking your recipients' enthusiasm.

The Dining Experience

In all cases, opt for selecting a menu that is appealing both visually and tastewise, evokes the senses, and connotes sumptuousness. While your black-tie event should have a theme, don't feel compelled to cater to the beat of a gimmick. **While theming certain lunches and dinners makes sense, a black-tie event stands separate.** For instance, the casual nature of a Southern picnic, a Mexican fiesta, or an Italian spaghetti dinner by their very nature seem to contrast the sophistication of everyone gathered in tuxes and gowns.

Serving

Consider serving in ways that lend elegance. For instance, wait staff passing hors d'oeuvres has more panache than guests gathering or crowding around buffet tables laden with appetizers. Similarly, having wait staff serve tables—rather than have tables called one by one to have guests serve themselves at a buffet—is a nicer touch. Review such niceties as formal dining service with your CSM, and review your options.

The Menu

Your menu will probably include appetizers, salad, an entrée with vegetables, and dessert. Depending on your site, and with your budget in hand, the CSM can provide you an array of choices that fit your needs. Strive for creativity with caution in your menu selection. The meal should be attractively presented and memorable and be suitable for most tastes. Still, you can veer narrowly outside the comfort zone if you think some of your audience will appreciate a new taste. While you shouldn't simply opt for baked chicken and mashed potatoes, you wouldn't want to offer veal cheeks and caramelized fennel either.

In addition, don't be afraid to ask questions when presented with the menu choices. Sometimes menu items can be illustratively and clearly described, and sometimes not. Occasionally several adjectives are covering up what's simply a hamburger. Try to sample some of the menu possibilities. If that's not offered and you are seriously considering the venue, ask for an opportunity to taste a selection of choices.

Alcohol

If you're trying to pare down costs, you can choose to go with a nice selection of beers and wines instead of an open bar. But for a black-tie event guests typically expect a fully stocked bar. Check the charts in Chapter 16 to find suggested guidelines for alcohol types and quantities.

Generally you'll need one bartender per seventy-five guests. Some venues allow you to bring your own bottles of alcohol, but ask if the venue assesses a corkage fee per bottle opened. If you're supplying the alcohol, you often pay less than a hotel's charge per bottle.

Types of liquor also comes in tiers of pricing at hotels and other venues: the *well* brand is what is typically poured; better varieties are known as *call*, *super-call*, or *premium* choices and cost more.

Black-tie events also may necessitate you eliminating certain beverage choices. For instance, you may want to take cranberry juice, tomato juice, and even red wine off the cocktail list if you're concerned about any spills that may stain elegant surroundings.

Extras to Add

In planning a gala you can easily become intensely focused on the event's infrastructure: squaring away the site, selecting the menu, and sending out the invitations. But don't forget that you or designated staff or committee members need to tend to details for your event to be a success. If those details are ignored, they could leave guests with a bad overall impression of the evening.

Creating a Glowing Buzz Upon Arrival

You may have noticed during a black-tie event—or seen coverage of one—that a huge reflecting light in the shape of a logo or special design heralds nighttime arrivals. A gobo has become standard equipment at many galas. A gobo (short for "goes before optics") is a template that, pierced by light, can project a huge image on a wall, building, or awning. Typically the image has to be custom made. You can learn more about creating or renting one for your event at an audio-visual company or through a party rentals facility.

Distilling the Evening

When you embark on the task of fleshing out your evening, scheduling it, and putting together the complete program, you need to go through your plan line by line to determine any special requirements or enhancements you'll need. For instance, if the evening includes awards, do you need to order plaques, certificates, or other recognition pieces? If so, you also need to build in time for inscribing (for plaques) or setting up calligraphy (for certificates).

Set the Scene

Make sure that as guests arrive they know from the get-go they are entering a rarefied experience. Don't just leave it to a hotel to announce and direct arrivals. Either have guests greeted by designated staff or committee members, or consider activities outside the ballroom that will be an instant draw.

If check-in is necessary, make sure that you have it staffed and set up to run smoothly and swiftly. That may mean, for instance, breaking down the check-in alphabetically, having each check-in staff member equipped to handle any arrival, or setting up several different areas (such as one for VIPs, another for media, one for internal staff members, and so on).

Valet Service

Many times black-tie events require valet service depending on your location and the available parking. You don't want people walking miles in tuxes and gowns to reach your party. In some locations you might have no choice but valet parking. If that's the case, double-check with the venue to make sure that they will have the proper staffing that night to accommodate the influx of vehicles for your event.

Just as importantly, have valet service so regimented that no one has to wait an excessive amount of time for a car to depart. Guests having to wait a long time for their car won't be left with a lasting, positive impression of the event.

Providing Entertainment

At a black-tie gala, entertainment can take on many forms before and during the event. Consider these possibilities:

Music—This is appropriate for before, such as a string quartet that greets guests, during, including a jazz ensemble for background during dinner, and afterward, such as a contemporary band for dancing.

Speaker—A speaker can be hired for entertainment after dinner and before dessert. Look at personalities from the fields of e-commerce, television, lifestyle, sports, or business.

Unconventional—The speakers don't have to fit within a mold. You can include a motivational personality, a well-known standup comic, or someone who you know would appeal to the majority of your guests.

Atmospheric—You can include strolling musicians, storytellers, or acrobats.

Entertainment shouldn't just be relegated to performers. At black-tie events you also have some leeway with entertaining activities as long as they're designed and delivered in good taste.

- *Beauty bar*—with tips on makeup for women and free samples of beauty products
- *Fortuneteller*—have a medium on hand who can read palms, cards, or a crystal ball
- *Photo booth*—offer guests the chance to sit, pose, and have pictures delivered within minutes
- *Retro arcade*—feature pinball machines and video games from another era
- *Chocolate or wine tastings*—staff with culinary experts and offer guests both tastes and educational information about their favorites

Favors and Gift Bags

Black-tie events and galas increasingly rely on providing elaborate favors or entire gift bags for guests at a soiree. Depending on your business and the attendees coming, you may be able to get items for a gift bag donated. Still, if you go the gift bag route, the contents should be relevant to the event and appreciated by guests. Don't just plan on stuffing a gift bag containing a hodgepodge of products simply to have one in each person's chair or to dole out at the end of the evening. Each article in it should have a logical tie-in.

Typically gift bags are placed on each attendee's seat. Alternatively they are handed out at the end of the evening. For some gatherings organizers have gone a step further: to free up their guests' hands valets place the gift bags in the attendees' cars.

If the event has a substantial attendance and the gift bags are coveted, plan to hand out a ticket or stub to each arriving guest that can be redeemed at the end of the evening as they depart.

▶▶ Test Drive

If you decided that a black-tie event was a fit for your company, what do you think would be the biggest obstacle in planning it for your company?

- ➲ Costs? If so, would it be possible to cohost the event with another company that wouldn't dilute but complement your company's branding?
- ➲ Time involved? If so, would you consider sharing responsibilities among staff members or temporarily hire someone to oversee the event?
- ➲ An impressive venue? If so, could you find some unconventional locations that could be outfitted to host such an event?

Deciding Your Purpose

Whereas dinner and cocktail parties offer a more formal flair, open houses and receptions have a more relaxed tone. Open houses usually occur during the day or early evening; Sunday afternoon is a popular time, for example. Often because of the time of the day it's held, the dress may be more casual and kids may be part of the mix.

Events known as receptions generally follow the same time frames unless they are associated with a larger evening event. In that case, they will adhere more to the guidelines for cocktail parties. Reasons for either an open house or reception include to:

➲ Celebrate an occasion, such as a promotion, your company receiving an award, or a holiday

➲ Showcase your place of business to community leaders and residents, particularly if you are new to the area, have just completed a remodel, have moved operations, or have added a new facility or showroom

➲ Introduce others in your company or in your community to new staff members

➲ Get acquainted in a relaxed atmosphere with others with whom your company works

➲ Offer tours of your place of business or an institution associated with your place of business

➲ Show appreciation for customers

Whatever reason you decide on for hosting an open house, make sure you've given it shape and purpose. **Don't quickly put together an event just to get it out of the way.** Determine beforehand how having this event will positively impact business. Make it part of your overall business and marketing plan.

Where's the Best Place?

An open house doesn't always occur in a house. It can be in an office, a school, or a church—whichever location matches your specific business and purpose. An open house is simply hosting an event in a place in which you want to showcase a specific entity. Likewise, a reception that your company hosts doesn't necessarily have to occur at your place of business. You can check out several possibilities for venues in Chapter 6.

Are Kids Part of the Mix?

If you've elected to include children at the open house or reception, realize that your tone may be less formal. In addition, plan to coordinate activities that appeal to kids, such as having art or building-block stations, hiring a face painter, or—if outdoors—providing sports equipment.

You also need to child-proof certain areas. For example, make sure swimming pools have fences around them and that any fragile items are on high shelves.

Co-opting an Open House

While you don't want to dilute your message, consider cohosting an open house with another entity to mitigate costs. For instance, shops that share a courtyard, strip mall, or stretch of street might hold a joint open house to welcome the holiday season. Or if you're a sole proprietor of a business, consider holding a reception with those in ancillary businesses; all of you may have clients that could benefit from your different services. For instance, a real-estate agent, lawyer, and accountant might cohost a "Getting Your Financial House in Order" event, or a publicist, graphic artist, and advertising copywriter might hold a "Marketing Mavens" reception.

Giving Your Event a Strategy

With its free-flowing atmosphere, an open house presents a challenge in that you must be constantly prepared during it. Since people may drop in at any time during an open house, you may have a small gathering initially then brace for a large crowd near the end. The ebb and flow of the crowd means that you have to ensure that food being served is replenished and drinks are continually stocked.

Further, you don't want guests to feel as if they've arrived too early or too late or somehow missed a part of the function. No matter if the event is at its beginning or end, always have staff present at appropriate posts: at the check-in table if applicable, handing out nametags, serving food, taking coats. You're striving for a seamless experience.

Typically open houses and receptions don't concentrate on having the event culminate in some way, such as with a PowerPoint presentation or awards ceremony. However, if you are showing off your business, plan to have tours that occur every ten or fifteen minutes. You may also consider having a visual set up, such as a presentation of computer-generated images that provides snapshots running on a continuous loop of your business' features.

Devising a Game Plan

Consult Chapter 3 for the responsibilities that need to be included in a timeline for carrying out your open house. The particulars you must begin with include:

- Determining the best date (and checking that it's a date for optimal attendance with no conflicts)
- Setting the budget
- Identifying the invitees
- Finding a location if it's not at your place of business
- Sending out invitations
- Planning for food and beverages

Repair, Refurbish, Replace

If the open house is at your place of business, immediately assess any repairs that need to be handled before the event, such as painting that should be done, furniture that should be purchased, or any other fixes that if left undone will detract from a polished place of business. Analyze the space ruthlessly. Are wires dangling needlessly? Is clutter overwhelming? Are drapes ripped or blinds bent?

Sometimes people become inured to their workspace. Have someone you trust take a look around and see what he or she points out that could give your workplace an unimpressive atmosphere. In addition, take digital snapshots of your offices or place of business. You'll be surprised to realize what a picture can point out or what draws your attention that your eyes might not notice otherwise. In addition, include a thorough cleaning as part of the timeline.

Deciding the Day and Hours

Most business open houses occur immediately after the workday, around 5:00–9:00 P.M., and most guests stay for about an hour. Stay away from Monday and Friday. Monday events can catch people off guard, and Fridays often find people leaving town early.

Avoid overcrowding—particularly if you're working in smaller confines or you're trying to coordinate tours of a building—by staggering the schedule. For instance, you might send two versions of the invitation. On one you invite family members and close friends for the first two hours, and on another invitation segue to industry colleagues for the last half of the event. Make sure that the groups you're separating are distinct enough that they won't be confused if they compare invitations. If you've got a particularly lengthy invitation list, consider splitting up groups and have the event on two nights.

Food

Open house and reception food tends toward cocktails and appetizers or coffee and dessert. Create a menu that can be easily replenished throughout the event. The menu items should be served in bite-sized portions that are easy to eat while standing. Depending on the tenor of your event, you can have the food selections served buffet style or have them passed, or you can use a combination of the two.

If the reception or open house is occurring in your place of business, figure out—preferably with the caterer—the best areas to serve the food and drink that will be easy for guests to maneuver around and won't create clogs in the traffic flow.

While it's acceptable to use and redress available tables and credenzas, you should move copiers and printers out of the way, or if that's not feasible drape them with fabric. Don't serve food off of them.

If this event is occurring in a home, do not concentrate all the food and drink in the kitchen. Use other areas. The kitchen will be command central for preparing and plating the food and trays; don't compound a space issue by also setting up serving stations there.

Station Possibilities

You can also take your open house or reception upscale by using carts or self-contained stations to serve your guests. Crepe makers, coffee carts, and chocolate fountain stations are all impressive yet reasonably priced offerings that add a sense of celebration to an event with a minimum of fuss. These types of services arrive at a predetermined time with all the equipment and food or beverage they need. As outlined in the catering guidelines provided in Chapter 16, get contract specifics down, including how many people they plan to serve, what menu items they offer, where they will set up, facilities (such as electrical outlets) they need, and references you can check out beforehand. You can visit *www.partypop.com* to get ideas of the options you have in this category and possible vendors in your area.

Accepting or Deflecting Alcohol

Alcohol lends a festive air to many events, but if you don't deem it appropriate or don't think it's consistent with your business practices, don't feel obligated to offer cocktails.

If you decide to have liquor on hand, a fully stocked bar isn't a necessity for open houses and receptions. You can serve beer and wine along with soft drinks, bottled water, and juices.

If serving alcohol will squeeze your budget, remember that an open house won't seem very hospitable if you ask people to pay for drinks. Instead, stick with nonalcoholic beverages and have a celebration punch.

Taking Other Particulars into Account

Just because an open house or reception takes on a more relaxed tone doesn't mean it's not orderly in its arrangement and execution. Make sure you're very specific in all the details you carry out.

What Will the Invitations Look Like?

Use the invitations to set the tone of the event, and make sure to include a start and end time. If you need to be out of your venue by a certain time (to avoid extra charges, for example) state an end time that will give you some leeway.

The invitations should include the dress code, which is always appreciated by invitees. The dress code can be along the lines of business or casual dress, or depending on the time of year even holiday attire.

As a courtesy, let your invitees know what food and beverages to expect. While you certainly don't have to include your menu on the invitation, give them a descriptor such as "light refreshments," "picnic fare," or "dessert bar."

Even though a reception or open house has more relaxed rules for punctuality, ask for an RSVP, and provide a phone number or e-mail guests can respond to and the date by which the invitee should respond.

The E-vite

Since open houses and receptions take on a more relaxed tone, they represent one event in which using an e-mail invitation may be appropriate. A wide selection of electronic invitations offered at *www.evite.com* includes hundreds of design options for parties, and you can even customize an invitation with your own uploaded images. And the site's a boon for the cost conscious: their e-vites are free. To take a look at some of the artwork available for a business-related invitation, go to "Invitations" on the main navigation bar, and click on "Professional Events" for the theme.

Nametags

Once you have your RSVP list, make nametags for those who will be attending. For anyone who arrives who doesn't have a nametag waiting for them, have someone at the registration or greeting table that will clearly print it out for them. Better yet, have a laptop and portable printer that can print it out. For strictly business events you may also include your guests' company name. At your own company events, give the name and title of your employees so that your guests can recognize them and put a face to a voice.

Your choices for nametags include self-adhesive, pin-back, or clear plastic pouches with lanyards. You can be creative without choosing the usual "My Name Is . . . " tag. Instead you can opt for having nametags cut out of heavy cardstock that has a light background pattern, or print tags that are laminated and hung on lanyards. Whichever route you go, use a large, readable font for the names for everyone's visual ease.

Give a Nametag Double Duty

Think outside the box and preprint the nametags with a fun design that features a graphic consistent with your open house or reception's theme, or include your company's logo in an eye-catching way. Consider having the nametags play a part in a festivity. For instance, perhaps they have been randomly assigned numbers, and winning numbers are called out at a predetermined time with winners receiving company products or other prizes. Or if you're trying to encourage mixing among your guests, have each nametag feature a number or symbol that matches or fits in with a similar mark on someone else's nametag.

Nose Check

Whether in the workplace or at a home, take note of the scents that someone might encounter upon entering your open house or reception. You may be inured to odors that may surprise, offend, or simply catch guests off guard. For instance, your place of business may have machinery or other equipment that emits an industrial smell.

To combat such a problem, fill the air with aromas that are memorably pleasing. You can try fresh floral arrangements, bowls of lemons, vases filled with lavender, scented candles, or aromatherapy burners. Real-estate agents who invite prospective buyers into homes for sale routinely bake cookies or simmer cinnamon sticks because of the warm, inviting feelings those scents conjure up.

Serving Needs

Since crystal and china aren't always necessary for an open house, this event marks an occasion where paper products and plastic cups are perfectly suitable. And since people will be roaming more than being seated, you can consider such products as a cocktail/party plate that accommodates a glass on the plate.

Clean Up

Particularly because of an open house or reception's constant flow, don't let the trash pile up. If it's an informal setting, have attractive (such as stainless steel) garbage pails visible for guests to toss their used plates and cups. Or keep the garbage pails hidden and have a few people assigned to throw refuse away so it doesn't clutter tables and ledges.

Executing the Event

Before hosting the event, check your layout to be sure that you've created a workable, comfortable environment for guests to feel welcome and enjoy each other's company. To that end, will everybody be standing? Or do you see where well-placed chairs can offer comfortable, spontaneous seating? Consider how you might set up conversation areas. Make sure that areas where people congregate won't restrict flow, overwhelm the buffet table, be in the way of servers, be near dangerous stairs or equipment, or be too close to where drinks are being poured. You might also consider overflow areas, such as an outdoor patio or veranda, where guests can gather.

As guests arrive greet them as soon as possible. Work with your fellow staff to make introductions, and do your best to keep mingling.

Tailoring the Event to Your Business

Sometimes open houses take on a different meaning when applied to your particular business. So use the tenets of an impressive open house, then add on components that will be beneficial and impressive for your needs.

For instance, real-estate agents and brokers plan and host open houses to showcase properties. The same rules for open houses discussed in this chapter apply to their focus. However, they would certainly

| Inside Track | Don't Forget Your Ambassadors |

More than likely you'll be working with your staff to make sure your open house or reception goes off without a hitch. Remember that whomever you select to work the event will be working as an ambassador for your company.

A real-estate broker was responsible for a few open houses one weekend at a new development of homes for sale. For these particular homes she had decided to offer light refreshments to those who visited to check them out. However, spread thin, she dispatched some employees to staff them and decided to float among the houses.

As she came to each of the houses, she was horrified to find how business under her name was being conducted. At one property guests who arrived before the start time had been admonished for appearing too soon. At another home guests had been greeted by a woman with a sour face who warned them to "Sign this sheet or I'll get in trouble." When the broker arrived at another model home she found an employee chatting with friends while prospective buyers came and went with no questions answered and stacks of used cups and plates littered the inside. Calmly she pulled employees aside and, upon speaking with each one, she realized she had improperly trained her employees to handle the flow of visitors and answer questions.

Before your open house begins, make sure your staff knows why you're holding the event, and brief them with questions they might be expected to answer. In advance of their arrival, they should also know the appropriate attire to wear. If during the event they don't know the answer to a question asked, make sure they know who can provide follow-up. Realize that depending on the length of the event and the responsibilities they have they may be entitled to breaks.

At an event your staff members are your PR people and goodwill ambassadors. If they don't come off as professional and hospitable, it reflects badly on your business.

add on such things as displaying literature pertinent to the house, including details of the home's features and the price. Instead of providing nametags for those who visit, agents offer a sign-in sheet to follow up with possible buyers.

Similarly entrepreneurs who are party-plan sellers (hosting parties to sell Tupperware, Pampered Chef, Southern Living Home, and the like) take an open-house tack in their preparations for holding the event, displaying and selling their company's goods. For those open house-type affairs, they may—taking some tips from product launches discussed in Chapter 19—figure out how to turn a home's atmosphere and features to their advantage. Certainly they send invitations and offer refreshments during the event. However, as part of their preparations they need to decide how they want their products showcased—such as presenting items on tables covered with tablecloths—and coordinate other arrangements and activities that will attractively spotlight their products for sale.

Even with just a regular open house or reception, make sure you've taken into account how you can portray your business in a flattering light to those assembled. Provide brochures or other information, and perhaps offer a token gift that has your company's logo on it. Open houses are a casual, inviting way for you to get to know customers or clients better, assimilate into the community, and show off your business' attributes in an accessible arena. Take advantage of its comfortable focus and relaxed aura to make the most for your business.

▶▶ **Test Drive**

If you wanted to host a reception or open house for your company, can you think of how the following might benefit your business and interest guests? Would one of these provide an appropriate forum for your organizing such an event?

- ➥ A tour of your company's offices or work facility
- ➥ A gathering of your employees' friends and relatives
- ➥ An informal get-together for current and potential clients
- ➥ An opportunity to spotlight an award or an honor bestowed on an employee

Events and Ideas With a Marketing Edge

PART **5**

The Varieties of Launches

Once you've got your product or service ready to go, or you have a new line of products or services that you're adding on, you need to design an event (or series of events) to introduce that product to the world. Only one in five products survives past its second birthday. For the industry it covers, *Software Marketing Journal* says that 45 percent of all product launches fail. That disappointing figure probably is linked to the fact that most products don't make a big enough impression or don't communicate their value to a wide audience. In one poll, *Corporate Event* magazine noted that 56 percent of 1,000 people surveyed couldn't recall one product launched in 2004, a 50 percent increase from what could be recalled for 2003 launches.

Since so many new products don't survive, having a successful product launch event serves your product well and helps its chances in beating the odds and being remembered and bought. This chapter introduces some of the traditional ways that companies bring products to the attention of targeted consumers. Some of the most popular methods include:

- Product and service sampling
- Taste tests
- Product demonstrations

And while this chapter addresses the how-to behind these launches, you have many other options to select from as well. Further methods such as guerrilla marketing techniques and Web-based initiatives are covered in Chapters 23 and 24.

Before You Begin

Make sure your product is ready before you initiate a product launch event. You don't want to put time and money behind a false start, generating sales that you can't fulfill. While the following information may not pertain to your particular product or service, the necessary tests, attributes, and evaluations of a product launch that are covered apply to any situation. Some of these are helpful or required to have—such as marketing materials for a launch at a trade show—as you conduct a product launch.

When your product doesn't meet these criteria, you lose credibility with your customer base and will have difficulty in earning customers' trust when or if you relaunch your product. Only launch the product when your service, sales, and distribution channels are ready. Put it through this twelve-point test:

1. Final packaging has been designed, ordered, and implemented.
2. Product performance has been evaluated and tested.
3. Sales channels have been identified and established.
4. Product forecasts and market demands have been documented.
5. The production processes have been developed and tested.
6. Any regulatory approvals have been obtained.
7. Needed materials are in stock.
8. Engineering, purchasing, and manufacturing personnel stand ready to address any issues that arise.
9. User documentation, operating manuals, and maintenance instructions have been completed.
10. Advertising, product brochures, marketing materials, press releases, and Web site pages have been prepared and are ready to distribute at the appropriate time.
11. Sales, service, and support personnel have been trained or a phased training program is underway.
12. The distribution pipeline is filled with the appropriate level of product.

Your Goals

When you conduct your product launch, what do you want to achieve? Are you trying to get a one-time sale, a commitment to buy on a periodic basis, or do you want customers to request more information about the product? State your goals beforehand so that you guide your efforts and the launch itself appropriately.

Who's Coming?

Who will comprise the audience you're most eager to have at your launch? Will it be potential customers, reporters from specific media outlets, executives from companies you want to be in business with, or a combination of all of those? For your event to be optimally effective, make sure you're aware of who your target audience is—who you're trying to woo, impress, or curry favor with at the product launch.

Particularly if the media is present, you want to have your potential target audience members there enthusiastically and excitedly trying out and responding to your product.

Other Preparations

Take the time to identify who is going to be on your front line with this product launch. Who needs to serve as a point of contact for questions, issues, and requests regarding the product? Is it a sales force, customer service representatives, or trained staff members? Whomever you decide, they need to be apprised of such particulars as, for instance, release dates, availability, and how to use it. These contacts must deliver the information in a way that's consistent with your company's image and brand.

Product and Service Sampling

In launching a product or service, let your audience know that it's something they can't possibly do without by actually letting them use it. For some products this practice could be prohibitively costly. If that's the case, you may consider having an array of your products set up at a conference or fair and allow potential customers to use them that way.

The Apple stores provide a prime example of how this strategy can work effectively. Every Apple store features much of their product line—computers, iPods, printers, cameras—set out expressly for you to fiddle with. For instance, with a computer you can see how you like the feel of the keyboard, how the mouse clicks and opens programs, and what the modem speed is. They even let you check your e-mail. What better way to prove to customers that an Apple model may be exactly what they need as their next computer?

Regardless of the event you design, keep in mind that sampling should somehow—if possible—be an integral component. For example, if it's too expensive to hand out regular-sized samples, consider manufacturing some trial-size or smaller ones to hand out. That way you can effectively demonstrate how your product or service changes the way people live or do business and why they need your product to bring success in their personal or professional life.

If your product is too expensive or cumbersome to hand out even trial sizes or if you have a service that can't necessarily be sampled, consider doling out promotional items that have a tie-in—such as a mouse pad if you manufacture computer parts—so that you can reinforce your brand and logo.

Methods and Ideas to Consider

As you assess and determine your target audience, brainstorm the types of events that will appeal to them, if it will be a single or multiple one, the location of the event(s)—both in venue and pinpointing the geographical area(s)—the number of people expected, the employees needed to staff, and how your product will be showcased. You'll need to answer:

➲ What's the target demographic for the product?
➲ Where, geographically, is the product available?
➲ How will the customer use this product?
➲ How will the customer benefit from this product?
➲ How does the price point and performance compare to the competition?
➲ Who are the primary competitors?
➲ What is this product's USP (unique selling proposition), or how is it unique in the marketplace?

Appeal to the Media

Certainly the media can play a tremendous part in getting your product seen and noticed, increasing your chances of survival. In crafting a product launch that you deem worthy of your product, brainstorm ways to attract the media's interest. In addition to staging the event in a city that has several media outlets and inviting as many media as you can that might be interested in your product and your event's approach, think about the angles that you can provide that highlight the news value, differences, or novelties of your product. Many members of the media have heard and seen everything; they'll be delighted by something presented to them that's new and different.

Further, think of dramatic ways that flaunt the product, which could include involving celebrities, featuring the product in a high-flying demonstration, and sending out eye-popping invitations.

Don't Forget about the Timing

As with other events, be cognizant of the time, day, and date you select for an initial launch or a series of launches. It should be at a time that a bulk of your media targets can attend. Check schedules in the area of your launch to ensure that you're not conflicting with any high-profile festivities that will draw media away from your endeavors.

Taste Tests

Even if your product can't be actually tasted, understanding how taste tests are put together can give valuable insights into how product launches can succeed. In a taste test, samples of the product are doled out to passersby, encouraging their desire to purchase it. The product should be attractively presented and have an aroma that is enticing. Further, the product may be featured in an array of uses. For example, a new salad dressing may be tossed with lettuce or pasta or served as a dip. Those who are offering the tastes (or samples) are enthusiastic about the product, giving informed answers to questions, and eager to show how the product can be enjoyed. Finally, an effective taste test might also offer a coupon as an additional incentive to buy the product.

Product Demonstrations

A product demonstration shows potential customers the ease and effectiveness with which your product works. When you conduct a

Introducing a Beverage and a Bike ■ Inside Track

If you can determine a way for your product to be effectively showcased (think of taste tests and product demonstrations), I find this method an indispensable part of any product launch, particularly when it's coupled with an enthusiastic, focused, well-trained staff.

I was on the team for the relaunch of a carbonated beverage that had just endured a well-publicized product recall and was determined to recapture its market share. With the reintroduction of the branded beverage, we organized public tastings in dozens of cities at malls, parks, outdoor shopping areas, and in front of grocery stores. The tastings worked in a twofold manner: they showed the product was back in full force and that the beverage was tasty and safe. In our appeal to consumers we stressed that the beverage was low calorie, healthy, and refreshing . . . all features that would evoke an emotional appeal.

Another client introduced a stunning new motorcycle with fireworks and fanfare as stunt riders took the models through some gravity-defying paces in front of a huge audience of automotive press and industry professionals. Then automotive industry writers were escorted to a track where they could hop on the bikes and ride to their heart's content. With both those launch components we expressed the product's prime attributes for customers: This was a vehicle that was eye-catching, with a high cool quotient, backed up by easy maneuverability and a smooth ride.

In both cases—the beverage and the bike—every aspect of the product launch was focused on an exact target audience we were trying to attract. In addition, we benefited from everyone involved with both those launches being rigorously trained to answer questions about all aspects of the product.

demonstration you must point out how a product's advantages or features benefit the customer. Think of it from this perspective: In the case of a product demonstration for a microwave, don't think of your mission as selling an appliance, think of presenting how that appliance cooks food fast for its buyers.

To find out what you should stress most in a demo answer these questions: What is it about your product that will make your customer or client's life easier? How will it impact that person's life the most?

Generating Other Ideas Outside the Box

While taste testings and demonstrations offer a couple of ready-made options, be as creative as you want in designing a product launch that will be perfect for your product. Remember, the more memorable you can bring an association to your product, the more likely you'll attract media and establish a profile and brand that will resonate with customers.

Unveilings

Certainly one of the most dramatic ways to launch a product is with an unveiling: building a significant buzz for what a product will look like or do, then revealing its identity to an audience that can then experience its features firsthand. **Unveilings are most effective when you've succeeding in creating interest and anticipation in the product—for instance, through a series of teaser mailings, billboards, blog postings, or a combination of those.** In these cases you must match the level of excitement you've built with a product that meets or exceeds expectations and an unveiling event that does both the buzz and the product justice.

If you don't have a big budget to pour into your launch, an unveiling may not be the best route. Still, that doesn't mean your product has to be the next Xbox. For instance, with a more limited endeavor you can take a grassroots approach—a community-by-community endeavor—to start off with a small introduction of your product, then grow sales and exposure from there.

Road Shows

Taking a new product on the road can reap considerable gains, especially because you're giving others—particularly media outlets—easy access to see and experience it firsthand. For instance, a sewing machine company with clients that included many smaller shops that didn't have the time to visit trade shows took a fifty-three-foot trailer with its most popular products to more than 100 cities during six months in 2005. As that example illustrates, road shows are actually a series of events. You have to take into account how to customize the event for each location, the audience size in each place, how you can control environmental factors, and, of course, travel costs.

Learning from the Shopping Channels

HSN and QVC can give you an idea of what it takes to drum up or deter interest in a new product. Watching these shopping channels gives you a sense of how the host and product spokesperson are touting a product's benefits and applications and whether they're connecting with the message. You may notice that they're appealing to a specific demographic and how their approach is working. You may also see how a little tweaking would make the pitch more powerful.

Rallies for a Cause

Products come in different forms. Sometimes the concept of a product launch needs to be turned upside down. If your product isn't a store-bought item but rather a philanthropic cause, rallies can be instrumental in disseminating your message and gathering support. In the most easily understood examples, you've assembled a crowd to shower support on finding a cure for a disease or to encourage others to continue good works, or to help launch a nonprofit initiative that has been recently formed. The hallmarks of successful rallies typically include:

- Large crowds
- A big venue
- Lots of movement and activity
- A defining moment, such as an arrival, a major announcement, or an unveiling
- Speakers addressing the crowd
- A commitment to better the lives of others through backing the cause or mission that everyone has gathered to celebrate or learn more about

Once you have your mission and budget allocated for a rally, you need to pay special attention to finding a venue large enough, making sure you have a sufficient amount of people in attendance to make the rally successful, and crafting an itinerary that includes celebrities, community leaders, or other newsworthy individuals who are capable of drawing attention to your message for its launch and beyond.

Other Arenas for Your Pitch

When you have decided on the method of your product launch, next think of what kind of atmosphere or venue is best suited for your product or cause. Think beyond a room. Obviously for taste tests or demos you may be limited by retail stores or trade shows, but not always and not necessarily.

Product launches have occurred in barns and silos, in wine cellars and atop skyscrapers, on carousels and roller coasters. Don't be afraid to consider any possibility. You need to ask:

- ➲ Is it easy to get to or can you make it easy to get to?
- ➲ Can you set the scene for a dramatic impact?
- ➲ Is the setting consistent with the image you're aiming for your company to project with this product?
- ➲ Will the venue be a bigger star than the product, or will the setting bolster and accentuate the product?

Even if it is in just a room, how can you make it so special that your product instantly has fawning fans? In 2003 TiVo launched its TiVo Series 2 model by transforming New York's Roxy Theater into a replica of the 1964 New York World's Fair with exhibits and pavilions like the TiVo Better Living Center, TiVo Progressland, and the TiVo Modern Living Room standing in for the yesteryear originals.

Costs Versus Value

In the case of a launch party or event, it's not always about having it at the hottest, hippest place in town. If securing a location like that swallows up your budget, think of ways that you could customize a more affordable location. If you're in a less swanky place, you may be able to make more of an impact with huge images of your logo, custom-printed banners and carpets, logo-bearing nametags for all of those in attendance, along with activities that give the event a cool factor.

In addition, when implementing the specifics of a product launch event, you have to figure out how the launch will sustain the product's profile. Launches shouldn't be regarded as one-shot situations where you spend money to showcase the product and that's the end of it.

Pay attention to how you can extend the value of the time and resources you commit to the launch. **A product launch that attracts widespread media is laudable, but how will it benefit your company past that initial media blitz.** In other words, will the exposure you receive justify the expenses? How will the launch continue to impact sales? If you can amortize the cost of the launch over a long, successful run of keeping your product front and center, the value will definitely outweigh the cost.

If you're convinced that the initial impact is all you need to get your product off and running, so be it. But more often than not deeper analysis will show that, particularly with small companies' new offerings, exposure must be stoked and nurtured.

Checking in with Your Customers

Post-launch, you should brainstorm and consider ways that you can check in on customer satisfaction with your new product and publicize positive results. At the time of a product's introduction or when a customer initially buys it, provide a survey (or even a hotline or e-mail address) that allows them to give feedback on the product. In so doing you give your company the chance to gather then release data on your product's success. If those statistics are particularly newsworthy or compelling, you may be giving your company the foundation for another event to celebrate the product's performance.

Did the Launch Service the Product and Sales?

As the launch of a product can make or break a company, it's only natural to conduct a final assessment as part of your plan. To find out whether the launch was successful and to guide your efforts when you face a similar challenge again, ask:

⮑ What was the reaction to your product?

⮑ If you consider the launch successful, how are you measuring that success?

⮑ If you consider the launch problematic, how did you come to that conclusion? Can you redirect the efforts toward another launch?

⮑ Did the venue(s) serve its purpose? How might it have been better adapted?

⮑ Did you receive questions, issues, concerns, or requests that you didn't expect? How can you be better prepared next time?

⮑ Since the launch occurred have you already received orders for the product, seen an increase in sales, or encountered problems in manufacturing and distribution?

⮑ Have you figured out a way for the launch to translate into more sales or more company success stories?

⮑ Even if you deem the event a success, can you name areas that need improvement or components you would have done differently?

▶▶ Test Drive

Think about a recent product launch. It can be from a competitor of yours or in a completely different field.

⮑ How did you hear about the launch? If it was a newspaper article, did it receive favorable coverage?

⮑ What was the driving event of the launch? Was it an original idea, or did it include activities you thought were unique?

⮑ Are you the target audience for the product? If so, why or why not is it appealing to you to actually purchase?

⮑ How would you have added to the launch to make it more effective?

What Is a Press Conference?

A press conference is an event that in some ways can be considered a living press release. However, press conferences must have some element that shows why the event isn't being handled in writing. In other words, why is your company's news being taken off the page and presented live?

With a press conference, a company deems some piece of information or an announcement important enough to gather the media in person to hear it and to ask questions of company officials or of spokespersons afterward. In a best-case scenario the media gathered are so impressed with the information they write a story that appears in a newspaper, on a well-trafficked Web site, or in a magazine, or they produce a report for that evening's television news.

During a press conference, company officials and sometimes others who add further validity to the announcement—for instance, a celebrity endorser or medical expert—make prepared remarks and then usually invite questions from the media in attendance. The conference can also include some aspect of a product launch, such as a demonstration or an impressive showcase that adds further credibility to the announcement.

What Is Being Announced?

The conference is being held to announce news. Assembling the media for routine goings-on or a nonevent will cost you on two fronts: the money you poured into a press conference that yielded no stories, and your credibility with the media for any event you want to have in the future.

A key announcement worthy of a press conference might include:

- ⤳ A merger or acquisition of a competitor
- ⤳ The findings of a substantial, groundbreaking poll
- ⤳ The introduction or launch of a new product that should be seen in person for its applications or uses to be understood or fully appreciated

➲ An agreement struck with a large corporation for a specific reason or cause that also positions your two companies as allies

➲ The signing of a celebrity, star, or key figure to further some cause or initiative for your company

➲ Presenting the current status of a crisis situation your company is facing

---

News Briefings

Have enough news for the media but not enough for a press conference? Consider a news briefing. In this less formal get-together you bring a few reporters in to give them an update on your company or fill them in on some new product information. You can also use the time to answer questions and let the press learn more about what you and your company do. You can hold a briefing in your company's conference room, over lunch at a restaurant, or at another comfortable location. This type of briefing might also be handled effectively with a conference call, though an in-person meeting will give your news greater import.

The Five Ws and an H

As with any sound and solid press release, the point of your press conference must be distilled into the five Ws and an H: who, what, when, where, why, and how. **Make sure your announcement contains all the pertinent information a journalist needs to file a story.** Clarity on those points is important as well since you will be providing written materials at the press conference for media to take with them. More information on those is presented later in this chapter.

The Message to Convey

Craft the messages you want to convey to the news conference so it comes across to the media in a pithy, accessible manner. Those speaking at the news conference must be primed beforehand and well versed in the comments they will deliver. While those speaking should be rehearsed, they should never appear canned or seem as if they're reading directly from pages on a podium.

Remember that the message you craft—and the overall theme you're intent on delivering—is the guiding force of your press conference. It is the focus that you want the media to concentrate on and informs all your actions: setting the schedule, identifying whom to invite, and deciding the content of both speeches and written materials.

Most press conferences contain a Q&A session in which the media can ask questions of those who have spoken. Your audience may represent several publications, each with its own content and point of view. Some may lob unexpected questions, so those speaking must be thoroughly prepared. Part of those preparations must include responses to questions that could throw them off. Make sure that company representatives know how to answer the questions posed but still make the points they need to.

You may wish to hold media training sessions with your spokespersons, depending on their experience. Put company officials in a mock interview setup where other employees posing as reporters ask questions. This practice helps the company officials gain insights and knowledge into how they're coming off, if they're clear in their responses, and if any questions make them uncomfortable.

You can try to prepare your key representatives for every possible question-and-answer scenario, but realize that it's impossible to know everything. It's perfectly acceptable for you or a spokesperson to issue an "I don't know," as long as it's not done to be evasive and you make clear to the press that you fully intend to have an answer forthcoming shortly. Make sure that media representatives receive the information or answers they requested.

Check Out the Politicians

Politicians—congressional and presidential candidates specifically—offer some amazing lessons in *bridging*. Bridging is taking a question that may be unrelated to your focus and figuring out how to answer it while also mentioning points that are important to the initiative you have underway. Some politicians use bridging to stay the course in providing a focused response when the media pose a question that could derail them from bringing across the points of their platform they need to during a campaign.

Who Will You Invite?

Invite a precise, targeted media list to the event, giving them details in an invitation or an e-mail. Determine the media that is most interested in your news, preferably through a list you've already compiled for your ongoing publicity efforts, adding other names from media outlets to the list that may be specifically interested in the news you'll be announcing. Then follow up with the media members to gauge interest and get an accurate head count for attendance.

The day before the event, help secure a good turnout by contacting the press via e-mail with a reminder of all the specifics—such as time and location.

When you send your reminder, offer contact information complete with a cell phone number, and give them details such as directions (particularly if it's a difficult location to find, though in the case of a press conference it shouldn't be!) and parking specifics (especially if parking is tight or they need credentials or a pass to get a space). With the media so often under deadline pressure, you'll build further goodwill with them by letting them know you have their best interests in mind and respect their time. That consideration also puts the media in a positive frame of mind as they arrive at your press conference. Keep a record of who attended so that you can follow up with them after the press conference and enlist their support for other company events.

Others to Invite

For a press conference, you may also want to put others on your invitation list—such as employees, volunteers, or another group with a vested interest in your company—to add verve to the proceedings. Depending on the announcement and who's involved, you may also find it appropriate to invite government representatives and community leaders.

Business Cards and Nametags

For those in the know at your event, such as company employees, have nametags ready for them to wear and instruct them beforehand to have business cards to hand out. Remember that a press conference

A Cautionary Tale

In some instances press conferences will involve your company working with others to distribute a message to the media. When that's the case, have all parties sit down beforehand to hammer out any concerns, differences, and agendas. Remember, even when you have a great message—and perhaps well-known celebrities who have agreed to speak on your behalf—once the press is present you're at the mercy of events in real time. Still, every event provides a lesson.

Two celebrities—one a talk-show host, the other a music icon—had joined forces for a cause in Los Angeles and wanted to announce their initiative to the press, who showed up in full force. A check presentation was also part of the news conference, which was to be held on the host's soundstage.

Unfortunately, although all parties had signed off on the message points and itinerary, the stars became intent on upstaging one another: The rock icon didn't like being on the talk-show host's turf, and the talk-show host wouldn't come out of his dressing room until the rock icon was in place on stage for the event. Sadly their behavior became the focal point of the press conference instead of the worthy charitable cause they were supporting.

When we set out to evaluate the event, we realized that a more effective solution would have been to hold the press conference on more neutral territory, such as one selected by the philanthropy, or to have been content with one star's participation instead of trying to make a now clearly unlikely alliance work.

is an ideal venue for all-around exposure for your company, particularly if you're disseminating positive news about your business. However, make sure reporters know the company designate to whom press inquiries should be directed. You don't want any employee becoming an unofficial spokesperson or unintentionally speaking on the record when you've prepped others to perfectly deliver the intended message for the news conference.

What Will They Do There?

Once you have gathered the media, you need to follow a precise schedule. As you set up your itinerary beforehand, ask yourself what is the meat of the press conference. Will the press sit in chairs in front of a panel? Will they stand in an IMAX theatre to watch a big-screen presentation? Will they roam through an exhibit before being called to another area to ask questions? You must plot out moment by moment how you want the press conference to unfold. You must know beforehand what equipment, arrangements, and furnishings are necessary for your venture.

Does the venue fulfill your expectations? Find an appropriate setting that serves your company, your guests, and your message. For instance, you may need:

- Chairs for panelists and reporters
- A podium or lectern
- A sound system
- A display area for company products
- Tables for press materials and other handouts
- Technological arrangements, such as access to PowerPoint
- A large screen
- A product demonstration area
- Oversized, mounted graphics displaying charts and statistics

Who and What Will They See?

In crafting your program, think about visual aspects that you can create or add. You need to identify the primary speakers for the event and designate the responsibilities for each one. Additionally, if you can create some flash that is integral to your product, company message, or both, by all means do so. That will most likely give your news even more impact. While your event may simply be a gathering of press and company officials, have your branding prominently displayed, such as a logo on a podium or on a banner behind a panel.

Survey the area to ensure the press won't be exposed to any unsightly views that might show up unflatteringly in photos or video. For instance, you wouldn't want an exit sign in the middle of the backdrop where your panel will be sitting or graffiti blasted across a wall where your table of press materials is.

Press Materials as Takeaways

Make sure you augment the presentation with press materials. While the press will be taking notes, they will need—and appreciate—take-away information that has the correct spellings of the names of company officials, as well as key figures and dates. In addition to a release concerning the news in the conference, have company fact sheets and executive bios available as well. You can also supply the releases on CD-ROM that includes photos and, if applicable, a DVD showcasing uses or applications of company product. Offer details on how any reporter present can access the information in a paperless way, such as on your company Web site.

Designate someone to either pass out the information or to staff the table with a fresh supply of the releases always on hand. That person should also be available to facilitate any media requests for more information or set up interviews with company officials.

Press Materials That Are Material

At the news conference, make sure you offer a selection of pieces that provide illuminating, interesting information. If there is complementary background that will be useful to the media, have that available as well. Don't furnish every release your company has ever produced, but aim to make the media as well informed as possible about the news being presented. For those media people who might not be interested or have the time to conduct a full-fledged interview afterward, have a complete Q&A already compiled for them with quotable answers from a key executive.

Refreshments

At the venue, offer light food and beverages such as bottled water, but don't go overboard unless your press conference has been folded into a more grandiose event or is the centerpiece of a food-oriented product launch. Often press will be rushing right from this press conference back to the newsroom or to cover another story, and a great deal of catering will, unfortunately, go to waste.

Will They Care?

Unfortunately many companies, big and small, tend to misuse press conferences. Small companies in particular may not have the money to make the press conference a big draw.

It Must Be Important to Others, Too

Be reasonable about your expectations and the news you are offering. While it may be important—even monumental—to you and generates excitement within your company, that importance doesn't always translate to the outside world and the press. The two words you never want to hear at a press conference are "So what?"

Before you hold a press conference, try this tack: If the information is proprietary, run the news by a trusted source outside your company and gauge his or her interest. (If necessary, have the person sign a nondisclosure agreement.) By bouncing the information off someone with an objective view, you can more accurately assess the importance of your news and the usefulness of holding a press conference to announce it.

Consider Other Possibilities

If you have doubts about whether to hold a press conference, investigate more effective and cost-conscious methods that might benefit your company and serve the message or news better. Those methods might include inviting a few key press people to a luncheon and giving them the news, making the news part of another event such as a splash at a trade show, or transforming it into another initiative entirely such as sending consumers a direct-mail piece announcing the news and offering a coupon for a product or service at your place of business.

Where and When Should It Be?

As discussed earlier, the location is of prime importance to your press conference. Is it possible to have it at your place of business? Is that convenient and attractive? Would a hotel ballroom or in front of a thrill ride at an amusement park be better? Take into consideration your best forum for relaying your message to the press that aids and abets and doesn't detract from the announcement you're making or news you're offering.

Do a site check of the location prior to the conference, even if it's a venue you already feel comfortable with. You don't want to be surprised the day of the event to see that the room actually is too small, or that new construction has blocked some entrances.

Outside or Inside

If the event is being held outside, make sure contingency plans are in place. Do you have tents or a standby shelter if it rains? Is the weather exceptionally hot or cold this time of year? Could that weather negatively affect turnout?

Security Measures

You need a location for your press conference that is easy to get to and easy to get in. Consider parking and directional signage to where the event is held. You don't want it be in an unsafe or unsecured venue, or allow anyone who's not invited to gain easy access. If the press conference is in a high-security location, how will media gain entry? Will you have a list prepared of those allowed inside? Do you need to let press members know they must have a driver's license or other form of identification to get inside?

Timing

Most press conferences take place midmorning. That gives reporters enough time to file their story later in the day. **Tuesdays, Wednesdays, and Thursdays are the best choices to maximize attendance.**

Check out the calendar in your community and the nation beforehand. You don't want to compete with a big event that could swipe a large part of your intended audience—such as your city's first day of school or the Super Bowl.

You may find that some media you had expected to attend your press conference were pulled onto another breaking news story. Depending on the importance of that event, you may have to postpone your press conference or find another way, such as a video news release or a Web cast, to get your news to the media.

How Long Should It Be?

Most newspeople would agree that the sooner you deliver the information during a press conference the better. Don't make it a drawn-out affair. Set a schedule that is well paced and leaves time for questions.

Take the time you need to get your message across. Just be sure that you're being economical with your words and schedule items. At the same time, don't make the media representatives feel rushed. Allow time for them to receive additional information, view product demonstrations, and conduct interviews with executives, officials, or celebrities.

What Do You Do When It's Over?

Just because the press conference is finished doesn't mean your company's role is finished. Designate a company representative to be responsible for following up with every press member who attended. Taking care of these tasks completes the event, making sure you met your goals. Ask these questions:

- ➲ Did media representatives get all the materials they needed?
- ➲ Did they request information that required you to follow up?
- ➲ Have they mentioned that a piece will run that features the announcement? If so, when?
- ➲ If not, is there any information you can supply or interview that you could offer that would make a piece possible?

If expected media didn't attend, follow up with them offering the news from the event and, if they are interested, opportunities to interview appropriate spokespeople. Then comes your chance to gauge the success of your press conference:

- ➲ How many placements were secured in magazines, newspapers, broadcast, or on the Web?
- ➲ Analyzing each placement, what is its tenor? Was the news and the press conference well received? Did it receive any criticism? Was that criticism justified?

For the event itself:

- ⟳ Did the message you wanted to convey come across?
- ⟳ Were all participants on point?
- ⟳ Did the expected number of media attend? If not, why?
- ⟳ What was the overall reaction of the media in attendance?
- ⟳ Did the program flow smoothly?
- ⟳ Was the space laid out appropriately?
- ⟳ Did A/V equipment work properly?
- ⟳ Did any glitches occur? How were they handled? Could they have been better addressed?

▶▶ Test Drive

Take a look at a national network morning or evening news program. Chances are that one story will feature a news conference. When watching that piece, answer these questions:

- ⟳ What was the news released at the press conference?
- ⟳ Why did the network choose to feature it as news?
- ⟳ Who was the featured speaker? Why was that person selected to speak?
- ⟳ Did you notice any branding, such as company signage, banners, or a logo, on a podium?

Putting an Incentive to Work for Your Business

An event doesn't always have to be a large venue with wine and food flowing, a series of seminars, or a vendors-only meeting. Sometimes an event acts as an enticement for customers or employees. For example, you could invite customers to a sale or make them feel important with a members-only card with special benefits. You could reward your employees with a trip for making their sales quota. While you may not consider each of these an event, the execution of any of these tactics requires event planning.

The incentive you promote for your business varies depending on the type of business you're in, but done the right way with specific goals in mind, incentives positively impact sales of your product or service.

In your business, can you think of ways your competitors use incentives to attract and keep customers? If not, think of a business completely unrelated to yours but one with which you are familiar as a customer. Do they conduct any initiatives that keep you coming back? What drew you to patronize them initially?

Why Go With an Incentive?

Different kinds of incentives are discussed in this chapter, and you can decide whether one will work for your business. As with other events, you have to assess what you expect it to do for your business. Think about these questions:

- ➲ To whom will the incentive appeal?
- ➲ What do you want to accomplish with the incentive?
- ➲ How will you measure that accomplishment?

Incentives for Your Customers

Incentives for customers generally fall into two categories: those intended to increase sales and those aimed at encouraging loyalty. The most obvious incentive event for a customer is a sale. The most common examples are sales you find at retail stores: white sale, anniversary sale, moonlight madness sale. Sales lure customers with promises of saving money, getting a good deal, being the first to buy a new season's offerings, or getting a sneak peek at a new product. Customers have an immediate idea of how a sale benefits them, so it's a clear-cut incentive.

You can be as inventive as you'd like with a sale. The calendar is full of hundreds of holidays and special occasions. You can easily find one that fits your sale and creates an interesting hook for your enterprise. Other customer incentives include loyalty cards, referrals, and coupons, all of which are discussed later in this chapter.

Take a Cue from Long-Distance Competition

If you're looking for ways to bring in more customers, think about conferring with businesses like yours that are located in other cities and don't offer direct competition. They might be willing to offer insights on their successes. For instance, a group of small chain grocery store owners—each with less than five stores—meets once a year (they talk and e-mail more often) to exchange ideas on loyalty cards, popular sales, and other incentives. The owners come from such diverse geographical areas as Richmond, Virginia, and Dublin, Ireland.

Incentives for Your Employees

Incentive programs can also reward employees, such as a sales force, for hitting a target or delivering an exceptional performance. For these types of incentive programs your reward can be such events as:

- Travel to an exciting destination
- Certificates for experiences such as free meals at restaurants or tickets to the theater
- Gifts ranging from gourmet cookies and sporting gear to electronics and sterling silver pens

Be very specific about what you want your employee incentives to do. That will be crucial to their success. Consider your answers to these questions:

- Why are you instituting this incentive program? Is it because of lackluster sales, lack of motivation, or a new product you're trying to push?

➲ What are the employees working toward? What is the reward? Are there different levels of rewards corresponding to goals achieved?

➲ What mission is each employee expected to accomplish to receive the reward?

➲ Is the reward attractive enough?

➲ How will you distribute information about the reward program for the employees?

➲ Do you have the rewards ready and arranged for? Is it possible that the rewards you're expecting to dole out may not come to fruition? If so, do you have an acceptable substitute as a backup?

The Importance of Calls to Action

Any incentive you put out there to potential customers isn't effective unless it entices them to buy your product or service or otherwise support your business. **In considering incentive programs for your business, think about initiatives that appeal to your core and target customers for your particular product or service.** In examining the following options, ascertain what excites your customers about patronizing your business.

Customer Cards

You can give your customers cards that they use at the point of purchase.

With **loyalty cards** (such as grocery store club cards), which came into wide use beginning in the mid 1990s, customers swipe a card that has a barcode or mag stripe. You as the retailer collect information about that customer. In turn, they receive deals on some of the products they buy.

A **rewards card** is punched, stamped, or otherwise marked each time the customer purchases a specific item. After a certain amount of times, the customer receives a free item (for example, a free cup of coffee after purchasing six cups of coffee, a free CD after purchasing ten music CDs, and so on).

A **dollars earned** or **points card** gives a customer a point for each dollar spent at your establishment (or in the case of airlines' frequent flier programs, a mile for each certain number of miles flown). After customers spend a predetermined amount of money, they could get 10 percent off their next purchase. Or points could be accrued for a bigger award or prize.

In each of these cases you are also gaining an opportunity to accumulate information about your customers and learn about their product preferences and shopping patterns. Because of the vast amount of information you receive—pertinent to shopping trends, product popularity, the effectiveness of certain sales—through these types of incentive programs, don't underestimate the value of instituting one of them.

Keep It Simple

When it comes to customer cards, keep the rewards simple for the customer. (Think about the customer cards you currently have in your wallet. Why are you keeping them?) If the points system of a loyalty card or rewards program is too complex, or customers are unsure of what they'll receive by redeeming it, then they're unlikely to use it or keep patronizing your business because of it. Simplicity doesn't mean you have to forsake inventiveness. In a twist on incentive programs, eBay at one time instituted the successful eBay Anything Points, which in effect allowed visitors to use reward points from companies such as airlines and hotels to make purchases on the site.

You can amass a veritable gold mine of information with loyalty cards:

- ➲ How many new customers your business is retaining.
- ➲ The percentage of sales that markdowns account for.
- ➲ Which products appeal the most to your core customers.

Offering your customers some type of card requires a commitment of resources that increases the more high tech you go. Depending on the card and how you want it to work for you, you may need to hire a consultant to help establish the program and set up software to collect information and make the program work optimally for your business.

To get an idea of the process involved in setting up an incentive card and if having such a program is right for your company, visit Web sites such as *www.ipccards.com* and *www.cardlogix.com*. These sites explain the costs involved and how incentive cards can be designed, manufactured, and tailored to your business' needs. To launch the customer card, consider an in-store event that sparks interest, points out customer advantages, and encourages sign-ups.

Customer Clubs

When you band customers together with loyalty cards or other incentives, you also get the opportunity to create a sense of community for your business. For example, you might plan member-only events that are specifically tied into your enterprise. If you have an athletic apparel store you could host runs or races for club customers and their friends. Or if you own a fabric store you might organize trips to quilting fairs for your card-carrying members. Those kinds of value-added events increase loyalty to your business and create experiences that encourage positive word of mouth about your business.

Referrals

Referrals offer you another chance to increase business with a pre-sold audience: those who already support and patronize your enterprise. By offering existing customers the incentive to refer new ones you can increase your business substantially. Make it worth their while to recommend your business. Pinpoint what rewards will encourage your existing customers or clients to refer new ones. Try a test program first with a few loyal customers. Connect to those you feel comfortable with, and find out what kind of offering would make it enticing for them to recommend your business. Don't blindly take a percentage off goods or give a free gift. Do some research first with a core group of customers. Find out what your competitors do as well. Some solid research will help make your referral program an instant success.

Turning Coupons into Sales

If you are having a sale, launching a new product in store, or you want someone to try your service, give him or her a reason: a coupon. In fact, don't distribute a sales piece without a coupon that reinforces the advantages of doing business with your company. Even more importantly, the coupon gives the recipient a reason to take action immediately to patronize your business. In designing a coupon for your business, give it a use by date, which increases the chance that the coupon will be used a timely manner.

Extending Coupons' Uses

Coupons can also be helpful when they are tied to an event that your company is hosting. For instance, if your company is having a sale, you might extend a coupon offering that allows for 10 percent off any purchases of items that have already been marked down.

Rebates

Rebates are a form of delayed coupons that customers also may consider as an incentive to purchase, even if their savings actually come later. Rebates tend to be used more often with higher-ticket items. If you offer a rebate to customers, make sure you relay clear instructions for how the customer will receive the rebate, for example, with a copy of the receipt or with a UPC packaging symbol and the customer's name and address. Give the specifics for where the customer should send the information and by what date. On the form, let the customer know how soon they can expect to receive a rebate, and conduct stringent follow-up and adhere to deadlines that you've set for getting the money back to the customer. Let the rebates be a positive transaction for the customer; if not, they can have an adverse effect and discourage rather than encourage further patronage.

Direct-Mail Pieces

Direct-mail pieces—cards or letters sent to a predetermined list of current or potential customers—can use incentives to draw attention to a newly launched product or service or offer details on an upcoming sale.

Drafting Effective Copy

When considering direct-mail pieces to advertise your incentive, consider the attributes that material should typically have. First off, it should follow the four-part mandate—A-I-D-A—of any direct-mail piece:

A for attention: The piece should attract the attention of the recipient with graphics and a snappy headline that can be clever but shouldn't warrant deep thought or be too complex to be quickly understood. An illustrative graphic should also be included. Gentle—not overt—humor may also be effective.

I for interest: The headline and a possible subhead should build interest into the copy, showing the recipient how the product can benefit him or her.

D for desire: The copy should suggest how the offer will change the life of the recipient for the better. This might involve saving time or money but also might concern appearance or esteem. Essentially this aspect conveys how they can't live without this product or service.

A for action: The copy should include a call to action within a set time frame.

Other Tips for Mailings

Direct-mail pieces that are personalized to your current or potential clients or customers generally have a greater response rate. Make sure your copy includes an additional incentive for coming to your place of business. For instance, offer someone who brings in the direct-mail piece a gift or an additional 10 percent off. If possible, and if it's cost-efficient for your business, consider a series of mailings to highlight products and keep in touch with customers.

Grand Opening, Grand Incentives

Inside Track

Incentives can be used in everyday business, for the duration of a sale, or as a tie-in for a main event. When I worked on the publicity team to open a new hotel in a burgeoning resort area, we relied on a bevy of incentive-oriented promotions to initiate and continue business.

Because this particular property also hosted upscale restaurants and a casino, we were able to provide incentives and, in some cases, cross-promote each distinct revenue-generating component. For instance, those who came to the grand opening of the casino could register for a loyalty card that gave them points to redeem later when they played the slots. A grand opening incentive on the rooms meant that you could stay two nights and get the third night free. Each restaurant had an incentive-based promotion that was tailored to its theme or cuisine: a free breakfast for the kids with paying adults at one cafe, a happy hour each afternoon for a week at the hotel's pub, and a deal on featured desserts at the French bakery.

All the guests' information was entered in a database for them to receive notices via direct-mail pieces about upcoming promotions for special hotel rates, casino theme nights, and a future wine tasting at the property's Italian restaurant.

Handouts and Flyers

In addition to mailings there are other ways to offer inexpensive incentives such as supplying handouts or flyers to other nearby businesses or at fairs or expos. **Make sure the handout and flyer gives someone a reason to pick it up.** Look for ways to include a coupon so that the piece holds resonance and has a better chance of keeping your business on that person's mind.

You can also make the handout or flyer part of the festivities at your business in another way. Perhaps it includes clues to finding special prizes or coupons in your place of business or otherwise spotlights a can't-miss event that promises big savings or one-of-a-kind offerings and the flyer is a ticket to have access.

Trade-Show Incentives

Direct-mail pieces are often distributed by companies before a show starts, and handouts and flyers are passed out during them. If you are trying to drive traffic to your booth with these materials, incentives are important—particularly with competition from the myriad other booths at the show.

Use these pieces to create a buzz that will prompt your intended audience to come visit your booth. You may be showcasing a new design, a new product, or be giving an exclusive, first-look peek at an upcoming service your company will provide. Have the handouts or mailings explain why your booth is worthwhile for visiting, and use that information to provide a further incentive with a discount, free shipping, or a gift offer for the first fifty people who visit the booth each day.

Depending on your budget, decide if you can host an enticing event inside the booth. Think about what in-booth event might relate to your business. Can you have robots that interact with guests? Are you promoting a service with a sense of humor and clowns could help out? Could you offer free music downloads to cell phones, or give out chocolate cupcakes?

Determine an event specific to your enterprise that will encourage a must-visit attitude among those you're trying to attract. Of course, once you have an event planned for inside your booth, make sure your direct-mail pieces say so.

Other Special Offers

While sales-based incentives may be the most common way to attract customers, you can be creative in coming up with other ideas. Think beyond the once-popular "open a bank account today and get a free toaster!" Taking a cue from the cosmetics industry, you may notice how they often offer a gift with a purchase for their products. Attractively packaged, these gifts almost always include something with a stylish appearance (such as a makeup kit case, an umbrella, or a purse), a perfect fit for the product they're providing an incentive to buy.

Can you think of a gift-with-purchase incentive that would complement your product or service? For instance, instead of a toaster, a bank branch could give out subscriptions to *Money* magazine or a one-year membership to a financial Web site. Remember that this type of incentive doesn't have to come in a box. Depending on your business and the product or service you're providing an incentive for, it might be an experience: a free consulting session from your company, or a session with a personal trainer or shopping expert.

Also consider tradeoffs that you could facilitate with nearby similar but noncompeting businesses that you respect and may already refer customers and clients to. A paint store might offer customers who buy five gallons or more a free one-hour consultation with a nearby interior designer, who gives her clients coupons for a free gallon of paint at the paint store. While product oriented, these types of tradeoffs also qualify as cross promotions, which are discussed further in the next chapter.

▶▶ Inside Track

What's an incentive that you've responded to for another business that might work for yours?

- ➲ Do you ever use coupons? Is that an enticement that might interest your customers or clients?
- ➲ Do you ever consider giveaways? Is there a cost-effective one that might tie in with an upcoming product push?
- ➲ Could you initiate some kind of customer loyalty program? If so, how can you track results to enhance and increase business further?
- ➲ Have you ever sent a direct-mail piece without including a coupon, a deadline, or some other incentive for the recipient? If so, will you alter your approach next time?

Building and Branding Ideas for Promotions

The concept of promotion can take on a broad definition in business. Promotion is an umbrella term that can really be used to describe any activity that keeps your product or service in front of your target audience. But promotions such as the ones discussed in this chapter are events that tie back in with advertising, publicity, and other marketing-related initiatives. Promotions here refer to events that embrace community service, sponsorships, cross promotions, contests, or some combination thereof, leveraging advertising to gain exposure unconventionally.

Promotion Objectives

Because promotions are such a broad category, opportunities for them are limitless. Before you consider the many options you have available for promotional events, review how one will benefit your company and not simply be the chance for a good time. Promotional events should fulfill one or more of the following four objectives:

1. Build awareness or create interest for your product or service, particularly if it's been recently launched, is brand new to your area, or is expanding its presence.
2. Provide information to your key demographic, giving them more details about your company and its products or services.
3. Stimulate demand for the product or service you provide.
4. Engender goodwill, keeping your name in the community as an entity that gives back to the residents it serves.

In all these instances your objective must also reinforce your brand. In other words, no matter what event you're undertaking in a promotional arena, it should be consistent with the goals you've set forth to establish or continue your brand and the ideals it strives to uphold.

As you structure a promotion to initiate or in which to participate, figure out how it will impact sales. How will this event promote a direct link to your business? What are the components that will elevate the status of your brand, endear you to customers, or spotlight a specific product or service? How can you measure the impact of the promotion

Distinctly Tying in

If you're involved with a promotion for a charitable cause or philanthropy, look for ways that promotional partners can both enhance the event and remain distinct. A national household product that had a teddy bear as its mascot was conducting a months-long promotion that involved embarking on a series of events across the country to get exposure. In many of the cities they sought out a charity that would be a natural fit, such as the building of a new bear exhibit at one city's wild animal park.

I was part of the special events team that organized a "Teddy Bear Affair" that the company sponsored at the park. With the product targeted toward moms, the event was perfect for families and included such activities as teddy bear make-and-dress-up workshops conducted by a craft store, cookie decorating with the pastry chef from an upscale hotel guiding youngsters and their parents to bake and decorate teddy bear-shaped cookies, and reading time that concentrated on teddy bear-themed books supplied by a local bookstore. The sponsoring company also had product samples available on site for families to take home. All of the companies involved received logo exposure on programs and tickets for the day of the event, signage on the property, and all advertising bought to publicize it.

The event was exceptionally well attended, and each participating business reported subsequent bumps in sales. Further, none of the companies' brands and products were muddled by the others; each complemented rather than detracted from each other's presence, all for the good of a unifying cause.

If presented or involved with an opportunity that sparks ideas for participants, don't assume that the more companies involved the less focus each one will receive. With the proper balance and a good measure of creative brainstorming you can find ways that a promotion will be more memorable and more results oriented for all concerned.

during or after it, such as with increased receipts, a surge in requests for information regarding your company's services, or an uptick in customer traffic?

Community Service

These types of promotions involve your company with a nonprofit organization to heighten your profile in the community. In these instances you may be providing financial resources or in-kind donations. (In-kind refers to contributions of products or services instead of money.) As a participant—and depending on the event—you're likely to get logo exposure, provide information about your products or services to a target audience in conjunction with the event, or offer your product for use or consumption at the event.

Similar to the charity events discussed in Chapter 14, work with the benefiting organization to detail how your involvement can be mutually beneficial. **When coordinating a promotion with a charity, think of ways you might increase your exposure while also offering assistance.** For instance, if your company can provide volunteers, you'll have ambassadors for your business engendering community goodwill. And if they wear T-shirts with your company's logo while they're helping out, they're creating a positive impact and giving your brand exposure.

Sponsorships

In this category of promotion you're providing company resources (in monetary contributions, services, or products) in exchange for your name and logo being associated with a large event or a community endeavor on a smaller scale. For instance, your name could be on Little League baseball uniforms, your company could host a PTA's back-to-school family picnic, or you could adopt an acre of a park or a mile of roadside to keep clean.

If you go the sponsorship route, stay involved with the cause both to continue your support and to make sure that it stays consistent with your company's values. If you're just signing a check to give money to an organization, that's a contribution, not a sponsorship linked to company promotion. For a sponsorship to be most effective for your company it requires your sustained commitment, input, and presence.

Contests

One of the most popular forms of promotional events is contests because they're easy to implement. Contests get your company's name out there while enticing patrons with exciting prizes. Generally speaking, people love to play games and win. The simplest contests for a company are "Drop your business card in a fishbowl for a free weekly drawing" or "Count the number of beans in this jar to win a prize." But you can take a more creative approach in considering contests that will work for your company, be consistent with your brand, and provide a recognizable link to your product or service. For example, in the aisles of the grocery store there are dozens of packages touting contests to win prizes by, for instance, mailing package UPC symbols or popping the top of a soda can to find a clue or a winning number for a bigger reward. In these cases consumer interest will spur sales and motivate them to keep buying the product for more chances to win.

Contests or sweepstakes can often generate more than consumer interest in your product. If your idea is unique enough, you may also attract media attention. Recently Häagen-Dazs and Ben & Jerry's have both received substantial publicity for contests to name and create new ice cream flavors. The winners were Sticky Toffee Pudding and Puttin' on the Ritz, respectively. Some possibilities for promotional contests that involve potential or existing customers vying for a prize include:

- Naming a new product
- Answering questions or trivia
- Creating a piece of artwork
- Devising a solution to a problem
- Coming up with an advertising jingle
- Submitting an original recipe
- Producing an amateur video for the company's Web site
- Participating in a treasure hunt with clues in physical or virtual locations

For contests to be their most compelling, you must make sure you're offering a prize that's worth someone's time to enter. The more attractive the prize, the more likely you'll generate interest and participation. But just as you'd link your contest's purpose to your stated goal, create a logical connection to the prize as well.

In addition, you'll need to carefully lay out the execution of your contest for not only the contest rules but how you'll be advertising it. If you've got products distributed to several stores, how will you add to or change your packaging to give contest details? If you're keeping the advertising confined to your place of business, what signage can you display that will attractively, effectively promote the contest?

Cross Promotions

This category, further delved into later in this chapter, is a popular choice because you align with a complementary, noncompeting business in a mutually beneficial promotional arrangement that could save money for both enterprises. For instance, you might take a contest to a new level with a cross promotion: a furniture store and a brewery offered a plasma-screen television and twelve cases of beer for a contest winner (who then gets to keep the television and the leftover beverages) to watch a hotly contested basketball game. While you both promote your business, you lower the financial commitment by sharing in costs for printing contest forms, signage, and advertising.

Executing Your Ideas

Whatever type of promotion you're pursuing, make sure it fits with your company's image. For instance, in the sponsorship or community service arena, just because you may be approached by an organization doesn't necessarily mean it's a perfect match. To entice your participation, many charities do their homework and build a case for your involvement with their cause. They cite statistics, information, and market analysis for why being involved with their cause will be in your company's best interest and looked favorably upon by your target audience.

Even when you're not involved with a promotional event that centers around a charitable cause or community service, you should do the same, making sure that your efforts effectively target your desired demographic and that your promotional ideas are unique enough to cut through the clutter and reach that audience.

To make the best use of the promotion, you must devise a comprehensive game plan that includes your company's objective(s), timing, staffing needs, budget, and action steps. (These components are extensively detailed in Chapters 1–6.)

In conducting or participating in a promotion, think about all the ways that you can extract the best use of giving your company and brand exposure. Plan on creating inexpensive items such as T-shirts, aprons, pens with your business logo and phone number, or other custom promotional products that can be given away during an event.

As mentioned previously, even if the event isn't yours alone, seek out opportunities for your logo to be present on banners, posters, flyers, and other signage.

Unusual, Unheard of, and Perfect

Some of the best ideas for promotions can come from the unlikeliest of places. Often your company may seem to be stuck in a rut, participating or conducting the same promotions. You may have become so accustomed to them, you may have forsaken measuring results or questioning if the promotional events are effective anymore.

Many events are so common that they lose resonance with your target audience. How often do you notice a chili cook-off, 5K race, or ticket giveaway happening in your area? At one time they were all novel ideas that spawned a slew of imitators.

Brainstorming

Conducting a brainstorming session is a worthwhile endeavor to make an ordinary promotion idea extraordinary. Gather a group eager to help your company succeed and, in an orderly fashion, everyone, stated mission in hand, contributes ideas to develop a fabulous promotion. **There should be two rules in your brainstorming session: no idea is a bad one, and costs at this point are not a concern.** In a natural progression, participants continually built upon ideas. At the meeting's conclusion, participants nominate their top choices for follow-through. See Chapter 7 for further details on implementing this type of meeting to spin ideas for your enterprise.

Putting a Twist on the Promotion

As well as brainstorming, consider what's "in," right now, or think about how a paradigm can be shifted to make your promotion more exciting. For instance, one philanthropic organization turned a 5K race into a night walk, replete with glowing balloons. Instead of hosting an awards ceremony to promote their newest product, a jewelry company that specialized in designing and manufacturing hand-carved agate cameos was considering raising their profile with Hollywood celebrities and stylists by hosting the Cameo Awards. That ceremony would award expensive pieces to those stars who had the most memorable, if brief, appearances in films that year. The next chapter covers guerrilla marketing techniques, unconventional events that can take promotions to the extreme, often in inexpensive ways.

Developing Radio Promotions

Radio continues to be one of the easiest media to venture into and provides ample opportunities for originality and creativity, particularly with its live, immediate feel and often light-hearted approach in communicating and connecting with an audience. If you already have a relationship with a radio station from which you buy advertising time, consider trying to work with their promotions department for an event.

Amp Up Your Promotion

If you're holding a promotional event and attracting large crowds for the event, many radio stations will—for a fee—send out one of their personalities and a station vehicle, passing out station swag and adding an element of excitement to an existing event. In addition, they may give your event mentions on the radio, which will help you create buzz, publicize the event and its purpose, and increase your attendance.

A car dealership may advertise on the radio, and for the morning drive show it may contribute a car for which the morning DJs will conduct a contest. For instance, every weekday morning during the month of February, the DJs could ask listeners for an answer to an auto-related question—for example, famous cars in the movies—in order to qualify for the final drawing. The last day of the month, all the winners are put into the drawing for the car.

The radio station may have a regular feature that your company can tie in to. Perhaps a personality conducts an afternoon "unscramble the word" contest each weekday during drive time. Your company could furnish the winning prize of free accounting services during tax season, a shopping spree in your place of business, or an office party lunch at your restaurant.

A Promotion in Good Taste

Sometimes in a bid to jolt or surprise listeners, DJs on certain radio stations carry promotions to the extremes, and their moves may not always be in your company's best interests. If you decide to embark on a radio promotion, be familiar with the station you're getting involved with. Partner up with a station that on air sounds consistent with an image you want to bring across about your company. Granted, radio is by its very nature spontaneous, and you won't ever have 100 percent control over what will happen on air. But being cognizant about how the station has conducted past promotions will give you foundation for, and good sense of, the station's mores.

Sporting Event Tie-ins

Because sporting events are so pervasive, they often can give you a ready-made opportunity to promote your business. Not every promotional effort has to center on the Super Bowl, World Series, or Olympics (though many often do).

Does your product or service have a logical tie-in with sports? Or, with a bit of brainstorming, can you make a good case for it? Organizations and businesses often find fun, easy-to-promote events such as runs, marathons, and golf, poker, and bowling tournaments.

While every city might not have a major league professional team, they often have Little Leagues, high school and college teams, and even farm clubs for the major leagues. You may be able to create a promotion for your company with the team for an afternoon or night game.

Name the night after your company: For a sponsorship fee, the evening is branded with your company's name and logo. This may include giveaways at the gate or contests during the game.

Pay for tickets: For a promotional price, your company arranges for a certain group—such as seniors, kids, ladies' night—to gain admittance to the game for free or at a discount.

Seat announcements: Those sitting in certain seats—with an announcement for fans to look under their seat at a predetermined time during the game—win a prize package from your company.

Give away your product: Your business provides your product as a natural tie-in with the game, for example, providing your company's sunscreen for fans during an afternoon match-up.

Give away a promotional item: Your company logo has been put on some giveaway, such as visors or footballs, and given away to fans.

Hooking up with Other Products

In this area, also known as cross promotions, you can stand out from the competition by joining forces with another business to market your products in a clever, credible way while cutting costs in executing an event and advertising it. Consider these possibilities for cross-promoting:

- Offer percentages off each other's products
- Buy a product from one and get a service from the other
- Provide a prize package for a contest that is a fit for each company
- Cosponsor a philanthropic event that provides an organic tie-in for both companies

Cross promotions don't have to limit themselves to the event itself; they can also build on it with extras. For instance, the companies may extend an event in such a way that you collaboratively publish resource booklets or produce how-to videos.

However you decide to combine forces, both companies, before proceeding, should answer the following questions to confirm that the arrangement will be mutually beneficial.

- ➲ Is the companies' fit natural or forced?
- ➲ Does each company gain credibility through the association or diminish it?
- ➲ Is each business bringing unique resources to the arrangement, or is there too much overlap?
- ➲ Would the promotion be bigger with both organizations involved or the same?

Consider Your Employees

If you're not sure that your promotion is a fit for your company, try it on employees. For instance, if you're interested in discounting a product for an extended time, test it by seeing what your employees think. If you try it out on them and they like it, you've not only got results that back up your idea but you've also got a built-in audience for publicizing the promotion before it starts.

▶▶ Test Drive

Next time you're in a grocery store, take a look at products that have shelf-talkers or are featured as part of in-store displays.

- ➲ What is the featured promotion? Is it a contest or sweepstakes?
- ➲ Does it have a catchy name?
- ➲ Is the promotion easy to understand?
- ➲ Are you enticed into participating? Why or why not?
- ➲ What will the reward be? Is it clearly described?
- ➲ Is it a promotion that could possibly work for your business? Why or why not?

PART 5
Events and Ideas With a Marketing Edge

What Is a Guerrilla Tactic?

With his book *Guerrilla Marketing: Secrets for Making Big Profits from Your Small Business*, author Jay Conrad Levinson launched an entirely new way of promoting businesses. Coining the phrase "guerrilla marketing," Levinson spawned a movement, primarily targeted to small businesses, to think of ingenious ways, on very tight budgets, to get the word out about companies. Particularly in its incarnation, guerrilla marketing actions were often referred to—accurately or not—as stunt events.

By its very nature a guerrilla tactic is rarely repeated; it's executed for surprise effect, so repeating it would be unwarranted and ineffective. Often guerrilla tactics are used to launch a product or Web site, create instant brand awareness, or feature a product in a compelling way.

Nearly twenty-five years after its inception, guerrilla marketing has grown beyond its small-business pitch. Corporations such as Nike, Citigroup, and Burger King have all adopted guerrilla marketing techniques in various guises, many of which became noted events.

The Guerrilla Goes Big Time

While guerrilla-style events are more closely associated with small company endeavors, even Fortune 500 companies can't deny the connection they can make with consumers. Some guerrilla tactics from big companies have included placing 16,000 butterfly stickers to dot outside walls in Manhattan for Microsoft, a midair soccer match for Adidas, and a woman sleeping on a bed in the middle of a crowded Hong Kong subway station for McDonald's.

The Guerrilla's Conceits

Despite guerrilla tactics' renegade roots, using them to influence or drive an initiative has become a routine course in brainstorming for events. Sometimes what might be categorized as novel or exciting gets labeled as guerrilla. In its purest sense, a guerrilla tactic depends on the following four components:

1. Spending little money
2. Using information and imagination to generate a big idea

3. Designing events or ploys that are so innovative or unusual they grab the media's attention

4. Captivating the consumer and taking him or her by surprise during his or her daily routine

Other Guerrilla Strategies

Because people have seen the effectiveness of certain guerrilla-centric events, guerrilla marketing is now synonymous for many marketing initiatives that also rely on surprise and thrill, such as:

Buzz marketing, which seeks to create word-of-mouth referrals with a "gotta know that" sensibility stimulated by outlandish events

Viral marketing, which taps into social networks such as MySpace (*www.myspace.com*) and YouTube (*www.youtube.com*) to attract attention and deliver messages by word of mouth

Experiential marketing, which calls on targeted consumers to interact with the product or service for a positive, emotional response

---

Guerrilla Marketing by the Books

If using guerrilla tactics in events for your company has you convinced that they can play an even bigger role in your enterprise's efforts, you can investigate other applications of guerrilla methods in such books as *Mastering Guerrilla Marketing*, *The Way of the Guerrilla*, and *The Guerrilla Marketing Handbook*, all by Levinson and Seth Goodson; as well as *Guerrilla Publicity*, by Levinson, Rick Frishman, and Jill Lublin.

The Unlikely Places You'll Go

Guerrilla marketing has a reputation for sparking zany ideas. Yet the most effective campaigns, however zany, have to be successful for your business. With guerrilla tactics and events you must be open to the possibility of a different method to increase sales or awareness for your product or service.

Consider the many guerrilla marketing events United Airlines used to launch their low-cost airline Ted. With nary a mention of it initially being an airline or part of United, the team embarked on a plan to give Ted a folksy, first-name approach in Denver, where the airline was starting a route. Their efforts—which are all events—included hiring temps to carve the name "Ted" in Halloween jack-o-lanterns, hiring fake fans to shout "Go Ted" at sporting events, and having "Ted" sponsor mysterious pizza and ice cream giveaways. Before anyone even realized who or what Ted actually was, name recognition was sky-high in a campaign that cost only tens of thousands of dollars.

Having gotten a feel for guerrilla marketing's milieu, decide if you want to embark on a like-minded initiative for your company. If so, what will be your goal in creating and producing a guerrilla event? Be very specific. Consider the following possibilities. Will your guerrilla event:

➲ Launch a product?
➲ Create brand awareness?
➲ Push a particular line of goods or services?
➲ Introduce your company to a city?
➲ Offer an incentive to customers?

How will you determine the response to your guerrilla tactic? Will it be increased sales or traffic? Orders written in the days after the event? Media coverage in daily and national newspapers? A sudden, measurable increase in logo recognition? (Refer to Chapter 19: Product Launches and Chapter 21: Incentive Programs for more details on the goal you're pursuing.)

Organize a brainstorming session once you have your objective firmly decided. Hopefully your brainstorming session will generate dozens of ideas from which to choose. Refer to Chapter 7 for the particulars of a successful brainstorming session.

Remember, in a brainstorming session there are two rules: no idea is a bad idea, and no idea can be cast aside because of monetary concerns. Those guidelines are necessary—particularly in the realm of guerrilla tactics—because one idea (even a perceived bad one) may be a springboard for someone else to come up with a truly great one. When par-

Signs of the Times

I worked for a famed Atlanta-based company that found a treasure trove of its history and a new connection to its consumers on the sides of brick walls.

One of the company's century-old advertisements—a fanciful design once painted in bright colors on the side of a pharmacy—had been discovered by an urban archeologist.

The company hired artists to restore the sign to its former glory, removing twenty-five layers of paint to reveal the original look. Further, the company was able to authenticate that the sign dated back to 1894. A press conference, attended by CNN, Associated Press, an NBC affiliate, and other media, was held to unveil the work of art.

Then the company hired artists (for a nominal fee) and sought out other buildings in towns across the South that had once hosted company advertisements. Each restoration and unveiling was met with a flurry of press, and with each newly painted sign the company gained long-time advertising practically for free on the sides of these buildings.

Hardly a traditional way to promote a company—in fact, we realized it had all the markings of a guerrilla campaign—the advertising signs evoked positive feelings among long-time customers and were a novelty for newer ones.

ticipants aren't reined in by budget restraints they tend to come up with bigger and better ideas, many of which may not seem financially feasible but, influenced and enhanced by guerrilla techniques, actually might be within your budget.

When Less Is Much More

With brainstorming ideas in hand, ask yourself which ones can be tailored or executed for very little cost. That precept is one of guerrilla marketing's biggest strengths: The lack of money will prompt a surfeit of imagination.

Begin by defining which of the ideas from the initial session are the most thrilling, alluring, exciting, and appealing. Then drill down into these ideas. Are the ones you're considering really novel or different, or are they a rehash or a reproduction of one that has already been done?

What can take your favorite ideas to the next level? What twist can you give it? What unusual component could be incorporated? In reviewing those aspects, determine which ideas are unique to your company and can bear real value for your company. You must also make sure that what you're finally considering is also economically feasible and budgetarily possible for your company.

For instance, say you're coming up with a guerrilla tactic to pump up sales in your product, which has been lagging since its introduction. The product is a reproduction of the Princess telephones of the 1960s, which come in an array of colors. The idea is to set up a game of Telephone, the childhood game wherein someone whispers a sentence to the next person and so on down the line until the last person utters the sentence and you take note of the difference between the initial and final sentences.

To make the idea truly unique, you could up with an actual game of Telephone—using your new product—where someone places a call to someone else across dozens of cities all around the world. Each person relays a "message" to the next person and, without repeating it back, calls the next person. The calls will cost, but the message will be brief—and not repeated—so no one will be on the phone for long. The last person gives the message he or she has been given, and it's compared with the initial one. You could then release the results to the media.

More Buzz-Generating Techniques

Guerrilla marketing events seek attention, hope to lure customers, keep current ones happy, or pursue all of those goals. With those objectives in mind, you will find that—despite guerrilla tactics' push for the new and different—often you can start with tried and true basics. What will make them different—or guerrilla-like—is the spin your own company will put on them.

Start the Chat

Say your company has developed the next version of a piece of software. You dispatch hundreds of college students around town. Each has a huge blue "2" that's been drawn on his or her forehead (which actually relates back to the new name, such as Versabrowser 2.0). In guerrilla-related event parlance, this practice is called *headvertising*. And it's been created as a way to get people talking.

In your thinking, imagining, and brainstorming, plant that seed in your mission: find ways that prompt people to ask "What is that?" with an answer that leads back to your product or service.

Freebies

Your attention-seeking mission doesn't always have to be outrageous. Some companies offer freebies to grab attention. Everyone seems to love a giveaway. And sometimes the freebie doesn't have a distinct link to the company's product or service, it's just different or clever, which is what prompts the attention. For instance, a florist could give away a rhubarb pie with every order over $50 during the month of July, a travel agent could pass out board games to customers taking a cruise to Alaska, or a gourmet grocer could dole out paint-by-number kits to shoppers who tried his new delivery service.

Common to Uncommon, Low-Cost Ideas

In the spirit of guerrilla tactics, many of the following ideas imbue a sense of humor and strike a self-deprecating tone for the business that endears itself to its clients and customers, which can even attract media interest. In addition, they can cost very little to implement.

A **contest** that has several winners, all of whom receive a product, service, or gesture of goodwill from your company. The contest can be for customers who wear the craziest pants in your store, clients with the best hair, or even simply patrons who smile. The contest should have a name commensurate with the contest's tenor.

A made-up, madcap **holiday** in which your company celebrates a day (or a week) by naming it something peculiar, out of the ordinary, or just fun, such as "It's Everybody's Birthday Day" or "Happy Rainbow Day." Of course, to extend the guerrilla technique, your business can commemorate the honor further with sales or other customer incentives (detailed further in Chapter 21).

An **award** your company receives that you conceive or create with another organization that spotlights some ridiculous feat, such as a business that has the most polite employees, or the enterprise that has received the "Year 2087 Award," having been recognized in the future as the most forward-thinking company of this current year.

A **cross promotion** (discussed in Chapter 22) with another company that might not seem related to your business and generates word-of-mouth because of it. For instance, a company that sells air conditioners could team up with a restaurant or bar in which the business provides the inspiration for a cold sandwich or frosty martini that gets named after it. In return, the air conditioning company gives away free meals at the restaurant to customers who keep their homes the coldest.

Accomplishing the Act

Once you've got your concept down, you have to set up a plan for executing your guerrilla tactic event. Note that in many instances planning a guerrilla-style event will necessitate different kinds of action steps, particularly in order to keep the budget lean and in check.

Regarding the Budget

Once you've got your fantastic, out-of-this-world guerrilla idea, you need to consider grassroots ways of keeping within your budget. Guerrilla ideas often trade money for manpower. Even though staffing can still cost, you can find ways to rein it in. For instance, rather than hiring staff at professional rates, you may be able to hire college students at more reasonable pay. In many cases companies have enlisted the assistance of college marketing classes to help with the event, which gives the business manpower and the class real-life experience.

Rather than paying for venues for your guerrilla event, remember that public places (as long as you've got the necessary permission and permits) can provide prime access to your audience and are available for little money. Keep other resources in mind as well. For example, while you don't want to dilute the message of your company, you may also get other companies to donate their services for the exposure they'll receive.

Logistics and Timing

With guerrilla events, which often will occur in a public place, keep in mind aspects you don't have control over. For instance, you may not be able to reserve the space at a public park's gazebo. In the throes of planning you may forget that a holiday may render a typically packed office building empty.

Even though guerrilla events are considered loose and imaginative, you still have to have your checklists in order. **The best guerrilla events benefit from a strict, organized perspective.** As many specifics as possible must be nailed down. While creativity should inspire the driving idea, don't let all the duties and responsibilities that will propel the idea to its fruition be left to the imagination.

Letting the Guerrilla Out at a Trade Show

When you're trying to get attention for your booth at a trade show, consider guerrilla techniques that aren't offensive but are attention grabbing. How can you attract people to your booth? Who or what can make an appearance at your booth that would make it a must visit? A ballerina, a lion tamer, a supermodel, a cover boy? Offer brownies that have your company name printed in frosting? Send a tall man out on stilts announcing your booth number, or have skateboarders cruise the aisles handing out your company's details?

Guerrilla tactics embrace and laud imagination and inventiveness, particularly in an arena such as a trade show where it seems as if everything's been done before. Brainstorm beforehand, but follow the rules for your trade show. (And if you're not sure if your plan meets the show's guidelines, get sign-off from the event organizer before you unleash the guerrilla.)

Keeping the Guerrilla Grounded

Even with all the excitement a guerrilla event can generate, don't let that enthusiasm cloud common sense or good judgment. While many successful and positive guerrilla initiatives can be discussed and analyzed, notorious examples exist too.

Guerrilla marketing—particularly in its infancy—even suffered from some backlash concerning its ethics and deceptions employed for certain efforts. As recently as 2007, guerrilla marketing received a fresh round of criticism. To promote an upcoming animated series on Cartoon Network, an ad agency that specialized in guerrilla marketing techniques had placed small blinking signs of the show's characters in Boston—among other cities. But the devices, though harmless, were mistaken for bombs, putting the city on high alert.

Tune in to Your Procedures

Don't let your guerrilla event suffer from a backlash or negative press. Once you've got the concept fleshed out, analyze each detail you expect to include for it from start to finish. Ask yourself if the event could somehow possibly be mistaken or misunderstood.

If you move forward, review all the steps of your action plan, paying attention to any possible inadvertent destructive scenarios. Have you done the necessary vetting of everyone who is involved with it? Have you mitigated any possible problems? Have you notified officials who should know of your plans beforehand? Do you have a well-thought-out plan in case of a crisis or emergency?

Guerrilla Warnings

With the guerrilla-style event you decide to implement, stay away from techniques that could backfire because they could be mistaken as dishonest. Several controversial methods have surfaced in guerrilla marketing, and though they've been used by other companies that doesn't mean they can positively contribute to yours. They include:

Bluejacking, in which the marketer temporarily hijacks consumers' mobile devices by anonymously texting or sending an image

Employing undercover marketing, which strives for subtle product placement but often in a deceitful manner, such as planting "normal" people (who are actually paid spokespeople) to talk about a product

Stealth marketing, in which a marketer manipulates consumers, such as a company paying online chat groups to promote a product, pretending these "fans" are letting others in on a secret product, service, or good deal

Determining the Event's Effectiveness

Even though a guerrilla event is often a one-shot endeavor, you should perform a debriefing:

- ➲ Could you have cut costs anywhere?
- ➲ Did the event go as planned?
- ➲ Are there aspects you could have been more creative with?
- ➲ Could you have put a more effective twist on the driving idea?
- ➲ What were the responses? Were they what you expected? Why or why not?
- ➲ If you had it to do over again, would you?
- ➲ Did the idea of implementing a guerrilla event match up to the results, or—looking back—were you more caught up in the excitement of trying out the concept?
- ➲ What has executing this event taught you about future guerrilla-style endeavors you may pursue?

▶▶ Test Drive

Do you think a guerrilla event would work for your company? Think about your customers or clients as you consider the possibilities. What about a guerrilla tactic would be most appealing in deciding to execute one for your business?

- ➲ Would the low cost allow you to use your creativity in place of huge funding for an initiative?
- ➲ Could you get media attention or get your company in the news with a truly outstanding, outlandish, but relevant idea?
- ➲ Can you shake up the norm and break out of your typical event planning to capitalize on a different approach?

Out of the Storefront and onto the Internet

Events don't have to be relegated to in-store happenings, vendor meetings in a restaurant, or a cocktail party with potential clients. While face time can never be underestimated, you can supplement your marketing efforts with a variety of Web-based events. To that end, discussion in this chapter is skewed both toward those with Web-only businesses and those with brick-and-mortar businesses who also maintain, or would like to increase, their Web business.

Many of the events discussed in this book can be adapted to work on the Web. If you're launching a Web site, you can have a grand opening event. If your company is introducing a new product, you can create buzz with bloggers and cross promotion with other sites. While you can't literally have a sit-down dinner on the Internet, you can invite participation in a conference or Webinar. And while trade shows will probably never find a counterpart on the Web, you're already aware of the importance the Internet plays in announcing and following up on conferences and conventions.

Consider the Web a player in your events: either for an event in and of itself or as a corollary component to an existing one. The Web can enhance, foment, and strengthen your efforts.

E-Mail Matters

To get the word out on the events you're conducting, e-mail will play an integral, necessary role. That being the case, take the time to learn how to compose the most effective e-mails for your business.

To announce events you're having, such as an online sale, make sure that your e-mails contain all the essential information in a pithy manner. Look out for grammar, misspellings, and punctuation. Errors will detract from the excitement you're trying to build.

Because Web users are getting their information in a quick manner, present your information in chunks. Rather than using paragraphs to explain a promotion being conducted at your Web site, use brief but coherent sentences or bullets. Enliven your message with a colorful company logo, as well as—if appropriate—images of the items that will be on sale. Or consider having an actual electronic ad or flyer designed for the e-mail.

In whichever case you decide, make sure you've chosen an expressive, easy-to-see-and-read format to convey the information. For instance, your message or images shouldn't be so long that the customer or client has to scroll down endlessly to get the gist of the particulars: the title and dates of the sale, and the products offered.

In addition, check to make sure the e-mail opens exactly as you intend it to. You don't want the recipient to open the e-mail and miss images, contain a picture that's too large to open, or have text mangled upon transmission. **Do a test first; send the e-mail to a friend or business associate so you can confirm how it looks before sending it to a wider audience.** And, of course, make sure that the e-mail contains a hyperlink by which the customer can automatically jump to your site to start shopping or communicating with you.

Newsletters

Newsletters become events on the Web in that they create another opportunity for you to routinely get in front of your regular and potential customers. While they don't have to necessarily tout a sale or coupon, they should provide news a customer or client can use, and they should always include a link to your site. Beware of hokey language or presentation. Keep your message upbeat but sincere. For instance, a vitamin store might give the latest news on an herbal supplement report, or an electronics store could offer tips on keeping your computer fine-tuned. Make sure that your newsletter doesn't drone on needlessly but rather contains easy-to-read, pertinent information that's quick to digest and is useful and attractively presented.

Announcements

Sales aside, you can use e-mails to make special announcements about your company, including a recap of a gala your company organized, details about money your business raised for a charity and a link to the charity's Web site, or follow-up information from a press conference or meeting you've held.

E-Conferences

While most of the discussion in this chapter involves Web-based events and promotions to attract and keep customers, you can also rely on the Web for conferencing with vendors, far-flung employees, and other people and organizations for needs that may arise. Many companies have embraced Web conferences as a way to save on travel and time while still accomplishing goals that require involvement from multiple parties. If you're also hoping for face time, you can use computers with cameras that show pictures of the participants, although adding this component will mean extra cost, setup, and equipment. Some of the reasons for a Web conference that may apply to your business include:

- ➲ Training for new employees or new products
- ➲ Offering sales presentations
- ➲ Conducting staff meetings
- ➲ Holding press conferences
- ➲ Implementing focus groups

Before You Begin

First of all, ascertain why you're calling the meeting, why you think a Web conference is the best solution, who should attend, and your goals for the meeting. (You might want to review Chapter 7: Having a Remarkable Meeting to double-check your approach.) In addition, for Web conferencing you'll also need a computer, browser, DSL or broadband connection, and a phone. You also need to select a service provider that can help you host a Web conference. You may subscribe to a service or have them supply Web conferencing software on an as-needed basis.

Visit such Web sites as *www.webex.com* and *www.gotomeeting.com*, both of which offer a free trial, to get a better idea of how you can work with a service provider to put a Web conference effectively and efficiently to work for your company in a secure Web environment.

Sharing Documents

The conferences can be set up for you to share documents online with others, documents everyone can view and edit, as well as offer PowerPoint presentations, audio or video presentations, and even have others join you on a visit to other Web sites.

If you opt to show a PowerPoint presentation, keep the messages clean and crisp, with no more than four bullets per slide in easy-to-grasp information chunks. Use a 24-point font in a nonserif style such as Helvetica for easy reading and recall during the Web meeting.

Troubleshooting

Beware of technical problems that may interfere with your Web conference or e-seminar. By virtue of the fact that you're assembling others via technology, you run the risk of hampering your efforts with hard-to-predict snafus. Being cognizant that you may encounter difficulties, make sure you have backup plans in place with your Web conferencing software provider so that problems can be quickly rectified. Many Web conference companies have personnel attending your event while everyone is online so that such difficulties, should they arise, can be swiftly dealt with and eliminated. Even if a tech person isn't in the conference with you, have a phone number for technical support handy should you need to call it. If possible—and particularly if you've never conducted a Web conference or e-seminar—consider holding a practice session so you're familiar with procedures and possible problems.

E-Seminars

Also known as Webinars, these are e-learning initiatives, lessons doled out over the Internet. They can be used to inform your employees about new procedures, policies, or products, or they can work to position your company as an expert in its field. Like Web conferencing, they also offer the possibility to shave money off a budget for traveling by linking employees, vendors, or clients.

You can plan them with the help of a service provider. They will provide you with a meeting place in the form of a Web site, as well as log-ins for you to e-mail to your attendees.

Finally, some Webinars can be set up so that your customers or clients can download them at their convenience to view and receive information about—or instructions on how to use—a product or service. To go this route you need to be well versed in technology or use a Web consultant to package the video and post it.

Setting up a Webinar

To begin you have to determine the overall program: the information you'll be presenting to participants, complete with the moderator who will be in charge of ensuring the program follows its preplanned components. In addition, make sure e-mails have been distributed beforehand to participants so that they are aware of the program's start time, duration, and content.

Whoever the moderator—you or a designate—make sure that person is thoroughly prepared beforehand and logs on before the session starts. The moderator should be well versed in the program schedule, the time allotted for each component, and the information to be distributed and discussed, and he or she should be keen to keep the Webinar flowing smoothly.

Webinars for Positioning

More than likely, someone from your company can offer his or her expertise on a variety of subjects. **Many companies elect to hold regular e-seminars as a way of strengthening their brand or positioning themselves as an expert in a particular field.** If this is an endeavor that fits in with your marketing strategies, then plot out what you could hold an e-seminar about. Remember that you want the seminar to provide relevant, useful information for participants. E-seminars can't just be a laundry list presentation of all the great business your company does or the accomplishments it achieves. Ask and answer the question, "What will participants get out of this e-seminar for themselves (or their company)?" In other words, have something to say that e-seminar attendees can instantly realize will benefit them personally or professionally, and your customers, both existing and potential ones, will be grateful, impressed, and inclined to patronize your business further.

Once You've Presented

After you've presented your information, you can complete the program by engaging in a question-and-answer session with your audience, either through instant chat or by phone.

After the Webinar, be sure to send a thank-you note or e-mail to participants who attended, particularly if the e-seminar was introducing or touting a product you're trying to sell. Further, if some you expected to attend didn't, record the e-seminar as a Flash file that you can distribute to them afterward. Send the file in an e-mail with a message that says you're sorry they missed the event but that doesn't mean they'll miss out on the information presented. Finally, if appropriate, you can also post the e-seminar on your Web site as an added value for others visiting your site.

Timing Is Everything

For both Web conferencing and e-seminars, think about timing for your event. You should consider time zones. For example, 3 P.M. on the East Coast will be lunchtime on the West Coast. Holding it on Monday won't provide the opportunity for a timely e-mail reminder, and Fridays may be the start of a long weekend for some. Also consider such possible conflicts as federal holidays, end-of-the-month quotas, and trade-show dates. Even so, once you've set a date, make sure to follow up with a reminder thanking the participants for registering as well as another reminder e-mail a few days before the e-seminar to confirm the time, date, and content. For a Web conference, follow meeting guidelines for the appropriate length; for a Webinar, keep it long enough to present useful, nonrepetitive information but short enough to maintain interest. Just like in a meeting or in-the-same-room seminar, you won't have participants' endless attention.

E-Promotions

Promotions on the Internet can take on a variety of formats, all of which should drive traffic to your site and increase sales.

Sales

The most popular online promotion is a sale. On your Web site you can offer customers Web-only deals and discounts. You should consider signage on your Web site in the form of banners and images, which clearly alert the site visitor that a sale is going on. Have a separate category on the navigation bar set up, plainly marked "Sales" or "Clearance," so that visitors know where to find the goods. Consider having a theme—a holiday, a one-of-a-kind-that's-left, a spring cleaning—that promotes excitement.

In addition, have start and end dates for the sale. While your Web site may have a permanent sales button on your navigation bar, the time for a sale needs to be defined or it will last forever.

As discussed earlier in this chapter, publicize your sale with an e-mail that contains images and the theme behind the event. Include a headline that sums up the sale in an enticing way, and make sure your copy includes the sale's start and end dates.

Snappy E-Mails, Sizzling Sales

If you've never attempted a sale on your Web site, investigate what retailers you admire do. They need not be in your same industry. In fact, a noncompetitor might give you a better view of what works and what doesn't on the Internet. A high-end retailer of home furnishings and purveyor of "happy chic," Jonathan Adler (at www.jonathanadler.com and with eight retail stores) announces a sale via e-mail with a colorfully designed page that contains a hyperlink to the sale pages. If you visit the home page during the sale it features a billboard—created in the same style as the e-mail page—with information about the sale and a link to the pages. Further, the banner on the main sale page is presented in the same artistic style as the e-mail page and home page billboard. Presenting graphics unique to the sale and creating such crossover and consistency among several Web-based formats lends freshness to the sale and works to position it as an event.

Coupons, Special Offers, and Other Incentives

As with sales you might announce, you can also provide existing and potential customers with opportunities to take advantage of percentages off for merchandise or services, or dole out a coupon code that they can use upon checkout. Although you can send coupons via e-mail, be mindful that taking another approach could also be fruitful. Often Web sites will advertise in magazines or through direct-mail pieces and offer a promotional code to enter when making purchases on the site.

Charitable Promotions

Another sales event you can consider is one that benefits nonprofit organizations. For instance, perhaps during the month of January you designate that a percentage of the profits from each sale will go to a charitable cause.

As an example, customers at the Web site *www.goodkarmal.com*, which sells beautifully packaged caramels that include inspirational inscriptions, know that proceeds from their purchases benefit a certain charity. Good Karmal's effort is an ongoing one that alternately features different charities. If you take up such a cause-related marketing event for your site, provide links to the charity you're tying in with, and let your site visitors know what their purchase is benefiting. (Good Karmal has a button on their navigation bar called "Karmal Causes" that gives information on the charity and provides a link to its site.)

Live Chats

Another way to promote your business is through live chats, which are question-and-answer sessions for site visitors. Set a time, date, compelling subject matter, and, if possible, a guest with an amazing story or expert advice to connect with your audience for a live session.

Live chats can incorporate many twists. For instance, American Express hosted an event for entrepreneurs about brand building where Web users could ask questions of style icons Kate and Andy Spade, cosmetics maven Bobbie Brown, and financial guru Jean Chatsky. The event's title and theme, "Making a Name for Yourself," focused on how these individuals were catapulted from small-business entrepreneurs to global forces. In this case the live chat was complementing a live panel discussion (and, actually, another event). Thousands attended the event live in Times Square at the Nokia Theater, with another 6,000 participating in the live simulcast over the Internet.

Taking another course, you may feature a celebrity on your site who can take questions. Or in a different vein, you can encourage site visitors to upload a video question to ask a question on your site that will then be given to an expert to answer. Taking that tack allows you to weed out impertinent questions and fine-tune answers for concise delivery.

Podcasts

The advent of the iPod has made podcasts de rigueur for many businesses. A podcast is an audio file that you create in an mp3 format. Along with an RSS (Really Simple Syndication) file, it's uploaded to a server (such as your Web site) so that people can listen to it at their own convenience on their mp3 device, such as an iPod, or through their computer. The basics you need are a computer with an Internet connection, a microphone, sound recording software, and an mp3 encoder (the latter two can be retrieved free over the Net).

Is a podcast a medium that will fit in with your business' practices and goals? Do you have information that you could routinely release or discuss that would benefit your current or potential customers or clients? If so, you can record podcasts that are posted on your Web site that visitors can hear or download for later. Not only can you catalog them on your site, you can also arrange to post your content on iTunes so that the iTunes Store can offer them to site visitors to download for free.

If you've got topics and content you think will be valuable to listeners, visit *www.apple.com/support/garageband/podcasts/recording/* to learn more about the guidelines for podcasts and receive instructions on recording them. You can also take a look at *http://audacity.sourceforge. net* for free software for recording and editing.

Cross Promotions with Other Sites

Cross promotions with complementary but noncompeting Web sites can provide you with a winning formula for Web events. A purchase on your Web site might give you a coupon code for a percentage off or a free product from another one.

Podcasts for Small-Business Owners

Author, speaker, and coach Libby Gill realized the value of podcasts for her business nearly two years ago. Each week she produces a podcast that features excerpts from her *Dallas Morning News* column "Traveling Hopefully," as well as the occasional interview.

With a podcast program and a microphone that she extensively tested (different voices have different mike requirements), Libby produces the pieces in her office with her assistant performing engineering duties. Each podcast can be heard on her site and can be downloaded from iTunes.

While she doesn't consider herself to be a techie, she describes the entire process as completely unintimidating. And it's had a significant impact on her business. She consistently gets positive feedback from site visitors and at speaking engagements from people who tell her they routinely download her podcast. She finds that the podcast extends her reach with a versatile approach to capture more clients: those who prefer listening to her advice and teachings over reading them and those outside the Dallas market. She also benefits from a cool factor by being on the cutting edge of Web technology with a regularly scheduled podcast.

To get an idea of the variety of podcasts and a sense of how one might work for your business, visit *www.podcasts.yahoo.com* for a listing of 100 popular ones. You can subscribe to any of them for free.

Another possibility for cross promotions are reciprocal links: You provide a link to another site on your site and vice versa.

Check Out the Other Site

Just like the cross promotions discussed in Chapter 22—for cross promotions or reciprocal links—make sure that those sites are reputable, and do your research:

- ➲ Are your target demographics comparable?
- ➲ Are your products truly complementary or could they actually be competitive?

➲ Will you expand your audience and potential customer base, or are you cannibalizing each other's share?

➲ Do you complement—or detract from—each other's message?

➲ Are your company images consistent with each other?

Content Possibilities

Depending on the type of Web site you have for your business, you may be constantly in need of fresh content. If that's the case, that presents another cross-promotional opportunity that you may be able to barter for. For instance, if you'd like exposure on a company's site to drive traffic to your business' site, you may be able to offer to write an expert article or provide tips that might appeal to their audience. In exchange for your input, that Web site could offer a link to yours.

Garnering Chat with Your Site

Blogging has become immensely popular and can often prompt visits to your Web site. You may consider a blog for your Web site, in which you offer insights and tips into topics particularly relevant to your business. For instance, a fabric store Web site has a blog that gives lessons on patterns and projects that worked and those that didn't. The blog keeps visitors on the store's site and offers inspiration for projects readers may want to pursue and for which they need fabric and sewing materials and guidance on the company's Web site.

Blogs often offer up news, details, and links to other blogs. You could well find your blog listed on someone else's. That, too, helps drive traffic to your site.

You always want visitors on your site to have the means to offer input, ask questions, and make suggestions. Blogs and the chat they generate offer just that: an unintimidating forum for existing and potential customers to weigh in on a variety of issues. This creates opportunities for you to form bonds with your customers, even if it's in a virtual atmosphere rather than a neighborhood storefront.

▶▶ Test Drive

Participate in a Webinar. If you're on the lookout, you'll realize you receive more invitations to them than you think. If there is a high-ticket product you're interested in purchasing—particularly in the technology or electronics category—you can probably find a Webinar that explains instructions for it. When participating, ask yourself:

⮕ How is it produced? Is there a moderator and a panel or simply an instructor?

⮕ Is the tack effective and interesting?

⮕ If not, do you think the presentation is missing any particular component?

⮕ Was the Webinar easy to access online?

⮕ Was the Webinar too long or too short?

⮕ Is this, ultimately, an event that could benefit your business or a service or product that your company sells?

Attracting and Keeping
Audiences and Customers

PART

Media Outlets for Your Endeavors

An event can usually take on a greater importance and can have more of an impact on your business when you attract media coverage for it. As you carve out the plans for your event, make sure to have a thriving media component present.

Start thinking about what might draw the media to your event. While you undoubtedly have interest in your own business and an attendant event, what will rouse theirs?

Putting Together a Media List

Compile a media list of prospective targets, or work with a public relations professional to do so. Hopefully you've been assembling names of reporters, columnists, and editors in the media as part of your routine communication plan. And you may already, in fact, have fans in the media who often cover your company's initiatives. But if you don't, fear not: now's the time to begin.

Know the media you want to target. If you add a publication to your list, be confident that it represents a real possibility for coverage. Lofty ambitions are fine, but pie-in-the-sky possibilities rarely pan out. For a media target, get a name, title, address, phone number, and e-mail address. Determine exactly what that reporter's beat is, or pinpoint exactly where you would like your coverage in the publication to be. It's a waste of a journalist's time, and yours, to approach her about a story that isn't a fit for her publication or isn't a topic she ever covers, and some will tell you so.

If you're unsure of where to begin in putting together a list, three resources you might try are *www.easymedialist.com*, which can compile lists specific to certain areas of interest; *www.burrellesluce.com*, which specializes in assembling media directories as well as media monitoring and tracking; and *www.bacons.com*, which can research media, contact them, and monitor coverage. In all instances fees are involved, so do your homework to find a company that fits your needs and budget.

If a list seems absolutely overwhelming or your company is short on staff, you can also rely on services such as *www.prnewswire.com*. With your input, they can come up with the media targets and distribute a release, media advisory, or other information about an event.

Keep a Running Media Log

Even if you've got a media list already compiled, never stop adding to it. No doubt you're constantly keeping up on information important to your business in consumer magazines (those that appeal to general consumer audiences and typically found on the newsstand), trade publications unique to your industry, and Web sites that cover pertinent subject matter to your business. On a weekly basis, continue putting outlets on your list that may be perfect to approach for your next event, which will make the task of compiling one at the last minute far less daunting. Include the outlet's title, the reporter or editor, a phone number and other particulars, and the date you've added it. (You will want to periodically reverify the media list contacts as publications sometimes change addresses and phone numbers, and reporters move into other roles and positions.)

Considering the Pitch

Once you've got your media list in hand, have your pitch clearly defined before you start calling or e-mailing the press. **Your pitch is the brief description of your event and why you think the media will be interested in covering it.** While news outlets are always looking for stories, remember they also have many people approaching them with pitches. Make yours compelling and a standout. You can make your pitch by mail, fax, phone, e-mail, or a combination of those.

For a pitch via e-mail, craft a subject line that includes the news of your event. In the e-mail message you can try a clever approach, but employ it sparingly, and don't use silly language. In some cases you also may paraphrase your release's headline, or even take it verbatim if it's not too long. For instance, suppose the Polka Paper company is launching a new wrapping paper line with a party to wrap presents for children at a shelter. The subject line might read "Wrap All Night with the Polka Paper Party 12/03." While the e-mail message would then include the event's details and the benefiting charity, you wouldn't want to include more words with multiple meanings or take it a step further and set up your copy as a rap refrain.

Make sure your e-mail contains the precise points of your pitch but doesn't go on for paragraphs. In fact, consider using bullet points in bringing your information across. Provide a contact phone number in case they have questions upon receiving your e-mail.

If you're making the pitch via phone (or conducting follow-up from the pitch letter or release), rehearse your cogent points beforehand. Of course, you don't want to blurt all your information out in one rambling delivery. Instead, be rehearsed (without sounding canned), giving your exact, engaging pitch without extraneous details. **Be warm, friendly, professional, and concise.** Plus be ready to answer any questions the reporter may have. If a reporter or producer takes a pass on your pitch, don't take it personally or be insistent that he give it a second consideration. If you think of another angle that may be of interest, consider a reapproach via e-mail.

Often companies will send out pitch letters giving the media information about the event, as well as a CD-ROM or DVD of product information. In these cases the letters should be on crisp letterhead and, if you have one, might be attached to a brochure or other literature for the event. Then you should follow up by e-mail or phone.

Print Media

Probably you have a community weekly newspaper that could cover your event. But think even bigger: What daily newspapers are in your area? Have you noticed what events they cover? What about national papers? Is your event newsworthy enough for national exposure?

Magazines may be a tougher sell for procuring coverage for your event simply because the long lead times of the monthlies mean that your event will be old news by the time the magazine comes out. However, you can publicize it ahead of time, giving magazine columnists or "Coming Up" pages a brief item about the event for an advance mention. Further, consider weeklies, such as *Time*, *People*, and *Entertainment Weekly*, but only if you know your story has an angle that fits in with a certain section of the magazine or if the event will produce images that will be amazing to their readers.

Radio

Unless you've invited a radio station to participate in your event with a DJ appearance or live remote, you may find it hard to entice a station to cover your event. However, radio news stations may perhaps find it fitting to send a reporter to your event if it contains of-the-moment action or a gripping human-interest angle. If you think a news radio station in your area should be invited, familiarize yourself with the station's newscasts and shows to determine where you think coverage of your event will fit in.

Television

For a television crew to be sent to cover your event, you have to design your event to be visual. Think ahead: How will a television news producer translate your event into a visual story, told to viewers in pictures and words. While balloons and banners may be appropriate for your event, they might not be enough to entice a crew. Think about the action your event holds: Are races being held, is a lineup of 100 soldiers putting on orange jumpsuits, are huge ice sculptures dotting a landscape, or 1,000 limes being pressed to make limeade? How can you elevate your event to attract television coverage?

The Internet

While you can certainly ask certain Web news outlets to come to your event, you may also succeed in providing other outlets with a story and images they can post. The Internet is the one arena of the media you'll pitch that never seems to be pressed for space: So many sites compete for so many eyeballs that they're always looking for content.

In that vein, and as a service to all the media outlets, make sure you've prepared a media advisory and release about the event. Hire a photographer to take pictures. (All these things are discussed later in this chapter.)

Having a Spokesperson

Further, make sure to have a company spokesperson on site who will be instantly available—and well-informed—to answer questions, provide more information, and in the case of television outlets, appear on camera.

Inside Track   In the Newsroom

Having worked in both the newsroom of a top ten market daily newspaper and a national television entertainment news magazine, I've been fortunate to gain substantial insights into the kinds of pitches and information that create excitement in editors and reporters to cover a story or event, and what dissuades them from taking someone's call or responding to an e-mail. The following tips are culled from assignment editors and reporters at those two outlets.

First off, realize you might be approaching an assignment editor first at a specific publication or station. That person's job is to serve as a filter for all the stories that particular media outlet is being approached about and determine which is a fit for their organization's reporting.

Whomever you're pitching—an assignment editor, producer, reporter, or editor—is almost always simultaneously flooded with several pitches, under deadline for stories they're already covering, and on the lookout for the next ones.

Your media contact will appreciate a pitch that gets to the meat of the matter quickly—either by phone or e-mail, and many now vastly prefer e-mail—and immediately catches his attention as a story that's unique and appropriate for his audience. Remember, often times you might have a great pitch for a solid story but offer it to the wrong person, as it doesn't fit the beat your contact covers or is the wrong publication.

Be respectful of your media contact's time and taste. Don't bombard him or her with phone calls and e-mails until you get a response. If you haven't heard from the reporter after an initial e-mail and appropriately timed follow-up, be objective about the story's merit and use common sense in following up. It could be that your media contact is out of town or your story has been handed off to another reporter. But typically, if the media are interested after you've conducted your initial pitch and follow-up, their representatives will contact you if they plan to cover the event.

Finally, away from the deadlines of your particular event, try to cultivate some friendly media contacts that can give you personal insights into what a target publication might like to cover. Offer them resources that might prove valuable to them in their everyday reporting, such as providing information on industry trends, contacts for stories they're covering, or leads to other stories.

Getting a Response

As you make your pitches to attract the media, remember most of them receive story ideas from many sources. When gathering your media list, find out if your media contacts prefer being pitched by phone, fax, mail, or via e-mail and act accordingly.

If you're approaching them by phone, you may be leaving a voice mail. Even so, resist the urge to ramble or give unnecessary details. If possible, and if they are amenable, follow up the call with written details by fax or e-mail. Don't call every day for days if they've told you they might be interested or need to run it by an editor. It's appropriate to call once more to double-check on their interest.

Press Releases and Media Advisories

As a follow-up to your media pitch, or as an accompaniment to it to begin with, you will need a press release for your event. A press release explains the five Ws and an H (who, what, when, where, why, and how) behind the event. Most conveniently, you can send it by e-mail as an attachment or pasted into the e-mail message as text. Writing press releases takes particular care and attention. It has to be brief enough to convey facts quickly but complete enough to have questions answered.

Press Release Preferences

Members of the press you're working with may have different preferences on how they like to receive information, so because of that you should be ready and willing to deliver it in any format they request. Some might prefer a hard copy of the release and other supplementary information you're providing at your event, while others may want it on CD-ROM or—paperless and disk free—posted on your company's Web site to be retrieved at their convenience. If you post it on your Web site, make sure the press has easy access to it (if, for instance, the information's in a password-protected area).

For more information on writing press releases that encourage and inform the media with captivating headlines and compelling lead paragraphs, check out my book *Streetwise® Business Communication*. For a detailed discussion of press releases, see Chapter 20. You'll also need to have a press release at the event itself to fill in background and details for media attending the event.

Closer to the event, you may need to provide the media with an advisory. A media advisory gives additional details such as dignitaries who you know are attending, activities that have been added to the program, or disclosures about unveilings or surprises. The advisory should include the time, date, place, name of the event, purpose for it, a media contact, and other pertinent up-to-date details. It shouldn't be longer than a page.

Confirmations

Once you have a media RSVP list, confirm their attendance with a reminder e-mail a day or two before the event. **In a clear and concise format, the e-mail should include the event's time, date, and location, as well as any special instructions reporters may need regarding parking or credentials.** If possible, also offer them a detailed map, or at least a link to *www.mapquest.com* or *maps.google.com* so that they can find the best route there.

Other Publicity Ideas for Your Event

In addition to the coverage you hope to get at the event itself, you have an array of other possibilities for publicity to spur attendance and to spark advance notice of the event.

- Post information on your company's Web site about the event.
- Take advantage of large gatherings—chamber of commerce, neighborhood, civic, and Rotary club meetings—to announce the event.
- Distribute tasteful, professionally designed flyers to be available for patrons at area businesses and in public locations such as libraries.
- Include details in professionally related newsletters.
- Send out a direct-mail piece to your customer mailing list.

➲ Send an e-mail to current and potential customers providing information about the event.

Inviting the Right People

While you want a crowd at your event, make sure that you've invited those who will make a positive impact for media coverage. In addition, you may also consider inviting city dignitaries or celebrities who may also generate additional media interest. While you don't want them taking all of the limelight, their inclusion—particularly if they have an appropriate, understandable connection to your business, product, or service—will usually heighten media interest and increase your coverage. If you know certain high-profile people will be attending, make sure the media knows. Update your media advisory accordingly to list who will be attending.

When the Media Shows Up

Make sure that no matter how many media arrive they get what they need. While you don't want to interfere with the job they're there to do, which is covering your company's event, you should supply them with releases, offer interviews, and provide your contact information for any follow-up they may need. Whether you have two media reporters present or a hundred (and you'll have an idea of how many through the follow-up you conduct), have staff present who can greet them and handle any of their inquiries.

Considering and Securing Media Sponsors

Depending on the scope of your event, you may want to investigate having a media sponsor be part of your activities and festivities. A media sponsor could be a local radio station, a magazine that covers topics that mesh with the theme of your event, or a well-trafficked Web site that has a target audience similar to yours. If they deem your event a worthwhile cause, a media sponsor will offer publicity through its forum to publicize your event. Therefore, most typically a media sponsor is involved and offers that exposure to nonprofit entities.

If the media has signed up as a sponsor for your event, remember that exposure works both ways. The media are providing a public service for your event; how can you help them? The media can be included in any publicity you can offer: placement on direct-mail pieces, banners, flyers, and the event's promotional T-shirts; a link on your Web site; and mentions in your press releases.

Really Making a Name for Your Event

How unique is your event? Is it offering a new and novel twist? In a quest to garner publicity, can you brainstorm ways to make your event stand out? Are there activities you can include that would provide attention-grabbing, picture-taking possibilities? Is there an unveiling that would pique interest? A surprise appearance that you could create anticipation for?

Year to Year

If the media don't seem interested in details of your event, can you come up with a relevant event component, distinguishing element, or change that will attract them? Take a look at today's newspaper. You'll most likely find coverage of some event. What was it that drew the media to write a story about it?

If your event has become an annual affair that initially attracted attention, devise ways that can keep it fresh from year to year. Are there components you can build in that change each year and that the audience comes to expect and anticipate? Don't blindly follow the template from last year. Find ways to tailor the event so it seems new while retaining the flavor and the popular features that made it a success in the past. Use attendee, participant, and audience feedback to shape your event from year to year, building upon the positive and weeding out the negative.

Of course, when you keep in mind that your company will need to pitch this, either in a letter, e-mail, or over the phone, to the media, you start thinking as the press might, looking for angles that will spark interest in a general audience and make for a good story.

What's in a Name?

Don't underestimate the power of the name you give the event. The name becomes an instant way to brand the event and, if it's catchy enough, makes your pitching to the media much easier.

While your event has to live up to whatever billing you give it, spend some time brainstorming a name that will give it excitement and resonance. Some national ones that have gained prominence include the Nike Run Hit Wonder, a 10K race that features bands at points along the race course; Coca-Cola Art of Harmony, a high school student art competition that encourages works promoting unity; and the multicity tour of aloft a-go-go, an Airstream trailer bedecked in the room design of the new aloft hotels, W's new select-service brand.

And consider these names. Without even knowing the company, organization, or cause that's behind them, they catch your interest: Litquake, Sophisticated Snoop, The Great Fruitcake Toss, Yacht Hop, The Cookies 'n Crime Tour: What Will You Make?, Frostbike, and Change Your Mind Day. Obviously the name can't be the extent of the appeal of your event, so make sure to have yours fulfill the promise of its moniker. Stuff it with appealing events, announcements, and activities commensurate with your target audience that are also media friendly. What Will You Make? was a Lego-sponsored tour allowing participants to build anything they wanted to out of the brightly colored plastic blocks. Frostbike is Quality Bicycle Products' annual educational, social, and sales event held in February at the company's Minnesota headquarters.

The Importance of Photography

Don't underestimate your need to have a photographer on hand to capture the event. Now, more than ever, getting photos taken is easy with digital cameras. Still, hire a professional to get the shots. Amateur photos will rarely give your event the look it deserves.

Depending on your event, you should also devise a shot list beforehand. The shot list is a breakdown of the photos you're intent on getting during the event. In this list you'll include executives you need to gather for group shots, dignitaries attending, and moments that are crucial to the event's success (such as customers racing into a store's grand open-ing, children using your products to build and decorate sandcastles, or capturing the crowd assembled during a presentation).

Also, make sure you take a wide variety of shots. Pictures that look great in the newspaper may not be as descriptive or impactful when downsized for your Web site.

Building Upon Media Placements

Once you've garnered coverage, capitalize on it to receive additional coverage. If you've gotten an article placed about your event in one publication, you can often use that article to generate interest in another outlet. Further, reporters read their competitors' publications and see and hear news reports. They're always looking for new stories and interest-ing angles. You may also find that coverage you receive takes an angle you hadn't thought of. If it's appealing to you, you might try to take that approach in luring additional media interest.

For any of the media who didn't attend, and particularly those you thought would, follow up by sending an e-mail lauding the event, and include images. Finally, invite media fans of this event to future ones. They may be interested in following your other initiatives and will cer-tainly make a worthy addition to your media list.

After the Event

Spend some time shortly after the event to analyze how the media inter-est you cultivated panned out.

- Did the media show up?
- Did their showing up translate into coverage? Why or why not?
- Did you miss any outlets that now you wish you had invited?
- How would you attract more media attention next time?

Also once the event is over, make sure to track any press clippings or broadcast coverage you receive. You can contract with a service such as

Burrelle's (*www.burrellesluce.com*). For a fee they will gather the coverage you received, complete with circulation and audience numbers.

Once your obtain the clips, don't just pile them in a file or box to look at some time later. Sit down with them soon after the event, read or watch them, review them, and analyze them. Ask and answer questions about the coverage:

- ➲ Was it favorable?
- ➲ Was it accurate? Did any coverage surprise you?
- ➲ Did most of the outlets cover the same angle?
- ➲ Did any media take a different approach? Why? Was the story they wrote or produced a better fit with their publication or broadcast audience?
- ➲ Will the coverage benefit your company by pointing out products, giving your business better name recognition, or engendering goodwill for your efforts?

Getting a bead on the coverage will help you frame future events to make sure they're giving you the maximum impact with the media. Of course, that maximum impact will make your time and financial commitments to an event even more worthwhile.

▶▶ Test Drive

Before your next event, try writing a press release and getting some coverage. Think about a piece of company news that a media outlet—even your local weekly newspaper—might find valuable.

- ➲ Craft a release with the pertinent details, such as an award your company received or a special sale you're having.
- ➲ From the release, create a pitch you can e-mail to a reporter.
- ➲ Follow up with the reporter to determine her interest.
- ➲ If a reporter didn't run a story, can you ascertain why it wasn't newsworthy enough?

PART 6

Attracting and Keeping Audiences and Customers

What Could Possibly Go Wrong?

Unfortunately, plenty. Where events are concerned, lots of things can and will invariably go wrong—just because so many logistical aspects are in play, there are so many people to depend on, so many participants are involved, there are several places to be at and manage, and you have a variety of equipment to coordinate. **Part of your responsibility in planning the event is to limit the impact of problems that pop up and deal with them swiftly.** Don't take an overconfident attitude that you've expertly handled every minute detail because, unfortunately, despite your preparation and competence, you won't be able to predict everything. However, the more prepared you are, the less likely you'll have to call on any of these last-minute fixes.

So pull out your action plan, timeline, staffing charts, equipment list, venue contracts, and vendor agreements. Scrutinize your event from start to finish. Ideally you'll have kept contingency components at the top of your mind throughout the planning stages. If not, double-check your answers to these ten questions in the week before an event:

1. Have the vendor commitments and times of delivery been reconfirmed?
2. Is your staff aware of responsibilities and start times for the day of the event?
3. Have you done a walk-through at the site?
4. Have you accurately mapped out the space?
5. If necessary, has directional signage been arranged for?
6. Have you set aside time for rehearsals for speakers and presentations and for run-throughs with equipment?
7. Have you reconfirmed meals and beverages?
8. Have remarks been prepared for speakers?
9. Have deposits been received for all of those entities that needed them prior to the event?
10. Do you have a sheet with contact cell phone numbers for your staff, site personnel, and emergency scenarios?

In addition:

Check the weather report. Weather concerns are discussed later in this chapter, but even if your event is indoors you should be aware of possible precipitation that could hamper arrival times and notify vendors and staff accordingly.

Get a snapshot of news events. Is there a possibility of looming news that could take news crews away from coverage or distract your audience's attention?

Recheck area calendars for possible event conflicts. Has there been a last-minute schedule change or addition that could deflate attendance?

Forewarned Is Forearmed

Your event has a far greater chance of averting crises by simply taking a few additional steps prior to the event's start.

On-site Communication

At the event itself, place a premium on communication. If necessary, rent walkie-talkies so that you and fellow staff members can quickly communicate with each other. At the very least, make sure everyone has a cell phone that is turned on and has been preprogrammed with everyone else's phone numbers.

Contracts, Permits, and Other Legalese

Have all the necessary paperwork you need in order and easily accessible during an event. If you have trouble with a vendor performing his or her duties on site, you can quickly refer to a contract he or she has signed. Similarly you may have a visit from a city official to check on your event and make sure that it's being held in accordance with regulations. Review all your binding legal agreements before an event to ensure that they are all in order and that your expectations won't be dashed by unpleasant surprises.

Security

Depending on the number of people you expect and the venue of your event, you may need security personnel. Don't give this aspect short shrift. Even if it isn't required by city ordinances or to receive a permit, use your best judgment. Paying for security often isn't a needless or extravagant expense. Remember: Once an event becomes rowdy, you'll find it difficult to return the atmosphere to normal.

Emergency Issues

Know where the nearest hospital or emergency medical center is in case someone is injured on site. Particularly for larger gatherings, you don't want to have someone collapse and ask, "Is there a doctor in the house?"

If you're at a hotel, find out what their standard procedure is for injuries or health crises. In addition, and especially if you're in charge of a convention or conference that will be longer than a day, make sure your registration packet for attendees includes getting information from them about whom to contact in case of an emergency.

Be Up on the Net

Obviously you'll have a cell phone on you during an event. But if possible, have a PDA or laptop with Wi-Fi capabilities so you can access the Internet at your event. At the last minute you may need to get a weather update, retrieve an e-mail with directions or other details, look up a map, or get additional information about your speaker. Having that kind of quick access can save time, headaches, and may even help deflect a coming crisis. In addition, if reporters there are on deadline and need information e-mailed, you can quickly, efficiently handle that too.

What to Do about the Weather

Weather, by its very nature, is unpredictable. When you start planning your outdoor event months out, you have no idea whether it will rain on the date you've selected. Even if your event is indoors, rain or snow

Confidence, Just in Case

One of the largest events I was ever involved in coordinating was a televised program that featured several standup comic and music performances in Los Angeles at the Hollywood Bowl, with a seating capacity of nearly 18,000.

While the event was on a tape delay, it was being televised the same day of the taping so any major crisis that occurred would cause substantial problems in the subsequent broadcast, which a network of syndicated stations were awaiting. In addition, we had a unique blend of superstar talent, nervous network executives, and mercurial producers that needed to be nurtured, not to mention a sold-out crowd that was expecting a blockbuster show.

In the weeks leading up to the show's start we had devised several scenarios, including talent not showing up, a security breach, crowd control, a natural disaster, and how we would contend with them. (We even put a hold on thousands of umbrellas in case it rained so that the audience wouldn't leave before the taping was over.) Simply, calmly, and deftly discussing those possibilities, and orchestrating what our subsequent actions would be, gave us all even more confidence in proceeding with the event.

That day the event was a thrilling triumph and went off without a hitch. While we had to deal with several minor incidents, deciding on our proactive stances if major problems arose encouraged clear thinking and an organized mindset that made handling those minicrises a snap.

could cause traffic snarls that delay attendees. So while you have no control over the weather, you can make contingency plans that will come in handy should inclement weather threaten your event's success.

If the event is being held outdoors, survey the venue beforehand to consider such a crisis. Could the event be easily moved and set up indoors? Where could you put a tent? If you've contracted with a party rental equipment company, they may rent tents or have access to a company that does. You may have to put a nonrefundable deposit down so that you can quickly procure the tent should you need it, but that investment could be worth it if your event's being held in the middle of a golf course or on an open field.

If the weather blindsides you, you'll have to assess your options: Does the whole event have to be scrapped, or can it be restructured? Don't wait until that actually happens. Give some careful consideration to your possible alternatives prior to the event to prevent having to make a rash decision that could prompt your event to be postponed or canceled.

Otherwise, try to have a sense of humor and think inventively. One advertising premium company distributed umbrellas at a client picnic. It was a just-in-case, though imaginative, gesture that proved handy when a shower did come, and it made their clients realize how useful promotional products actually can be.

What if No One Shows Up?

As part of your action plan for most events discussed in Chapter 3, you must make sure that your schedule allows for some invitations to be mailed and e-mail reminders to be sent. If appropriate and depending on the event, include response cards to be returned or an RSVP line established to take attendee confirmations. With that setup you're likely to get a fairly accurate idea of how many to expect.

Even with that careful attention to details, you still may be faced with a low turnout. If low attendance made your event a failure, a thorough debriefing is immediately necessary. Consider:

➲ Did invitations, flyers, calendar items, direct-mail pieces, or other collateral devised to attract attention get delivered or posted?

➲ Were there any mistakes you can detect from gathering RSVPs or attendee confirmations?

➲ Did a catastrophic news story dominate people's minds and deter attention?

➲ Did your date conflict with another major event in town?

You must at this point also evaluate your entire event plan to determine what might have been avoided or changed in advance. For instance, did the event target the wrong audience? If the event was poorly received or suffered from an unexpected mistake in planning, can you salvage the event another way? Can you restage it at another time in the near future with a minimum of cost? Can you change locations or downsize it? Can you invite a limited guest list, and encourage attendance of fewer at a smaller venue?

What if Too Many People Are There?

Conversely you may have to unexpectedly contend with an abundance of people for your event. Being ill-equipped for massive crowds can be its own crisis. Even if you've made arrangements to host the largest number of people possible, perhaps your RSVP list far exceeds the venue's capacity.

In this case, is there spillover room available? If not, do you have security in place to keep crowds at bay? Or perhaps you should be ready to set out barriers, guiding people to wait in line to get in and then—in an orderly fashion—have them enter as others exit.

If too many people are gathered in too crowded a space, the fire department or other city officials will possibly show up and shut your event down. If you've prepared backup plans and devised scenarios to respond to and receive overflow crowds beforehand, your business will avoid the embarrassment, costs, and confusion of ending an event prematurely.

When Translation Is Needed

In this country's multicultural society you should be prepared to have translation services at your event. If you have any question about the language of speakers or participants in your event, take care to find out beforehand. Embarrassment will be the watchword for your event if you should have translators for speakers and don't.

Depending on the language, you may have a rough time in trying to procure an interpreter at the last minute. While Spanish and Japanese are commonly spoken in parts of the country by many who also know English, finding someone who knows either Finnish or Lithuanian and English will be a tougher assignment.

You may also need to make arrangements to have a sign language interpreter for hearing-impaired members of your audience. Again, check beforehand to see if this is necessary or required.

It's Not Optimal, But . . .

If it's last-minute, and you're in need of a few sentences translated, you can get some translation free online, particularly for more popular languages such as Spanish, French, German, Portuguese, Dutch, and Russian. Sites such as *www.freetranslation.com* can translate sentences or a block of text from English to another language (or vice versa, if you're trying to understand someone else's Dutch, for instance). However, remember: If you're doing the speaking in a language you're not accustomed to, you will still need assistance with pronunciation and inflection.

Remaining Calm under Pressure

Even when a crisis is looming and even if your event may appear to be headed toward disaster, don't lose hope. At least not yet. Getting caught up in the hysteria will only make matters worse. Others will look to you as the event planner for direction and will, most likely, follow your lead. That means that if you're losing your cool, so will everyone else. However, if you maintain composure, others will stay level-headed, too. **By remaining calm and focused you'll have a better chance of figuring out and implementing the best options for contending with the crisis at hand.**

Degrees of Crises

Crises have degrees of severity. A banner that doesn't arrive isn't nearly as serious as a food poisoning outbreak. Consider some crises that could happen. In reviewing these, realize that some have far greater import than others. Some will need apologies or be media magnets; others will be serious because of health concerns; and others are certainly instantly easily surmountable. Have the wisdom to figure out which are which.

➲ An entertainer doesn't arrive
➲ Malfunctioning equipment interferes with a presentation

- A speaker makes a racial slur on stage
- A participant suffers a heart attack
- The meal results in food poisoning
- Attendees imbibe too much alcohol
- A fire breaks out
- A chandelier crashes down
- Phone lines go down or Internet service is interrupted
- A staff member quits on the spot

If you see a crisis beginning to unfold, assess the situation quickly with an eye toward collecting all the facts. Then gather your team and download what you know. From that point you may need to wait for more information to properly deal with the matter, or you may be able to start brainstorming options. Just as you need to keep your cool to maintain the dignity and integrity of your company, ask the same of all your employees, staff members, vendors, and volunteers.

Call Times

Sometimes crises begin because people don't show up on time and a domino effect ensues. To prevent such an occurrence, issue a call sheet for all your staff members. This chart will include a column each for name, position, responsibilities, cell phone number, and the call time—the time each staff person is expected to arrive. As the event planner, help your cause by building in a time cushion for that arrival time to take into account someone arriving late. Further, a call sheet amps up personal responsibility: Everyone on the sheet realizes that each person has a job to do, and many are dependent on others getting their responsibilities done to fulfill their own.

Have a Crisis Plan

Businesses of all sizes are urged to create crisis plans so that they can relay information and next steps to customers, clients, investors, the media, and other audiences, and minimize the negative impact on their company. An event that your company is organizing, hosting, or sponsoring falls under your business' purview and, in effect, must also be scrutinized for crisis communication procedures.

For the big picture, how are your company's internal communications? In the event of any crisis that may affect your company, do you have a plan in place? For instance, do you have the services of a public relations professional or a legal team lined up in the event of a crisis? Have you designated a point person who will talk to the media?

Have a contact list of those who should first be notified and who can advise you appropriately. Select a spokesperson who will be able to respond to the media should a crisis arises. Finally, in the unfortunate event of a crisis don't feel as if you have to have all the answers right away. Only give out information that you know, and respond responsibly and as soon as possible. If you don't have all the answers the media and others are seeking, you can say "I don't know" for now. But be timely and dutiful in getting back to them with answers as you know them. You can find out more information about crafting a crisis communications plan in my book *Streetwise® Business Communication*.

How to Avert a Crisis the Next Time

The advantage of dealing with a crisis at an event is that the experience prepares you for the next time you may have to face one.

Avoiding the Most Common Mistakes

Crises or mishaps often occur from the same problems or mistakes. Fortunately these aren't usually life threatening, but, particularly when they spiral out of control, they reflect poorly on your company, lead to diminished presence or sales at an event, or render the event problematic in a host of other ways. Knowing about these mistakes and how to prevent them can keep them out of your next event.

Missing materials—If you're traveling to another city, ship materials—for example, samples for a trade show, collateral for a tour, signage for a reception, auction items for a gala—way ahead of time, and make sure to get a tracking number. If possible, have them checked on the receiving end to make sure they arrived completely and in good shape. If there are items that are absolutely essential, if at all possible take them on the plane with you. In a time crunch, waiting for lost luggage is maddening, unpredictable, and—unfortunately—sometimes futile.

Problems with food or drink (particularly for a dignitary, celebrity, or guest of honor)—Scrupulously review your banquet event order; make sure you've included a small overage for additional, or unexpected, attendees. Plan to have options for those who might be vegan, vegetarian, or lactose intolerant. To handle surprises that may occur once the meal begins, have a contact at the facility and a plan in place for last-minute requests.

Untrained staff—Participants in your event will easily get a bad impression if staff members are standing around not contributing to activities underway, seem uninformed when asked a question, or appear to be unenthusiastic about being there. If that's the case, you're also probably handling many responsibilities that others should be doing for you. Take the time or appoint someone to make sure the staff at an event is well rehearsed, knowledgeable about company initiatives, and eager to present your company in a flattering way.

No spokesperson—If the media are there and interested in your event, make sure their questions are answered. Decide beforehand whom you want your spokesperson to be. Don't hold a reporter at bay while you decide who should be interviewed. If you do that, the media will pick someone themselves, who might not be the best person to get your message across, or lose interest in the story and leave.

Not confirming—Reconfirm as many details as possible before the event, including transportation, itineraries, staff and entertainment call times, security staff and responsibilities, and contingency plans.

Equipment malfunctions—Try out all equipment (for video and Power-Point presentations, Web conferencing, sound mixers for speakers, a DVD screening) prior to the event. See and hear for yourself or assign a trusted staffer to make sure that all technology is in working order.

Unclear goals—Though your mission for an event may seem obvious, put it into words. It's the driving force behind all your plans and will inform each and every aspect, subtly or overtly. Make sure your event presents a unifying image and message that does your company proud.

Learn from Event Experience

If your event was struck by a crisis, gather all those involved in your efforts and discuss how the crisis was handled. Set an agenda and a time limit for the meeting to conduct this all-important analysis. Don't use this session to assign blame. Try to extract information regarding communication, responsibilities, and the aftermath, which will be beneficial in holding your next event.

Remember, just because a crisis happened doesn't mean the event was for naught. In fact, it may have presented your company with a chance to shine in the face of adversity. No matter the experience, positive or negative, always use what you've learned to make your next event—whatever it may be—a rousing success.

▶▶ **Test Drive**

Does your company have a crisis communications plan in place? If not, devising one will prepare you for a crisis at your next event. Consider the following:

- ➲ For a past event, or one you currently have under consideration, what are possible scenarios unique to your event that might prompt a crisis?
- ➲ If a crisis hit, is there a lawyer you could put on standby to help sort through the scenario?
- ➲ Some crises may never have media involvement, but if yours attracted media attention, do you know who would serve as company spokesperson?
- ➲ Assemble a list of all those you would need to call on a moment's notice if a crisis loomed.

Appendix A
Sample Forms

This comprehensive list will allow you to take stock of the various areas you may need to financially plan for. Remember that each event is different: line items for an open house won't be the same as those for a trade show. Use these as a guideline, brainstorming throughout your entire event to add and subtract the appropriate items within each category.

Budget Worksheet	
VENUE/FACILITY	
Rental fees for meeting, reception, or event room	
Setup fees	
Cleanup fees	
SUBTOTAL	
EQUIPMENT RENTALS	
Tables	
Chairs	
Furniture	
Pipe and drape	
Carpeting/flooring	
Staging	
Stanchions/ropes	
Lecterns	
Booths	
Heaters	
Fans	
Portable restrooms	
Tents/canopies	
Easels	
Risers	
Trash receptacles	
Lighting	
SUBTOTAL	

Budget Worksheet

DÉCOR/DECORATIONS

Stage décor	
Booth décor	
Table centerpieces	
Flowers	
Plants and other greenery	
Balloons	
Candles	
Chair covers	
Photo backdrops	
Props	
SUBTOTAL	

FOOD AND BEVERAGE (CATERING)

Fill out separately for each food-related event if more than one, such as coffee break, lunch, dinner, cocktails, dessert buffet, and so on.

Food	
Beverages (coffee, tea, water, soft drinks)	
Liquor	
Bartender	
Bar setup and glassware	
Ice/condiments	
Linens	
China	
Glasses	
Utensils	
Wait staff and servers	
Gratuities	
Service charges	
SUBTOTAL	

Budget Worksheet

PARKING AND TRANSPORTATION

Parking permits	
Limousine/car rentals	
Shuttles/valet service	
Road or area barricades	
SUBTOTAL	

AUDIO/VISUAL

Television monitors	
DVDs/VCRs	
Computers and computer interfaces	
Digital cameras	
Speaker system	
Sound mixer	
Flipcharts	
Blackboards	
Overhead projectors and/or LCD/DPL projectors	
Laser pointers	
Teleconferencing capabilities	
Walkie-talkies	
Extension cords	
Projector carts	
Technicians	
SUBTOTAL	

ENTERTAINMENT

Music	
Speaker	
Models	
Other talent (such as celebrities, magicians, and the like)	
Booking fees	
Travel fees	
SUBTOTAL	

Budget Worksheet	
DESIGN AND PRINTING	
Logo design	
Letterhead/envelopes	
Brochures	
Media kit	
Registration packets	
Invitations and response cards	
Tickets	
Program	
Signage and/or flyers	
Nametag holders	
Credentials	
Premiums	
Graphic designer fees	
SUBTOTAL	
ADVERTISING	
Newspapers	
Magazines	
Radio	
TV	
Banners	
Advertising agency fees	
Production house fees	
SUBTOTAL	
PUBLICITY AND MARKETING	
Web site design	
Photographer	
Videographer	
Publicity agency or publicist fees	
Press room equipment (fax, copiers, computers, DSL or wireless capabilities)	
SUBTOTAL	

Budget Worksheet

STAFF TRAVEL AND ACCOMMODATIONS	
Airfare	
Car rentals	
Hotel	
Meal Expenses	
SUBTOTAL	
ADMINISTRATION	
Postage	
Shipping	
Courier	
Office supplies	
Insurance	
Legal fees	
Accounting fees	
SUBTOTAL	
SECURITY	
Venue	
Private	
SUBTOTAL	
EMERGENCY CONTINGENCY PLANS	
Medical staff	
Tent	
Lawyer Fees	
SUBTOTAL	
TOTAL BUDGET	

Setting up a system to follow neatly delineates the responsibilities an event needs to be successful, and it encourages accountability and teamwork in working toward a single vision. You could use this to-do grid as is or tailor it precisely to your event. You may need to be even more specific with some of these entries, though they are meant to flow in a chronological order. Ultimately these tasks would be organized according to the timetable you've ascribed to planning your event.

To-Do Grid			
TASK	**DATE ASSIGNED**	**PERSON RESPONSIBLE**	**DEADLINE**
Determine your event's purpose			
Decide upon a theme			
Determine rough outline of event schedule			
List needs for each component of event			
Brainstorm locations			
Visit potential sites			
Gather estimates for venues			
Gather estimates for food and beverage			
Gather estimates for entertainment			
Gather estimates for design and printing			
Gather estimates for A/V equipment			
Finalize event elements			
Draft the budget			
Finalize budget			
Track budget weekly			
Determine venue, secure date and contract			
Determine and compile mailing list for invitees			
Select graphic artist			
Begin invitation design			
Create logo			
Order save-the-date cards			
Set schedule for advertising			
Secure URL for Web site or create pages specifically for event			
Investigate needs for permits, licenses, and insurance			
Assign committees			

To-Do Grid			
TASK	DATE ASSIGNED	PERSON RESPONSIBLE	DEADLINE
Distribute save-the-date cards			
Finalize venue details, such as meeting spaces and ballrooms			
Set menu with caterer for all food and beverages			
Review invitations and other collateral			
Finalize contract(s) for entertainment			
Finalize all components of the event that will require A/V resources			
Determine A/V equipment needed			
Secure A/V vendor and finalize contract			
Draft and begin implementing publicity plan			
Finalize mailing lists			
Secure permits and insurance			
Assess needed rentals			
Assess needed decorations			
Secure vendor for rentals			
Secure vendors for decorations			
Place orders for rentals			
Place orders for decorations			
Set tentative timeline for event			
Conduct walk-through at venue			
Finalize travel and accommodations for entertainment			
Finalize travel and accommodations for staff involved			
Review needs for signs at registration table			
Order signage			
Draft releases announcing event			
Finalize and distribute releases			
Distribute periodic e-mail blasts			
Determine all staffing needs for day of event			
Sign up additional staff or recruit volunteers			

To-Do Grid

TASK	DATE ASSIGNED	PERSON RESPONSIBLE	DEADLINE
Finalize invitation distribution			
Give food and beverage estimates to caterer			
Confirm details of all entertainment's participation			
Prepare itineraries for all travel and accommodations			
Confirm A/V list			
Confirm rentals and decorations list			
Set final agenda			
Write necessary scripts			
Determine welcome packet contents and assemble			
Place newspaper ads			
Follow up with news media			
Confirm staff/volunteer participation			
Meet with outside vendors to coordinate all final details			
Follow up on invitation list to track attendance			
Compose complete day-of itinerary			
Confirm number attending			
Hold final walk-through of venue			
Schedule and conduct rehearsal			
Schedule pickups and deliveries of rentals			
Schedule pickups and deliveries of decorations			
Schedule pickups and deliveries of A/V equipment			
Finalize catering guarantee			
Distribute final e-mail blast			
Distribute timelines, itineraries, and scripts to program participants			
Confirm media attendance			
Prepare checks for vendors			
Send thank-you notes			
Conduct debriefing session			

Trade Show Checklist	
	Receive and complete application form
	E-mail/snail mail application form
	Submit deposit
	Submit balance
	Request booth location
	Receive exhibitor package
	Outline and determine needs and responsibilities for booth: table, chairs, additional furniture, electricity, carpeting
	Brainstorm promotion possibilities for show to encourage traffic
	Devise promotions
	Ascertain needs to conduct promotion
	Publicize promotion to attendees via, for example, e-mail blasts
	Design premiums
	Order premiums
	Create press materials
	Create lead sheet
	Make travel arrangements for staff attending
	Follow up to finalize all booth arrangements
	Pack up all on-site necessities: press releases, lead sheets, extension cords, return shipping labels, contact lists, essential office supplies
	Coordinate shipping
	Confirm all shipping arrangements
	Conduct postshow follow-up with leads, fulfilling info and product requests

Silent Bid Auction	
Name of Auction	
To Benefit	
Item Description	
Donor	
Retail Value	$
Minimum Bid	$
Bid Increments *The minimum increase needed for each subsequent bid*	$
NAME (OR BIDDER NUMBER)	**BID**

Appendix B
Resources

As the planner of an upcoming event, review these resources to generate ideas and leads, get advice, find possible vendors, and brainstorm.

AUDIO-VISUAL NEEDS
www.meetingtomorrow.com offers services nationwide and provides a lists of equipment you may need for projectors, computers, or other audio and visual components.

Go to *www.corbis.com* and *www.flickr.com* for images that can add lively graphics to programs, collateral, or presentations.

Atkinson, Cliff. *Beyond Bullet Points*. Redmond, WA.: Microsoft Press, 2005.

BUSINESS COMMUNICATIONS
LoCicero, Joe. *Streetwise Business Communication*. Avon, MA: Adams Media, 2007.

DECORATIONS AND DETAILS
www.justlanyards.com
www.1-800-flowers.com
www.proflowers.com
www.nametag.com
www.nametagsource.com

ENTERTAINING
Spade, Kate. *Occasions*. New York: Simon & Schuster, 2004.

Pulitzer, Lilly, and Jay Mulvaney. *Essentially Lilly*. New York: HarperCollins, 2004.

Rowley, Cynthia, and Ilene Rosenzweig. *The Swell Dressed Party*. New York: Atria Books, 2005.

FOOD & BEVERAGE
www.webeventplanner.com has listings regarding hotel catering packages (as well as banquet and ballroom space).

Aloni, Nicole. *Secrets from a Caterer's Kitchen: The Indispensable Guide for Planning a Party*. New York: HP Trade, 2001.

Weiss, Edith and Hal Weiss. *Catering Handbook*. New York: John Wiley & Sons, 2004.

GUERRILLA MARKETING
Levinson, Jay Conrad. *Guerrilla Marketing: Secrets for Making Big Profits from Your Small Business*. Boston: Houghton Mifflin Company, 1998.

Levinson, Jay Conrad, and Seth Goodson. *Mastering Guerrilla Marketing*. Boston: Houghton Mifflin Company, 1999.

——*The Way of the Guerrilla*. Boston: Houghton Mifflin Company, 1997.

——*The Guerrilla Marketing Handbook*. Boston: Houghton Mifflin Company, 1994.

Levinson, Jay Conrad, Rick Frishman, and Jill Lublin. *Guerrilla Publicity*. Avon, MA: Adams Media, 2002.

IDEAS
Expo magazine (*www.expoweb.com*) boasts "strategies and solutions for trade show, convention and corporate event management."

Event Solutions magazine (*www.event-solutions.com*) "for successful meetings, events and incentives."

Special Events magazine (*www.specialevents. com*) touts itself as the "international resource for special event professionals."

www.forbes.com and *www.inc.com* profile companies that designed an event so ingeniously it attracted news coverage.

MEDIA/LISTS, MONITORING, TRACKING, AND DIRECTORIES
www.easymedialist.com
www.burrellesluce.com
www.bacons.com
www.prnewswire.com

NEGOTIATING
Fisher, Roger, William L. Ury, and Bruce Patton. *Getting to Yes*. New York: Penguin, 1991.

Shell, G. Richard. *Bargaining for Advantage: Negotiation Strategies for Reasonable People.* New York: Penguin, 2006.

PRINTING AND INVITATIONS
www.vistaprint.com
www.4by6.com
www.crane.com
www.swoozies.com
www.papyrusonline.com
www.paperstyle.com
www.katespaperie.com

PODCASTS
www.apple.com/support/garageband/podcasts/recording/

RENTALS
www.classicpartyrentals.com will give you an idea of the categories and specific items you may need for your event.

www.gatheringguide.com provides state-by-state listings of rental companies in your area for corporate event needs.

SPEAKERS
National Speakers Association
www.nsaspeakers.org

Premiere Speakers Bureau
www. Premierespeakers.com

International Speakers Bureau
www.internationalspeakers.com

TRADE SHOW DISPLAYS AND QUOTES
www.buyerzone.com
www.lazerquick.com

WEB CONFERENCING
www.webex.com
www.gotomeeting.com

INDEX

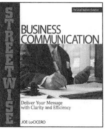

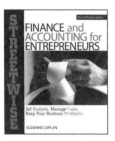

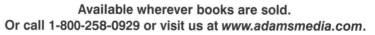

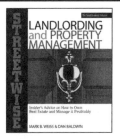

**Streetwise® Landlording &
Property Management**
Weiss & Baldwin
$19.95; ISBN 10: 1-58062-766-8

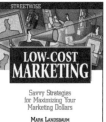

Streetwise® Low-Cost Marketing
Mark Landsbaum
$19.95; ISBN 10: 1-58062-858-3

**Streetwise® Low-Cost
Web Site Promotion**
Barry Feig
$19.95; ISBN 10: 1-58062-501-0

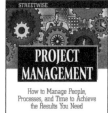

Streetwise® Managing a Nonprofit
John Riddle
$19.95; ISBN 10: 1-58062-698-X

Streetwise® Marketing Plan
Don Debelak
$19.95; ISBN 10: 1-58062-268-2

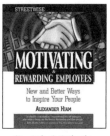

**Streetwise® Meeting and Event
Planning**
Joe LoCicero
$19.95; ISBN 10: 1-59869-271-2

**Streetwise® Motivating
& Rewarding Employees**
Alexander Hiam
$19.95; ISBN 10: 1-58062-130-9

**Streetwise® Project
Management**
Michael Dobson
$19.95; ISBN 10: 1-58062-770-6

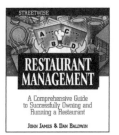

**Streetwise® Restaurant
Management**
John James & Dan Baldwin
$19.95; ISBN 10: 1-58062-781-1

**Streetwise® Sales Letters
with CD**
Reynard & Weiss
$29.95; ISBN 10: 1-58062-440-5

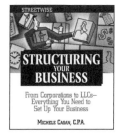

Streetwise® Selling on eBay®
Sonia Weiss
$19.95; ISBN 10: 1-59337-610-3

**Streetwise®
Small Business Book of Lists**
Edited by Gene Marks
$19.95; ISBN 10: 1-59337-684-7

Streetwise® Small Business Start-Up
Bob Adams
$19.95; ISBN 10: 1-55850-581-4

**Streetwise® Start Your Own
Business Workbook**
Gina Marie Mangiamele
$9.95; ISBN 10: 1-58062-506-1

**Streetwise® Structuring Your
Business**
Michele Cagan
$19.95; ISBN 10: 1-59337-177-2

Streetwise® Time Management
Marshall Cook
$19.95; ISBN 10: 1-58062-131-7

About the Author

As a Los Angeles–based writer, marketing consultant, event planner, and entrepreneur, JOE LoCICERO has been integrally involved with designing, orchestrating, and spearheading numerous events for *Fortune* 500 companies, entertainment conglomerates, hospitality chains, restaurants, retail stores, nonprofit organizations, tourist attractions, and startups. His clients have included such corporate icons as The Coca-Cola Company, Marriott, Turner Broadcasting, and Disney. His events have canvassed grand openings, product launches, company anniversaries, film screenings, press tours and conferences, and Web-only promotions, among hundreds of others.

Most recently, he has put his event-planning skills to work for his own enterprise, the lifestyle brand Practical Whimsy™, a company that celebrates family style with reversible products for baby and home. His business also presents recipes and tips for entertaining, offers ideas for gifts and home decorating, and conducts speaking engagements nationwide.

As part of his own company's efforts, he currently is the "Do-Dad" food and craft expert for disneyfamily.com; he writes the column "Practical Whimsy: Southern Hospitality, Hollywood Style" for *Y'ALL: The Magazine of Southern People*; he is a regular columnist for momready.com; and he keeps up with the commerce on his company's Web site (practical whimsy.com) and supplies select retailers with Practical Whimsy™ goods.

LoCicero and his advice have been featured in *Cosmopolitan, Woman's World,* and daily newspapers in the United States and Canada, and on Sirius' Martha Stewart Living Radio, Los Angeles' top-rated "The KTLA Morning Show," and Atlanta's "Good Day, L.A." (FOX). His books include *Streetwise® Business Communication, The Complete Idiot's Guide to Clear Thinking,* and *Cake Decorating for Dummies.*